CONTENDING

FOR THE

CONSTITUTION

Recalling the Christian Influence on the
Writing of the Constitution and the
Biblical Basis of American Law and
Liberty

Mark A. Beliles
and
Douglas S. Anderson

PROVIDENCE FOUNDATION
CHARLOTTESVILLE, VIRGINIA

Contending for the Constitution
Recalling the Christian Influence on the Writing of the Constitution and the
Biblical Basis of American Law and Liberty

Copyright © 2005 by Mark A. Beliles and Douglas S. Anderson

Published by:
Providence Foundation
PO Box 6759
Charlottesville, VA 22906
434-978-4535
Website: www.providencefoundation.com
E-mail: info@providencefoundation.com

For additional copies of this book, or for information on other books and materials contact the Providence Foundation.

The Providence Foundation is a Christian educational organization whose mission is to spread liberty, justice, and prosperity among the nations by educating individuals in a Biblical worldview. The Foundation studies the relationship between religion and public life and offers numerous seminars, presentations, books, tapes, and other materials on the subject.

Printed in the United States of America

ISBN: 1-887456-19-8
ISBN13: 978-1-8874546-19-7

Table of Contents

Acknowledgements

The authors wish to give special thanks to Stephen McDowell, President of the Providence Foundation, for his time and willingness to provide advice, and input on the draft and in preparing the manuscript for publication.

We also would like to thank Nicole Cober-Lake for her valuable editing of the manuscript, along with helpful comments from Daniel Driesbach, Dave Sullivan, and Laura Anderson who generously agreed to review the draft and provided valuable comments to improve it. Additionally, we want to thank Michelle Atchley for many hours of her time to layout and format the book to get it ready for printing.

We also are deeply grateful for the scholarship and excellence of Dr. Gary Amos' volume *Defending the Declaration*, that we so highly value as the foundation and inspiration for this book.

Finally, it is our deepest hope and prayer that the contents of this book give great honor to our Lord Jesus Christ who made this project possible and whose principles and truths are responsible for the liberties our nation has so richly enjoyed.

INTRODUCTION

Encased behind sealed protective glass, closely guarded in the National Archives Building, is one of this nation's most revered treasures: the Constitution of the United States of America. It has been described as "the greatest document ever written for the benefit and blessing of mankind other than the Holy Bible."[1] Today the ink on that historic document is largely faded, and its words are difficult to read. Yet fortunately, a great effort has been expended to preserve and protect the words so carefully scripted on simple parchment more than 200 years ago. Not only has the original document been protected in the National Archives, but numerous copies of it have been made, with new ink and more legible print to ensure that its words will never be lost.

But what about the spirit behind the words? What about the principles, intent, and ideological foundation upon which the words were cemented? What happens when the spirit behind the words begins to fade from our memories? Absent some reminders of what that spirit was, absent some "copies of the original," the spirit behind America's Constitution will be lost forever, and all that will be left will be the words without context. When that happens, our national treasure will be nothing more than a hollow shell, devoid of its original, dynamic meaning.

Sadly, we have not been as careful to preserve the spirit of our Constitution as we have its words. As a result, the spirit of our Constitution is badly faded, almost beyond recognition. Americans have been largely unfaithful in teaching their children and their children's children what the true spirit of America's Constitution is. We have faltered in our responsibility and in our duty as citizens. It is no wonder, then, that today we are in grave danger of allowing historians with other agendas to completely blot out the rich spiritual precepts upon which our Constitution rests and which set America's Constitution apart from all other constitutions in the world.

Our Constitutional heritage is worth preserving because it provides, better than any other, a government framework in which liberty can flourish. However, it can only provide such a framework if we ensure that its words are not separated from the context in which they were written and from their intended interpretation. That context was best articulated by President John

Adams when he stated that "[o]ur Constitution was made only for a moral and religious people. It is wholly inadequate to the government of any other." America's Constitution must therefore be construed through the lens of a moral and religious world view. To interpret it any other way would be inconsistent with the intent of the Founders.

There is a Biblical principle that states that you can determine the type of tree by the fruit it bears, and this is every bit as true today as it was when it was written nearly 2,000 years ago. The principle applies not only to individuals, but to societies and nations as well. America, despite its relatively brief existence as a nation, has astounded the world with its ability to produce the fruit of liberty. America is a nation where liberty and freedom have thrived to a degree far greater than anywhere else in the world. The Statue of Liberty stands proudly in New York's harbor as a symbolic testament to that fact.

The principles of liberty and freedom have been allowed to flourish through America's Constitution, but not merely because of the words written across its parchment. The former Soviet Union had a constitution with many similar words and noble sounding phrases, yet the fruit produced by that nation was completely contrary to that seen in America because the spirit behind the words was completely different. Constitutions consist of more than just inspiring language; behind the words is a spirit that reflects that of the nation which authors them. An agnostic or atheistic spirit cannot produce the spirit of liberty anymore than an apple tree can produce pears. America's Constitution incorporated a spirit of liberty derived from Biblical principles that our Founders brought to these shores nearly 200 years before its words were written. Unlike the founders of the former Soviet Union, who relied on the teachings of Karl Marx and sought the fruit of the Communist Manifesto, America's founders believed that true liberty could only be born out of a spirit of truth found in the Bible. The beliefs of America's founders have proven to be correct.

John Adams, who greatly influenced the ratification of the Constitution by writing *A Defense of the Constitutions of the Government of the United States,* had much to say about the positive influence of the Bible and religion on a nation. Consider this diary entry of February 22, 1756:

> Suppose a nation in some distant region should take the Bible for their only law book, and every member should regulate his conduct by the precepts there exhibited! Every member would be obliged in conscience, to temperance, frugality, and industry; to justice, kindness, and charity towards his fellow men; and to piety, love, and reverence toward Almighty God . . . . What a Eutopia, what a Paradise would this region be.[2]

John Adams understood the connection between the Bible and liberty, and so did the great majority of his fellow founders.

It is therefore appropriate that we recall the words from that Holy writ. The book of 2 Corinthians says: "[w]here the Spirit of the Lord is, there is liberty."[3] America's Constitution, like the Corinthian church the apostle Paul was referring to, was in many ways "written not with ink, but with the Spirit of the living God."

The spirit behind it is the Spirit of the Lord based upon a Biblical world view. Our founders, who authored the Declaration of Independence and the Constitution 11 years later, were filled with an attitude of dependency on God. They looked to Him as the source of their strength and the hope of their success in all major endeavors. The words of Paul might be indicative of the Founders' thoughts:

> And such trust have we through Christ to God-ward: Not that we are sufficient of ourselves to think any thing as of ourselves; but our sufficiency is of God; Who also hath made us able ministers of the new testament; not of the letter, but of the spirit: for the letter killeth, but the spirit giveth life.[4]

Constitutional scholars who focus primarily on the words of the Constitution, and interpret those words from a current secular perspective, cannot possibly understand them accurately. Nor can judges who refuse to consider any religious intent, despite overwhelming evidence of its existence. Accurate legal interpretation of the Constitution must not only give the words the meanings their founders intended them to carry, but also seek to understand them in light of the spirit behind them. We are thus presented with a problem. The Holy Scripture and its spirit of truth and liberty are the foundation stones of the Constitution, yet many Constitutional scholars insist on ignoring those Biblical foundations when interpreting its provisions. The result is nothing short of a disaster when Supreme Court decisions interpret the document in ways that directly contradict the Biblical principles upon which it was founded. As the scripture passage above illustrates, words and letters on their own cannot bring life. Only when those words are read in the context of the spirit behind them does our Constitution come alive to bring forth liberty.

In the historical account found in Part I of this book, you will encounter an amazing sequence of events that led up to the formation of our Constitution. Those events can only be explained in one of two ways: either they were completely coincidental, involving extraordinary luck, or they were divinely orchestrated by a sovereign God. There is simply no other logical explanation.

Secular scholars, afraid to admit the existence of any supernatural explanation for an historical event, will insist on the first explanation of mere coincidence. Their secular bias precludes them from even considering any other explanation. But a conclusion that our Constitution is a byproduct of coincidence is contrary to both our experience and reason, which tell us that when luck or coincidence is involved, there is no pattern or consistent direction to the events. There is neither "rhyme nor reason" to luck. Thus, when we see events that appear to be helter skelter in nature, with no consistent path or direction, then it is reasonable to ascribe the result to coincidence.

However, when a sequence of amazing events all point to one ultimate direction and result, and that result is consistent with the word of God, experience and reason tell us that God Himself is directing the events for a particular purpose. As noted above, few historical accounts even consider the possibility of divine intervention. Indeed, many historians would say that a consideration of divine intervention is beyond the bounds of good scholarship. We disagree. Our examination of the events leading up to the Constitutional Convention lead us to conclude that God intervened in the formation of America's Constitution and that such a conclusion is consistent with good historical scholarship. We will show in Part I that there were just too many improbable events that came together in just the right time and manner, geared towards one coherent outcome consistent with God's word, for them to be attributed to anything less than the product of a sovereign God directing human events.

Not only does a supernatural intervention coincide with the facts, it also is consistent with the conclusions of the participants themselves! Their conclusion, as those who saw the events unfold, was that God supernaturally intervened in this event of history. Moreover, their statements, such as that of President Adams mentioned earlier, reveal their belief that God's assistance was directly responsible for the success of their endeavor. Recall the words of President Washington in his Inaugural speech of April 30, 1789:

> No people can be bound to acknowledge and adore the Invisible Hand which conducts the affairs of men more than the people of the United States. Every step by which they have advanced to the character of an independent nation seems to have been distinguished by some token of providential agency.[5]

In Part II of this book, you will discover the Biblical principles that were intended to be the foundation of our Constitution and to provide the context in which the words and phrases were to be construed. No historic document is written in a vacuum, nor was this one. America's Constitution was the byproduct of a Biblical world view which had become a part of our heritage long before. In this part of the book, we will trace that heritage to provide you with a contextual background against which to measure the words contained in the Constitution. It is within this part of the book that we can remind ourselves of the real spirit behind America's Constitution: the spirit that led to true liberty and freedom to become what our nation is known for. It is here that we try to "copy" the spirit of this document as others have copied its words; to preserve for our posterity the true source of its greatness.

In Part III, you will see how that spirit has faded. Just as time has worked unmercifully upon the legibility of the Constitution's words, so too has time worked against its spirit. Indeed, time has been much harsher in the latter case. We will show how the original interpretation of the words has changed their meaning through a systematic undermining of the Biblical spirit upon which they once rested.

In the final section, we seek to outline a means of restoration directed at returning the hearts and minds of Americans to the Biblical world view which was so widely held by our Founders, and which produced the principles of liberty upon which our Constitution rests. A theocracy is not the goal. Instead, we seek to restore our democratic republic as it was originally created, one sealed with the glue of Christian virtue and the truths set forth in the Bible. That does not mean that every citizen must become a Christian, any more than it did during our founding era. In 1787 not every American was a Christian. Then, as now, there was divergence and freedom of beliefs. Yet even great leaders such as Thomas Jefferson, Benjamin Franklin, and others like them, who did not accept Jesus Christ as their Lord or Savior, nonetheless accepted and adhered to Biblical principles for the health and well-being of the nation. They knew to do so was the best means of protecting the Constitution and allowing liberty and freedom to thrive.

This book seeks to remind us of what our Founders understood all too well: that our Constitution was based on Biblical principles and was designed for a nation that adheres to them. We have tried, in the words of Thomas Jefferson, to ". . . carry ourselves back to the time in which the Constitution was adopted, [and to] recollect the spirit manifested in the debates."[6] We hope to create for you an atmosphere, not of discovery, for the principles we discuss were well known and acknowledged by our founders, but one of rediscovery. We hope you will be able to see anew the same perspective that our founders saw so clearly. In that light, the spirit of the Constitution is rediscovered when one reads the writings of the founders themselves. It is rediscovered in tracing the origins of their ideas. It is rediscovered in the "truths" held by our founders in other foundational documents. But most of all, that spirit is rediscovered in the discerning observation made by Benjamin Franklin at that historic Philadelphia Convention, "that God governs in the affairs of men."

PART I

THE STORY OF PROVIDENTIAL ASSISTANCE IN THE FORMING OF AMERICA'S CONSTITUTION

ONE

"PULLING AGAINST EACH OTHER:"
Prelude to the Constitutional Convention

Great dramas always begin in a cloud of obscurity. So must this one. In the months preceding that grand performance known as the Constitutional Convention of 1787, life gave no hint of coming drama. To the farmers and the store clerks, the bankers and the shoemakers, life in the spring of the year was nothing out of the ordinary, unless you consider the growing frustrations that were brewing.

Talk at the corner taverns, outside the local cobbler's shop, and just about anywhere else that people gathered often turned to politics. Generally, the tone was angry. It had only been six autumns prior that they had celebrated the news that the British regulars had surrendered to General Washington on the fields of Yorktown, Virginia. Yet the excitement of that moment was quickly forgotten in the growing realization that they had exchanged the shackles of foreign government tyranny for the cackles of their own government's incompetence. The new national government, under the Articles of Confederation, seemed incapable of doing anything right. It seemed that everyone had their own story of government ineptitude that they couldn't wait to share. Each of them could have given a different reason why the document didn't work, but almost everyone agreed that the governing system contained in the Articles of Confederation was a poor way to run a country. As a result, you could often hear a mixture of angry shouting and roars of laughter as the townsfolk and farmers took turns telling their tales. It didn't seem like a script from which great dramas could unfold.

So what was the problem with this first attempt at governing ourselves as a new nation? Perhaps a little background is in order to understand the strong feelings Americans held in the spring of 1787.

America's First Attempt at National Governance

Once America announced its "independence" on the steps of what is now called Independence Hall, we had immediately launched ourselves into the deep water. Severed from the governing authority of Britain, we had no national government of our own. We stood on the threshold of liberty, proclaiming great and historic truths, but we stood ill equipped, with no constitution. Nationally, you might say we were in over our heads.

Hence, work was commenced in earnest to create a ship of state without too many leaks. John Dickinson had the honor of drafting our first governing document, and in fairness, he did an admirable job. But the Continental Congress felt it was too strong.[1] Over the course of several months, they commenced to haggle, argue, and wrestle with the proposed Articles of Confederation, weakening them with each modification they made. Their final version was so watered down[2] that it practically ensured a leaky future.

The confederation between colonies was little more than a league of friendship necessitated by our need for national cooperation to win the War for Independence. It provided for a central government and emphasized "perpetual union," but it allowed for the 13 colonies to be mostly independent and separate. It ensured that the national government would have little power or authority to enforce its laws over the individual states, one of many fundamental flaws which became apparent in those crucial years during our fight for liberty from Great Britain.[3]

These flaws all pointed to a fatal lack of national power. The framers of the Articles were fearful of centralizing power in a chief executive or national legislature such as they had experienced under King George III and Parliament. Both were tyrannical and oppressive and did not respect their inalienable rights. Therefore, the Articles made each state legislature supreme in authority and gave no power to the Continental Congress to levy a tax, raise a soldier, control commerce, or enforce its policies on the states short of going to war with them. It had no executive or judicial branch whatsoever. In short, it was a ship of state with many leaks.

No one recognized these deficiencies more than General George Washington and the Continental Army that he commanded. He was convinced that the war might have been won much sooner had there not been a lack of supreme national authority. Many of the hardships experienced at Valley Forge in particular, and throughout the war effort in general, were a result of this flaw. The army's lack of weapons, food, clothing, and pay was in large measure the result of the refusal of various states to comply with the requisitions of Congress. When they did comply, it was often only on a partial basis, and even then usually quite late. The Continental Congress could do nothing to enforce state cooperation under the Articles of Confederation, even during a time when the nation's existence depended on it. Indeed, the Congress was so powerless that heads of foreign governments frequently bypassed it and went straight to General Washington!

It was a period of immense national humiliation that only an eyewitness can describe. Alexander Hamilton, a loyal patriot to America's cause, had reached the zenith of his tolerance when he let loose with a long and abusive criticism of the Articles of Confederation. Only the first portion of his invective is quoted here.

> We may indeed with propriety be said to have reached
> almost the last stage of national humiliation. There is scarcely
> anything that can wound the pride or degrade the character of an
> independent nation which we do not experience.[4]

Such humiliation was causing many people to realize the need for a stronger national government. Something had to be done to either strengthen or replace the Articles of Confederation. Alexander Hamilton did his part. In a forceful 17 page letter written in 1780, he was one of the first to assert that the only remedy for such a weak confederation was to call a convention of the states. Despite the wisdom of his suggestion, the "half-formed American Union"[5] was not ready for it. The angry shouting and roars of laughter down at the corner taverns would continue for a while longer.

Washington's Character Subdues an Insurgency

Although ultimately successful in winning our independence on the battlefield, after the war the Continental Army and its officers were still very frustrated by the federal government's inherent weaknesses. Many of them had not yet been paid for their military service. Some officers believed the desperate times justified desperate measures. Thus, Colonel Lewis Nicola wrote a letter to General Washington in May, 1782, endeavoring to persuade Washington to become king, by the voice of the army, as a necessity of national survival.[6] Their proposal was akin to a military dictatorship, by way of a military coup, and some of the soldiers who fought for independence saw it as their only hope.

Other nations, past and present, have fallen for this temptation, only to regret it later. Fortunately for America, God made sure that a man of Washington's character would receive such a request, for few men could sniff the aroma of power such a proposal offered and respond as unselfishly and ad-

mirably as did Washington. His response to Colonel Nicola was unequivo-
cal.

> [N]o occurrence in the course of the war has given me more painful sensa-
> tion, than information of there being such ideas existing in the army. . . I am
> much at a loss to conceive what part of my conduct could have given en-
> couragement to an address, which to me seems big with the greatest
> mischiefs, that can befall my country. If I am not deceived in the knowledge
> of myself, you could not have found a person to whom your schemes are
> more disagreeable. At the same time. . . no man possesses a more sincere
> wish to see ample justice done to the army than I do. . . [but only] in a consti-
> tutional way.[7]

Washington had indeed sniffed at the tempting and selfish aroma of
power and fame, yet chose what he knew was best for the country. Had it not
been for Washington's noble response, America's heritage today might be
like that of many other nations - government instability from rule by successive military coups.

Our country was sitting in a precarious position at this time in its history,
and the danger was not over. Again in 1783, the continued irritation of the
soldiers over lack of pay and other grievances led some officers to propose
an outright military coup, only this time without Washington's support.[8] A
letter to that end was circulating within the army. When Washington caught
wind of the idea, he again intervened to halt the insurrection.

Wisely, he called for a meeting of all his officers at Newburgh, New
York for the 15th of March. At that meeting, he listened to their grievances
and, in a "most eloquent and touching speech,"[9] expressed his earnest desire
to help them in any means other than civil discord, but he also made it clear
that he was opposed to anyone who attempted to "deluge our rising empire in
blood."[10] When he was through, he looked out upon the many loyal officers
he had led into battle. He saw that they remained sullen, quiet, and unconvinced. At this point Washington may have been the only person standing
between military revolt and the swift ending to our experiment in liberty.
The admiration from his fellow officers was considerable, and the fact they
all knew he had refused to take any pay himself gave his words added credi-
bility.[11] Still, it is not an exaggeration to say that our constitutional future
hung in the balance. The drama of the moment was worthy of a Hollywood
script.

He tried one more approach. He told his officers that there were many
Congressmen who understood their frustrations and were willing to help. He
pulled out a letter from one of those concerned Congressmen and offered to
read it to them. The General stood there looking at the sheet of paper, yet

reading nothing. He seemed hesitant, uncertain and ill at ease. At last, Washington began to fumble in his waistcoat pocket for something, something none of them had ever seen him wear - a pair of eye glasses. His failing eyesight prevented him from reading the letter unaided. In all the years his soldiers had known him, few had ever seen him wear glasses, yet now, as an aging warrior and patriot, he needed them to read a simple letter. As he pulled out that pair of spectacles for the first time in public, he seemed embarrassed. In humble apology he tried to explain.

> Gentlemen, you will permit me to put on my spectacles, for I have not only grown gray but almost blind in the service of my country.[12]

Truly no one had even come close to patiently sacrificing the way their Commander had. The officers were instantly overcome with tears by their Commander's strength of character and unselfish devotion to his country. They knew that what he said was true. After quietly reading the letter, he walked out of the hall, mounted his horse, and disappeared from view. That was all it took. The officers voted unanimously to support Washington for a peaceful, constructive solution.[13]

Washington's Appeal to Save the Union

On June 3, 1783, as Washington was preparing to retire from public life, he drafted a letter to the governors of the thirteen states describing fully what he thought needed to be done. He called this letter his "Legacy," mistakenly thinking it would be his final public act. In his letter he said that "[t]hirteen sovereignties pulling against each other, and all tugging at the federal head, will soon bring ruin on the whole . . . . I do not conceive we can exist long as a nation without having lodged somewhere a power which will pervade the whole union." Unless adequate authority were granted to a national government, he said, "it will become a matter of regret that so much blood and treasure have been lavished to no purpose, that so many sacrifices have been made in vain."[14] His lengthy 4,000 word letter continued:

> In less time, and with much less expense than has been incurred, the war might have been brought to the same happy conclusion, if the resources of the continent could have been properly drawn forth. The distresses and disappointments, which have very often occurred, have, in too many instances, resulted not from a deficiency of means in the particular States, but more from the want of an adequate authority in the supreme power, or from a partial compliance with the requisitions of Congress in some of the States, and from a failure of punctuality in others; . . . . If, after all, a spirit of disunion, or a temper of obstinacy and perverseness should manifest itself in any of the

States; if such an ungracious disposition should attempt to frustrate all the happy effects that might be expected to flow from the Union; if there should be a refusal to comply with the requisition for funds to discharge the annual interest of the public debts; . . . [then] Congress . . . will stand justified in the sight of God and man; and the State alone which puts itself in opposition to the aggregate wisdom of the continent, and follows such mistaken and pernicious counsels, will be responsible for all the consequences.[15]

As persuasive and admired as Washington's opinions were, they were not received favorably this time. His warnings would go unheeded by the states, which were still suspicious and fearful of the centralization of power.

America's Precarious Condition

It was not long before prejudices, ambitions and selfishness in these thirteen little "nations" began to rear their ugly heads. The war debts caused much inflation and taxation, and, without an authority to regulate commerce between states, there was no common standard of monetary exchange. Seven states began to print their own paper money, as did Congress, and a money crisis ensued. Nine states retained their own navies, and the rivalry and animosity between the states was like that of several quarreling foreign nations.[16] It was a dangerous time. The thin thread of liberty, won at such great hardship, was unraveling, and many of the founders knew it.

Reflection upon this period in our history leads many historians to realize how much God's hand was upon our nation at this time to preserve the flickering light of liberty He wanted to flame across the world.[17] The thirteen states were on the brink of going their separate ways. Had they done so, they would have been too weak to withstand the opportunistic invasions from European nations that would likely have occurred. Spain, England, and France were all waiting in the wings, waiting for the right moment to pounce.[18] Even those leaders who did understand the importance of maintaining a union, could not agree on the form that union should take. Centralized power in a federal government was seen as dangerous.

The anti-federal sentiment was so strong at this time that it was miraculous that we ever had a Constitutional Convention at all. The states were weary from six years of fighting to rid themselves of a powerful Parliament that burdened and oppressed them to the point of war. It made no sense to win their freedom from such bondage at the heavy price of blood and life, only to voluntarily relinquish that freedom to a new federal power that could control their lives. They wanted most of all to govern themselves. Typical of their feeling at that time was the proclamation voted back in 1776 by the town of Ashfield, Massachusetts that stated, "we do not want any Governor but the Governor of the universe."[19] Which was worse, being governed oppressively by the British Parliament, or governing themselves? The answer wasn't clear. While the colonies understood the sin of too much centralized power, they still needed convincing of the sin of anarchy which results from too little centralized power.

Most of the bickering between the states was based on commercial trade differences. Virginia and Maryland had particular difficulties resolving these issues. Especially the conflict over which one possessed the navigation rights to the Potomac River. Once again, George Washington attempted to reconcile the situation. Seeing an opportunity to encourage union, he arranged for delegates from the two states to have a conference at his home in Mount Vernon on March 28, 1785.[20] His idea blossomed! These delegates called for another conference to be held in Annapolis on September 11, 1786. At this convention, three more states sent delegates, including James Madison from Virginia and Alexander Hamilton from New York. This convention proposed yet another which would involve every state in order to solve their common commercial problems and regulate trade relations.

Momentum Builds Towards a Constitutional Convention

While momentum was clearly gathering for a federal convention, the Continental Congress refused to endorse the idea just yet. One more incident would be required to trigger their change of mind. That incident was an armed rebellion of eleven hundred farmers in western Massachusetts led by Daniel Shays in January, 1787.[21] The rebellion was sparked by the monetary crisis, heavy taxation, and the inability of the Continental Congress to repay debts it owned to its citizens.

Actually, in hindsight, that rebellion served a heavenly purpose. It forced Americans to consider the reality that many were fearful of — a civil war between the states over differences in trade and commercial relations. That fear, in turn, finally induced the Continental Congress to call for a Federal Convention on February 21, 1787. Remarkably, even through all of this, the Congressional call for change was a very limited one. Their vote to hold a Federal Convention in Philadelphia was "for the sole and express purpose" of *revising*, not doing away with, the Articles of Confederation. This modest, cautious step towards a stronger federal system was made with the still clear recollection of British abuses of centralized power.

Men may plan one thing, but Providential purposes and timing determine the outcome. Among the many gems of wisdom contained in the book of Ecclesiastes is this one: "To every thing there is a season, and a time to every purpose under the heaven."[22] It was certainly true in this case, for the timing of this Convention could not have been more Providential. Had it been held five years earlier, the states would still have been unconvinced of the need for a stronger federal union and never would have risked making substantial changes to the Articles of Confederation. Had the Convention been held five years later, news of the bloody anarchy of the French Revolution would probably have made them equally fearful of changing anything in their present system. Many leaders of the day were beginning to sense God's hand in the coming drama. Though invisible, it was clearly felt.

Preparations began for this historic gathering, although no one anticipated just how historic it would be. After all, the original purpose of this Convention was not to write a whole new Constitution, but merely to amend what they already had. Twelve states proceeded to appoint a total of seventy-four delegates. Rhode Island was the only hold-out, refusing to appoint or send any delegates. Of those attending, most delegates had to personally finance their trip to, and stay in, Philadelphia, since their home states did not have sufficient funds in their treasuries to pay for the endeavor. Given the long duration of the convention, this financial burden was not a light one. Little wonder, then, that only fifty-five delegates actually arrived at the Convention.[23]

Unique Qualifications of the Convention Delegates

While this group of fifty-five delegates was relatively small, their selection was no act of mere coincidence. It was apparent that God also played a role in the selection of this particular group of men for this particular event in history. He alone knew what was necessary for success, and it seems God made sure the players were ready for the task at hand. There are several pieces of evidence to support this conclusion of Providential involvement.

First, they were extremely well educated. Twenty-nine of the men were university trained, graduates of Harvard, Yale, Columbia, Princeton, William and Mary, Oxford, Glasgow, and Edinburgh.[24] Among the men who were not university trained were the likes of George Washington and Benjamin Franklin. Half of the delegates were lawyers by profession. Of these, there was James Wilson of Pennsylvania, born and educated in Scotland, and "one of the most learned jurists this country has ever seen."[25] Likewise, Oliver Ellsworth of Connecticut, who later became Chief Justice of the Supreme Court, "was one of the ablest lawyers of his time."[26]

A second fact which demonstrated these men were prepared for the task at hand was that they had strong experience in serving their country. Seven delegates had been state governors, eight had signed the Declaration of Independence, twenty-one had fought in the War for Independence with the Continental Army, and almost three quarters of them had already served in the Continental Congress.[27]

Third, they had extensive experience in writing legislative documents. Many had helped to write their own state constitutions in the five years following independence from Britain. Virtually all served in their state legislatures. These men were proven leaders who were willing to serve their country. Even the names of the participants read like a Who's Who of American History. Most people are aware of the likes of George Washington, Benjamin Franklin, James Madison, and Alexander Hamilton. Indeed, one historian said of the thirty-six year old Madison and the thirty year old Hamilton that "these two men must be ranked in the same order with Aristotle, Montesquieu, and Locke" as the most profound and original thinkers.[28] God had truly brought together an impressive group for an awesome task. After reading the list of delegates attending the Convention, Thomas Jefferson remarked in a letter to John Adams, "It is really an assembly of demigods."[29] He would later write, "A more able assembly never sat in America."[30] Many believe that a more able assembly has never met since.[31]

However, their most important quality was that they were well-versed in Biblical principles. All but two were regular members of Christian churches, and three were active clergy. Reverend Hugh Williamson was a licensed preacher of the Presbyterian Church who conducted regular church services in North Carolina. Reverend W. Samuel Johnson of Connecticut was the President of Columbia University when he was appointed to the Convention. Finally, the third member of the clergy, Reverend Abraham Baldwin, was a typical colonial clergyman who combined religion and politics: he was a lawyer, a chaplain in the war, a member of the Georgia legislature, and a member of the Continental Congress before becoming Georgia's delegate to the Convention. Afterwards, he was elected to the U.S. House and the U.S. Senate, and founded the University of Georgia.

The faith of these men would prove important for many reasons. The significance of George Washington's faith alone was apparent to Isaac Potts, Washington's temporary landlord during the ordeal at Valley Forge ten years earlier. After he came upon Washington at prayer in the woods, he told his wife, "If George Washington be not a man of God, I am greatly deceived - and still more shall I be deceived, if God does not, through him, work out a great salvation for America.[32] This was a critical time in our young nation's history. A wrong turn at this point, and union might never have been achieved. Even a cursory review of this period is enough to show that America stood at a precipice. God's hand of protection was busy shielding us from imminent destruction during this time of national weakness and vulnerability. The faith of these men that God would get them through, the faithfulness of God to direct them and the events surrounding them to preserve the delicate liberty that had been forged, would make the difference between the outcome of America's Constitutional Convention and the outcome of all other similar conventions of other nations throughout history. All the nations had brilliant and talented leaders, but no other nation's leaders sought God's aid in drafting their constitutions to the degree evidenced by America's founders.

A Providential Influence?

Considering all the fears and animosities that had to be overcome just for the delegates to agree to meet at such a Convention, the mere efforts of mortal men could not have accomplished such a feat. Even the great stature and persuasive skills of men like Washington, Madison and Hamilton had proven to be insufficient. The events that transpired to bring fifty-five delegates to Philadelphia with one common purpose required more than what men could provide. Too many things had to come together at the proper time and in the proper manner to chalk up the explanation to coincidence. Had it not been for the obvious intervention of God Himself, the Federal Convention of 1787 might never have met at all. God did His part.

Thanks to God, all was Providentially set in place to raise the curtain on the drama that was soon to transpire. But you would never have known it in the spring of 1787. Life seemed ordinary to the farmers and the store clerks, the bankers and the shoe makers. There was no hint of coming drama; but then, why should there be? After all, great dramas always begin in a cloud of obscurity.

TWO

"IN THE HANDS OF GOD:"
The Constitutional Convention

The meeting place for the great drama of the Convention would be a familiar one for many of the delegates. Thirteen years earlier, on July 4, 1774, some of these same men had sat together in this same historic room of the Pennsylvania State House and pledged their "lives, fortunes and sacred honor" for the sake of a new, fledgling nation. That State House would later be renamed Independence Hall for their heroic act, and that historic document we now know as The Declaration of Independence. It was a glorious moment in America's history, and no doubt the building would bring back many fond memories for some of those same delegates meeting there once again.

But the Constitutional Convention had a less auspicious beginning. On the scheduled opening day of the Convention, May 14, 1787, only the Virginia and Pennsylvania delegations had arrived. Moreover, it rained that day and that whole first week. Roads were deep in mud and difficult to travel on, so the first order of Convention business was to exercise patience and wait as the other delegations began to straggle into town.

As the delegates arrived, they began to hear about the ambitious plan the Virginia delegation was preparing. These rumors of thorough and complete reform created early hesitancy, fear, and doubt amongst many of the newly arriving delegates who thought they were there solely to make small adjustments to the Articles of Confederation. They were not ready for major reforms.[1] Many of them believed that half measures would be far more acceptable in the eyes of the people — any drastic change was sure to fail. The Constitutional Convention was on the brink of failure and it hadn't even started!

The first of many critical junctures was already at hand. George Washington chose this occasion to rise and address the skeptical Convention attendees who had arrived thus far in a brief, but "immortal speech."[2] He let them know that he, too, agreed with what must have been on their hearts; that it was "too probable that no plan we propose will be adopted."[3] If that were the case, then he believed that it was entirely possible that they would have to endure another dreadful war. But, he continued with what proved to be wisdom for the ages:

> If, to please the people, we offer what we ourselves disapprove, how can we afterward defend our work? Let us raise a standard to which the wise and the honest can repair; the event is in the hand of God.[4]

This noble and inspiring appeal by Washington proved decisive during the first ten days of the Convention. It served to remind the newly arriving delegates of their lofty mission and helped to solidify wavering attitudes in the early going. But Washington's speech was important for another reason. He reminded the delegates that they were not alone in this effort. In one of the most important historical moments, Washington made sure these men, who would soon be part of history, understood that their efforts were not their own, that they would receive heavenly assistance, and that God was ultimately in control of this event. Washington's statement was not just an inspirational reflection, it was prophetic.

The Convention Begins

While May 14, 1787, was the scheduled opening of the Convention, a quorum of states would not be represented for eleven more days.[5] The interval served two vital purposes. First, it divinely provided time for many of the delegates with widely differing opinions to get acquainted with each other and cultivate a spirit of unity and friendship.[6] Second, it gave George Washington, James Madison, and the other Virginia delegates time to convince a number of the others to work for an entirely new constitution.

Once the delegates from New Jersey arrived, the Convention finally had a quorum. It officially opened on Friday, May 25, 1787, with the New Jersey delegation joining those from Virginia, Pennsylvania, South Carolina, North Carolina, New York, and Delaware.

Under a unique set of rules, their discussions would be kept secret to encourage free and full deliberation;[7] each state would have one vote regardless of how many delegates it had; and everyone had to address the president of the Convention — never one another — to help temper emotions.[8] Moreover, the president could not express his own views while moderating from the chair. Only when they called for a "committee of the whole" would free discussion be allowed for all. Their goal was to achieve not merely a majority vote, but a genuine consensus on the issues.

Choosing the Convention Leader

One of the more crucial decisions for the delegates early on was to choose the right leader for this shaky Convention. History shows that they chose well. While James Madison is called the "Father of the Constitution" for his role in drafting the Virginia Plan, and many cite the indirect influence of Thomas Jefferson on the Constitution, without doubt the most dominant influence before, during, and after the Convention was the man who should be recognized as the chief architect of America's Constitution — George Washington. He is commonly recognized for his leadership in the War for Independence and as our first President, but few realize that there never would have been a Constitutional Convention and subsequent constitutional government without the leadership of George Washington.

His election to the chair of the Convention by the delegates was unanimous.[9] No others were even nominated! As president and moderator, he was prevented from expressing his views during formal sessions of the Convention, yet his biographers have noted that he showed his sentiments by smiling or frowning and that many a convert was won to his viewpoint during mealtimes.

Washington's Faith is Critical to the Convention

Washington's Christian character was clearly beneficial to the proceedings. It was not only evident, but became an effective influence upon all the delegates in the Convention. Historian William H. Wilbur noted that "the readiness to listen, the willingness to allow every person to express himself completely, and the patient temperament which permitted a delegate to reopen the same subject as many times as wished — these qualities began to have a noticeable effect. Just as Washington himself was always willing to listen to any person's ideas, so the members of the Convention found themselves listening to each other, trying to understand each other's viewpoint."[10]

The virtue of Washington was a product of his vibrant faith. As both Commander of the Continental Army and our first President, he took pains to consistently acknowledge and glorify God in every venture. He was a devout Episcopalian who regularly rode the ten miles to church while living at Mount Vernon. Faithful church attendance continued even while he served as President, unless he was sick or reasonably detained. On those occasions when he was unable to attend church services, he conducted them himself at his home.[11] His diary for an eight month period, for example, between October 1, 1789, and May 9, 1790, shows him attending church twenty-five of thirty-two Sundays plus three other weekly occasions.[12] Some Sundays he attended twice. His personal habit while President was to retire at 9 p.m. each day for prayer and Bible reading. He also would read a sermon or some Biblical passage aloud to the family each Sunday evening.[13]

His Christian character and faith have been praised by various denominations. For example, the General Assembly of the Presbyterian church in the U.S.A. sent a letter to the new President on May 26, 1789, which referred to Washington's Christian reputation as follows:

> We esteem it a peculiar happiness to behold in our Chief Magistrate, a steady, uniform, avowed friend of the Christian religion; who has commenced his administration in rational and exalted sentiments of piety; and who, in his private conduct, adorns the doctrines of the gospel of Christ; and on the most public and solemn occasions, devoutly acknowledges the government of Divine Providence.[14]

Congregational ministers of Connecticut, including Ezra Stiles and James Dana, similarly wrote President Washington in 1789:

> As ministers of the blessed Jesus, the Prince of Peace, we rejoice and have inexpressible pleasure in the demonstrations you have given of your sincere assertion toward that holy religion which is the glory of Christian States, and will become the glory of the world itself . . . . that . . . . the new and rising republic [may] become under your auspices, the most glorious . . and happy administration of government, that ever appeared on earth; and may you, sir, having finished a course of distinguished usefulness, receive the rewards of public virtue in the Kingdom of eternal glory.[15]

Many people recognized and admired Washington's faith and character. It was essential to the success of the Convention. However, as the Convention progressed, Washington's Christian faith would be severely tested. Fortunately for all Americans, his strength of character never broke and God's intervening hand never forsook him.

The Virginia Plan Presented to the Convention

Within four days of the official start of the Convention, delegates from Massachusetts, Maryland, and Connecticut arrived to bring the total number of participating states to ten. There would never be more than eleven state delegations present at any one time during the entire Convention.[16] Of these ten, five delegations were already suspicious of any major changes and resistant to any diminishing of state powers. They wanted to stay within their charter directed by the Continental Congress, comprehensive change was not their idea.

Despite this expected resistance to major change, on Tuesday morning, May 29, Governor Edmond Randolph of Virginia opened the main business of the Convention by presenting what became known as the Virginia Plan.[17] For the next three to four hours, the thirty-three year old governor stood on his feet carefully outlining the nature of and reasons for the proposal.[18] It represented a significant departure from the initial mission of the Convention to modify the Articles of Confederation. The Virginia Plan initially consisted of fifteen separate resolutions for change. In reality, it was a blueprint for a new constitution, with a framework for a national government containing separate legislative, executive, and judicial branches. The Virginia delegation was pushing for a more radical agenda, but they were unsure if the other delegates were ready for it.

Indeed, as first presented, it went much further toward national consolidation of power than the final ratified Constitution would later go.[19] Under the Virginia Plan, the national legislature would be composed of two houses, like those of the states. Members of the lower house would be chosen directly by the people, while members of the upper house would be elected by persons nominated by the state legislatures.[20] Votes in both chambers would be votes of individuals, not of states as was the current practice in the Continental Congress.

The most controversial provision however, was its proposal for representation. The Virginia Plan provided for representation based on state wealth or the number of its free inhabitants. Such a proposal would give Virginia, the most populous state at that time, sixteen representatives and leave Georgia, the least populous state, with only one.[21]

When presented to the Convention, the plan sent an immediate ripple through the delegations in attendance. John Dickinson, a delegate from Delaware, said the plan was "pushing things altogether too far."[22] Other delegates considered it to be far too audacious. George Reed hinted that the Delaware delegation might feel obliged to withdraw from the convention altogether, especially given their concerns on the representation issue.[23]

In order to have any hope of succeeding, the Virginia Plan needed to be voted on issue by issue, and the first was the most critical. Should this Federal Convention abandon their original purpose in meeting, which was merely to fashion amendments to the present Articles of Confederation, or should the Convention abolish the Articles completely and substitute them with a scheme for stronger national government?

On Thursday, May 31, following open debate in the Committee on the Whole the previous day,[24] Washington brought the pivotal proposal to a vote: Resolved "that it is the opinion of this Committee that a national government ought to be established consisting of a supreme Legislative, Judiciary, and Executive."[25] The Virginia delegates had been struggling to convince the other delegates of the merits of this resolution since they arrived. Although this vote would be non-binding, it would determine the early direction of the Convention from which it might never veer away. Thus the outcome of the Convention partially rested on this early pivotal vote.

Some Heavenly Assistance

Had the delegations from Rhode Island and New Hampshire been present, the Virginia Plan would have been dead on arrival, for both delegations opposed the plan. Their absence at this point was probably less coincidental than it was divinely arranged. Yet even in the absence of these two delegations, the Convention expected an evenly split vote between the ten state delegations present. More heavenly assistance would be necessary if this Convention was to provide meaningful change from the greatly disliked Articles of Confederation. The secret nature of the proceedings meant that America's citizens were not aware that, in some respects, the future of their country hung in the balance of this vote. They didn't realize how close the Convention was to failure, nor how close their nation was to complete dissolution through bickering and disunity between the states if a solution could not be produced at the Convention.

Yet God would not let the Convention fail. There were too many faithful believers He had in this fledgling nation who were seeking His aid and blessing on that Convention through prayer. When the vote was taken on the Virginia Plan, the result was completely unforeseen. The anticipated 5 to 5 outcome would have meant defeat. Yet, for no apparent reason, and without any prior indications, the Delaware delegation reversed its opposition to the Plan and voted along with its other proponents.[26] This was a remarkable turn-around from the delegation that had earlier threatened to withdraw from the Convention due to its strong opposition to the Virginia Plan! Additionally, the New Jersey delegation, which was also in opposition to the Virginians, for reasons not stated, lacked a quorum that day, preventing them from voting. Thus, in the first significant vote cast in the Convention, the delegates chose the more ambitious proposal of creating something new rather than revising something old. Although the vote was non-binding from the

Committee of the Whole, it was significant because it lent early legitimacy to the agenda of a new Constitution. God's hand over this Convention was beginning to be noticed.

The Representation Roadblock

The goal of a new Constitution was now set, but it was still tenuous at best, and many problems remained. As the delegates began to discuss a fair means of representation for both large and small states in the new Congress, disagreement and frustration arose. Predictably, the small states wanted an equal vote, as they currently enjoyed in the Continental Congress under the Articles of Confederation. The large states wanted a proportional vote calculated by population or wealth. For three weeks the delegates remained deadlocked on this issue. A major temptation again arose to retreat from their goal of devising an entirely new Constitution. That temptation became concrete on Friday, June 15, when William Paterson of New Jersey presented the Convention with an alternative proposal called the New Jersey Plan. This plan was nothing more than an amendment to the present Articles of Confederation.

The New Jersey Plan provided for a one-branch legislature, a plural executive branch in the form of a council chosen by Congress, and a weakened judiciary with no inferior courts.[27] While it created a few additional federal powers not granted by the Articles of Confederation, it continued to lack an effective enforcement mechanism. Thus, it had the same inherent weakness as the Articles it sought to amend.

The issue before the Convention was again clear: either keep working on the Virginia Plan by creating a whole new federal government system or switch to the New Jersey Plan. As before, the debate was heated, with a tinge of nervousness in the delegates as the scheduled June 19 vote approached. According to Luther Martin, one of the Maryland delegates, "[t]he convention was on the verge of dissolution, scarce held together by the strength of a hair."[28] Once again, the Convention was at a critical juncture, a crossroads between success and failure.

James Madison had previously urged the delegates to work for a constitution that would stand the test of time and be a model for the entire world. He set out for them their challenge, yet how the delegates would respond remained uncertain. The Convention's second pivotal vote in less than three weeks was at hand, and this time Delaware would not be an ally to the cause of a new Federal Constitution. Assistance was desperately needed from some other delegation.

With a marvelous flair for perfect timing, the long detained Georgia delegation finally arrived. Trumpeting cavalry reinforcements could not have been more welcome to the proponents of the Virginia Plan than the sight of the Georgia delegates' arrival in Philadelphia. They were well known supporters of the goal of a stronger national government. With their dramatic and timely arrival, along with another unexpected vote switch by Connecticut, the Virginia Plan once again won support. This time the vote was 7 to 3 with Maryland divided.[29] Two pivotal votes - two divinely orchestrated victories. From this point on, it would be only the Virginia Plan the delegates would work on, giving them a more singular focus. To those involved, it was becoming clearer that more then mere coincidence or good luck was involved in these Convention victories.

The Convention Officially Seeks God's Intervention

Despite these victories, they still had no agreed upon plan for state representation. The delegates pressed forward in their deliberations for nine more days, but the battle lines were drawn. The small states refused to accept a Congress where representatives were seated according to population; it would put them at a distinct disadvantage. Yet the large states refused to yield. They did not favor a system where each state had an equal vote; this would give the small states a type of "veto power" to block initiatives by the large states.

For over a month the delegates wrestled with this issue of representation with no breakthroughs, and now patience was wearing thin; emotions were on edge. A somber George Washington, presiding over the assembly, began to despair of seeing success in this Convention. Tempers were short, consensus was evaporating, and the mood was gloomy. The division between delegations was serious.[30] On June 28, 1787, the Convention was again on the verge of a complete rupture, and with it, our nation's future.

At this juncture, one of the most dramatic moments in the Convention occurred. The oldest delegate in attendance, Dr. Benjamin Franklin, asked for permission to speak. This alone was remarkable. At this point in his life, Franklin was eighty-one years old, with a body weak and infirm. Because of this, he had previously chosen to write out his remarks and have someone else read them. But this time he was stirred to rise and address the delegates himself, in what would be one of the more important speeches in America's early history. As Franklin began to speak, and his words began to filter through that historic Convention Hall, the delegates listened attentively. They knew this great statesman had something that weighed heavily on his heart. They sensed that this was an historic moment. Franklin's words were piercing:

> The small progress we have made after four or five weeks . . . with each other . . . is methinks a melancholy proof of the imperfection of the human understanding. . . . In this situation of this Assembly, groping as it were in the dark to find political truth, and scarce able to distinguish it when presented to us, how has it happened, Sir, that we have not hitherto once thought of humbly applying to the Father of lights to illuminate our understandings?
>
> In the beginning of the contest with Great Britain, when we were sensible of danger, we had daily prayer in this room for the Divine protection. Our prayers, Sir, were heard and they were graciously answered. All of us who were engaged in the struggle must have observed frequent instances of a superintending Providence in our favor. . . . Have we now forgotten that powerful Friend? Or do we imagine we no longer need His assistance?
>
> I have lived, Sir, a long time, and the longer I live, the more convincing proofs I see of this truth: that God governs in the affairs of men. And if a sparrow cannot fall to the ground without his notice, is it probable that an empire can rise without His aid? We have been assured, Sir, in the Sacred Writings that 'except the Lord build the house, they labor in vain that build it (Psalm 127:1).' I firmly believe this, and I also believe that without His concurring aid we shall succeed in this political building no better than the builders of Babel. We shall be divided by our little partial local interests; our projects will be confounded and we ourselves shall become a reproach and bye word down to future ages. I therefore beg leave to move that, henceforth, prayers imploring the assistance of Heaven and its blessing on our deliberation be held in this assembly every morning. . . and that one or more of the clergy of this city be requested to officiate in that service.[31]

His words hit their target with full impact. A delegate from New Jersey, Mr. Dayton, wrote: "The doctor sat down; and never did I behold a countenance at once so dignified and delighted as was that of Washington at the close of the address; nor were the members of the convention generally less affected. The words of the venerable Franklin fell upon our ears with a weight and authority even greater than we may suppose an oracle to have had in the Roman Senate."[32]

While the Christian faithful outside the Convention were steadfastly praying for the success of these men at this important gathering, and some delegates were perhaps doing likewise in private, it took the so-called deist to remind them of their need to publicly seek God's aid. Private prayers are certainly essential, but public prayer uttered by the lips of the participants themselves has an extra significance. It shows the world that these great leaders knew the true source of their success and their recognition that God, not man, is in ultimate control of the destiny of nations and governments.

Franklin's motion contained two parts. The first part, his motion for prayer and a special religious service, was seconded by Mr. Sherman and in effect passed without an official vote. But the second request, to procure the regular services of a clergyman or permanent chaplain, was not acted on because the Convention had no budget for it.[33] Delegate Williamson, being himself a clergyman, pointed out that this was the reason they had initially omitted requesting clergy to officiate in prayer services.[34] However, the sentiment was clearly behind Franklin's thoughts, and a few days later, volunteer clergy were found to lead the Convention delegates in prayer. Although Madison's notes on the Convention do not record a vote on Franklin's motions, the notes of other attending delegates did so. Jonathan Dayton of New Jersey said that "the motion for appointing a chaplain was instantly seconded and carried."[35] Much later Madison said that the matter was sent to a committee. A permanent chaplain was never adopted, but it is certain that prayers began to be held on a volunteer basis by clergymen. Some modern secularists try to argue that the delegates were not favorable to the idea of prayers at the Convention by selectively using Madison's first version of his notes without citing his and other's later comments. But the evidence proves the contrary, that the delegates did indeed respond with religious services and prayers as Benjamin Franklin had requested.

Those prayers made an immediate impact and the delegates noticed a profound difference! While the disagreements remained, their attitudes had significantly changed. According to Mr. Jonathan Dayton, the delegate from New Jersey, "every unfriendly feeling had been expelled; and a spirit of conciliation had been cultivated, which promised, at least, a calm and dispassionate reconsideration" of the representation issue.[36]

It was not coincidental therefore, that on that same day, July 2, then again officially on July 5, Roger Sherman of Connecticut proposed a new idea that would eventually resolve the entire representation dispute. Under the proposal Mr. Sherman presented, the states would be given proportional representation in one branch of the legislature and equal representation in the other. Although the delegates did not immediately recognize the Connecticut proposal as providing their solution, their temporary blindness did not change the reality that a breakthrough was on its way. Like a planted seed that must first germinate before sprouting into view, this new idea would take time to grow and be seen.

Delegate Pressures to Return Home

In the meantime, new problems arose as delegates began to feel pressure to take care of personal business back home. By July 3, many delegates who had neglected their personal business for the two months since the Convention began felt they needed to leave. If they did, the valuable momentum they had gathered would be lost and a re-gathering might never occur. If the delegates left now, in all likelihood, the hope of a new Constitution would be over. George Mason of Virginia tried to urge them to stay, reminding them that "no man here could possibly be hurting financially more than me, but I would rather bury my bones in this city than leave without success!"[37]

It was time to seek God's divine assistance once again. The delegates chose to worship together on July 4, 1787. The entire Convention went as a body to the Reformed Lutheran Church in Philadelphia and heard a sermon by Rev. William Rogers. Following the sermon, Rev. Rogers offered the following prayer on behalf of the convention delegates:

> As this is a period, O Lord, big with events impenetrable by any human scrutiny, we fervently recommend to thy fatherly notice that august body, assembled in this city, who compose our federal convention. Will it please thee, O thou Eternal I Am! O favor them from day to day, with thy inspiring presence; be their wisdom and strength; enable them to devise such measures as may prove happy instruments in healing all divisions and prove the good of the great whole; incline the hearts of all the people to receive with pleasure combined with a determination to carry into execution, whatever these thy servants may wisely recommend; that the United States of America may form one example of a free and virtuous government, which shall be the result of human mutual deliberation, and which shall not, like other governments, whether ancient or modern, spring out of mere chance or be established by force. May we trust in the cheering prospect of being a country delivered from anarchy, and continue under the influence of republican virtue, to partake of all the blessings of cultivated and Christian society.[38]

That prayer stirred many of their hearts and provided renewed vigor for the challenges that faced them. Yet the rift was not over. Within a week, two of the delegates from New York left the Convention, not only in frustration, but also in protest of the whole goal. On that day, one of the officers who had served under Washington saw him coming from the State House and wrote, "The look on his face reminded me of its expression during the terrible months we were in Valley Forge Camp."[39] In a letter to Hamilton that night, July 10, Washington himself wrote, "I almost despair of seeing a favorable issue to the proceedings of the Convention, and do therefore repent having had any agency in the business."[40]

It was a time that called for faith, steadfastness, and prayer. A short adjournment in the proceedings provided them that opportunity. Washington used those few days of adjournment to visit Valley Forge and remember how God had supernaturally provided the Continental army with the food and moral strength to survive. During those dark, bleak months, Washington had sought God earnestly on his knees in prayer, and God did not let him down. Perhaps Washington again called for God's providential intervention in his present period of darkness and despair. To have done so certainly would have been in his character.

The Connecticut Compromise

Washington's supplications, and others like his, were no doubt heard and answered, for two major breakthroughs came. Both involved the earlier proposed Connecticut Compromise. As previously noted, the Connecticut plan called for the House of Representatives to be based on population, thereby representing the interests of the larger states, while the Senate would feature equal representation to better represent the interests of the smaller states. One further safeguard was added,— Senators would not be elected by the people, but rather would be appointed by the state legislatures in order to protect the rights of the states even further. This helped convince those states concerned about giving Congress excessive powers to support the Constitution.

A portion of that compromise, the equality of votes for each state in the Senate, was put to a vote. Eleven state delegations were present. After ten delegations had stood to announce their vote, five states had voted against the Connecticut compromise (Massachusetts, Pennsylvania, Virginia, North Carolina, and South Carolina), and five states had voted in favor of it (Connecticut, New York, New Jersey, Delaware, and Maryland). The last state to vote was Georgia, its vote would determine the outcome. Georgia had four delegates. Two of them voted against the Compromise and another one voted for it. That left Reverend Abraham Baldwin, who was personally opposed to the Compromise. Yet he knew a negative vote by him would "in all probability have broken up the convention."[41] Historian John Fiske captured the drama of the moment:

> His state was the last to vote, and the house was hushed in anxious expectation, when this brave and wise young man yielded his private conviction to what he saw to be the paramount necessity of keeping the convention together.[42]

His vote in favor of the compromise made the Georgia vote a 2-2 nullity and preserved a tie vote on the issue. The result was in favor of the Compromise, since a tie vote was sufficient to refer the issue to a committee to work out the details.

After the committee reported back with a draft in favor of the Compromise, fresh objections arose as the larger, more populous states began to have second thoughts. The Compromise made sense, but a majority of delegates were becoming skeptical again. As the Convention met to decide the issue afresh on July 16, the Compromise appeared headed for certain defeat. It was yet another critical vote.

Once again, a providential event occurred that altered what appeared at the time to be certain defeat. On the day of the vote, Luther Martin, a Maryland delegate, arrived at the Convention. Maryland was prepared to vote against the Connecticut Compromise, but Luther Martin was somehow able to persuade his state delegation to change their vote. Their switch made the difference in the 5 to 4 vote in favor of the compromise plan.[43] What is now known by historians as the "great compromise" can be found in our Constitution in Article I, sections 2 and 3. Perhaps instead, it should be remembered as one of God's many miracles at this Convention.

An ironic twist occurred a few days later. Luther Martin, whom God used to secure that needed victory on the Connecticut Compromise, began to grow increasingly angry as he saw more and more state power transferred to the national government. Ultimately, he left the Convention in disgust, vowing to have nothing more to do with the project.[44] He would become one of the delegates that attended the Convention, yet refused to sign the final version of the Constitution, yet it was his action on the Compromise that enabled the Constitutional Convention to provide that final version.

The Slavery Issue

There was still one big obstacle left to deal with: how to handle the issue of slavery. Although most of the delegates were opposed to the continuance of slavery, the Framers believed that the national government should not be the means for dealing with social and moral problems. They therefore drafted the Constitution in such a way as to delegate no such power to the national government — it was reserved to the state governments, working with the churches.

However, the slavery issue came to the forefront in another context — in the debate on the power of the national government to regulate commerce.

At the time, some states were still importing slaves, and that was a commercial policy that the national government could regulate.

All the state delegations agreed that the importation of slaves should cease. The question was, when? North Carolina, South Carolina, and Georgia felt that their economies were so dependent on slavery that there should be a period of gradual elimination or else they would be financially ruined altogether. Anti-slavery forces were insistent upon a policy of immediate elimination. Moreover, having been joined in convention by the recent arrival of delegates from New Hampshire on July 23, they had the majority to invoke the immediate elimination of the slave trade. Nonetheless, Georgia and the two Carolinas made it clear that if they were required to eliminate slavery immediately, the people in their states probably would not support the Constitution and they would never join the Union.

This idea of disunion was terrifying to the other states. If there was another small nation to their south, the other ten states feared that the European empires could take advantage of it and use it to destroy all of their hard-earned liberty. Madison believed that dismemberment of the Union would be worse than allowing the evil of slavery to continue, for then they would not have the political freedom to deal with the institution at all. Moreover, it was not at all clear whether there would be enough states to ratify whatever constitution they voted on. Losing South Carolina, Georgia, and North Carolina on this issue would likely end any chance of those states ratifying the Constitution. New York and Rhode Island were already known to be bitterly opposed to the Constitution as it was.[45]

Again, a compromise for the sake of holding the nation together, was desperately needed, and again, it was obtained. The anti-slavery delegates agreed to allow the foreign slave trade to continue for another twenty years (until 1808) if the three southern states would agree to allow Congress to regulate commerce by a simple majority of votes.[46] The Union and the Constitution, through this compromise, were again preserved.

Today's criticism of our founding fathers on the issue of slavery should be tempered by certain historical perspectives. First, the consensus of our founders was that slavery was a sin, and that, in the words of James Madison, "[t]he whole Bible is against slavery."[47] If anything, their opposition to slavery was strengthened by their Biblical focus. Second, at the time, slavery was legal in virtually every nation on earth.[48] What the founders achieved in the Constitution is actually quite remarkable — the first government initiated restriction, coupled with a date for complete elimination of the slave trade. That was unprecedented at this point in history. Most of the leading anti-slavery delegates treasured the Constitutional guarantee to abolish the slave trade as the most precious paragraph of the entire document. James Madison, known as the Father of the Constitution, said, "The whole clause . . . ought to be considered as a great point gained in favor of humanity that a period of 20 years may terminate [slavery] forever, within these States."[49] Since slavery had been slowly dying out for nearly fifty years,[50] it was reasonable to expect that this compromise would be kept.

Nonetheless, not all the delegates could accept this compromise. One of them, George Mason of Virginia, did not feel such an accomplishment was enough. He passionately declared that allowing slavery to continue would bring the "judgment of heaven on their country because Providence punishes national sins by national calamities." He further noted that since "nations cannot be rewarded or punished in the next world, they must be in this."[51] He would become another of the Convention delegates that chose not to sign its final document.[52]

Despite the elimination of the slave trade, by the Constitutional provision, ending the slave trade and ending slavery were two different things. One does not necessitate the other, nor did the Founders think it would. Slavery did not actually end until 1808, due in large part to the invention of the cotton gin in 1793 and a moving away from Biblical principles by the people of America. By the 1830's, after all our Founders had passed away, slavery itself began to be justified and defended as moral for the first time. These radical changes from the trends toward abolition existing during the Convention could not possibly have been foreseen at the time of the Convention. Our national sin of slavery cost us the Civil War, a war unlike any other that our nation had ever been or would ever be involved in. More American lives were lost in that war than in any others, greater property destruction occurred to American households, and devastation to the American spirit was wreaked that continues even today. It probably was not a coincidence that Georgia, South Carolina, and North Carolina were the states most devastated by the Civil War, for they were the states that failed to keep their commitment to the spirit of the Constitutional Convention that intended to ultimately end all slavery sometime after the foreign slave trade was stopped.

The Convention Winds Down

With the slavery issue temporarily resolved, the Convention began to finalize its discussions in the months of August and September 1787. At times the Bible was quoted by delegates when they sought answers for their new frame of government. One example occurred in August while they were discussing the qualifications and payments of elected officials in the new national government. Of all people to quote the Bible, it was the man today's scholars widely claim as a deist, Benjamin Franklin, who said: "Remember, the Scripture requires in rulers that they should be men hating covetousness (Exodus 18:21)." Based on this Biblical principle, Franklin urged that the salaries of elected officials not be too high.[53]

The Preamble and final draft of the Constitution was written by Gouverneur Morris of Pennsylvania, and it was presented to the Convention on September 12. As the grand document awaited the delegates' signatures, the elder statesman Franklin pulled out a piece of paper for someone to read to the Convention for him since his voice was so weak. He told them that he did not approve of some parts of the Constitution, but "he was astonished to find it so nearly perfect. Whatever opinion he had of its errors he would sacrifice to the public good, and he hoped that every member of the convention who still had objections would on this occasion doubt a little of his own infallibility, and for the sake of unanimity put his name to this instrument."[54] For the most part, the delegates honored Franklin's request, but three of the members present that day, Governor Randolph, George Mason, and Elbridge Gerry, would continue their refusal to sign.

When the signing of the document was completed, many of the delegates expressed awe at the event. They had been through a lot together. Many probably never imagined they would successfully reach this point. Four months of hot summer toil, which witnessed numerous objections and disagreements that brought the Convention to the verge of dissolution on many occasions, were now completed. It was an enormous accomplishment. Despite the intensity of their disagreements at times, the delegates always maintained an honorable decorum amongst themselves that was, itself, remarkable. Now their seemingly impossible endeavor was completed. The relief of the delegates after such difficult work must have been overwhelming.

But the emotional impact of the moment for one delegate surpassed the feelings of them all. For when Hamilton was not yet born, Madison was just an infant, and Washington was a young lad, Ben Franklin was working to draft the Albany Plan of 1754, the first complete outline of a federal constitution ever made for America.[55] He, more than any other delegate, had spent his energies, hopes, and dreams on bringing the thirteen separate states into one harmonious and working federal union. For him, this day was a culmination of thirty-three years of struggle toward his dream. It is little wonder then, that after placing his signature to that document he had worked so hard for, the grand statesman began to weep. Through his tears of consummate joy,

Franklin pointed to the engraving on the back of Washington's chair, and said: "I have watched that sun on the president's chair and wondered if it was rising or setting — now I am happy to know it is a rising sun!"[56]

Historian John Fiske summed it up well:

> Thus after four months of anxious toil, through the whole of a scorching Philadelphia summer, after earnest but sometimes bitter discussion, in which more than once the meeting had seemed on the point of breaking up, a colossal work had at last been accomplished, the results of which were most powerfully to affect the whole human race so long as it shall dwell upon the earth.[57]

For Ben Franklin and his co-laborers in that historic Convention Hall in Philadelphia, this was a moment they would cherish in their bosoms forever.

THREE

"SUSPENDED BY A THREAD:" The Struggle For Ratification

The federal convention concluded on September 17, 1787, aglow in the satisfaction of having produced a Constitution that was not just completely new, but distinctively unequaled in its framework for preserving liberty. That satisfaction would be fleeting, however, for ahead lay an equally daunting task — convincing a skeptical country to ratify their work.

At this juncture, the mood of the country was much like it was when the convention began. The citizenry was fiercely independent minded, thinking of themselves first as Virginians, Georgians, or New Yorkers, rather than Americans. Strong national government was still something to be feared rather than embraced, and the general public could be expected to be quite skeptical of a document that departed significantly from the governmental structure they had previously had. Unlike the convention delegates who authored this new federal framework, the citizens of the thirteen sovereign states did not have the benefit of daily debates and ponderings to help them digest, bite by bite, the many changes this new document contained.

Considering this climate, the ensuing struggle to ratify the exhausting efforts of the convention delegates could have been monumental, if not overwhelming. The fact that it was not is a testimony to that unseen influence that had been guiding the delegates all along. God had brought them too far at this point to let their labors wither and die on the vine of non-ratification.

For the convention delegates, this must have been a time of extreme apprehension. To them, the proposed Constitution was more than just a document; it was a precious creation born out of a great sacrifice of their time and money. It involved extreme intellectual rigor and entailed a roller coaster of emotional experiences running the full gamut of frustration to hope, hope to despair, and despair to exhilaration, only to be repeated several times over. Sadly, today's history books do not capture the fullness of this commitment. Farm and business enterprises went unattended for months. Families were separated for long periods of time, and the lives of many influential leaders were put on hold. The delegates to the Constitutional Convention were not spoiled, pampered elitists protecting their riches. Quite the contrary. They were committed patriots of their country, willing to make extreme sacrifices for the sake of future liberty in the nation they loved. The actions those delegates took during the summer of 1787 proved far more than any words could say. It is important, therefore, that we understand that this period of presenting their hard work to the state legislatures for approval was more than just a simple moment in history; it was a period filled with anticipation far greater than many of us today can even imagine.

The ratification process was officially initiated on September 20, 1787, only three days after the federal convention concluded, when George Washington presented the Constitution to the Continental Congress.[1] They acted with a promptness not frequently seen in today's legislative bodies. On September 28, a scant eight days after its receipt, Congress voted to allow the Constitution to be submitted to the states for ratification.[2] This first procedural hurdle, a not insignificant one, was passed in little more than one week's time. While such a rapid start was no doubt gratifying to the convention signers, state ratification would prove more difficult and time consuming. Support for the proposed Constitution still needed to be garnered.

Efforts to Obtain Support for the Constitution

Although officially the ratification process started on September 20, unofficially the process had begun five days earlier, when the Convention delegates initiated organizational efforts to persuade the public that the new Constitution should be adopted. A number of delegates went to Noah Webster to ask him to write an essay in support of their plan. He agreed, and two days later produced a 55-page work that our founders disseminated throughout the country to rally support for the Constitution.[3] Additionally, James Madison, Alexander Hamilton, and John Jay began to contribute essays that were published in New York newspapers and eventually compiled to form what became known as *The Federalist Papers*.

These and other efforts were critical in the drive to ratify the Constitution, because the nation as a whole still distrusted centralization of national power. Almost immediately, two rival groups formed to oppose each other in a great and continuing debate to persuade the general public to either accept or reject the Constitution. Supporters of the Constitution were known as federalists, and those who opposed its ratification came to be known simply as the anti-federalists.

While the names of the opposing camps were simple, their debate was not. The arguments on both sides were passionate and well-reasoned. Arguments by the anti-federalists emphasized the fallen, carnal nature of man that could not be trusted to properly handle power exercised in a strong national union provided for under the proposed Constitution. The federalists also acknowledged the sinful nature of man, yet they chose to emphasize the modifying influence of Christian character, virtue, and morality upon the rulers of a nation that delegated limited powers under the Constitution.[4] Whenever government power is to be granted at the national level, a great deal more wisdom and trust is required. The Constitution created a delicate balance of government power in two separate ways: first, horizontally between the three branches of government at the national level, and second, vertically between the national level and that of the state and local governments. This balance can only be preserved by government leaders and citizens who are both virtuous and well informed. Unlike today's debates, both sides on this issue argued from the same world view — one based on Biblical principles!

The debate between the federalists and the anti-federalists was intense, but it was also a divine blessing. It was based on substantive issues and not empty partisan rhetoric, and as such it allowed citizens to carefully consider the crux of the problem before legislative votes were cast. George Washington astutely recognized the importance of this consideration when he wrote: "I doubt whether the opposition to the Constitution will not ultimately be productive of more good than evil....They have given the rights of man a full and fair discussion, and explained them in so clear and forcible a manner, as cannot fail to make a lasting impression."[5] Indeed, even though the federalist perspective would prevail in the ultimate ratification of the Constitution, many of the anti-federalists positions were incorporated into its structures and became a significant part of our heritage. Most notably, the anti-federalists insisted on a Bill of Rights to specify some of the individual liberties that were protected by the Constitution. That addition brought a balance of both Biblical perspectives into the Constitution.

Until this solution of a Bill of Rights was reached, however, the passion and eloquence of the anti-federalists posed a grave threat to the possibility of ratification. The group was led by the three convention delegates who refused to sign the Constitution, and they were joined in their opposition by such influential leaders as Samuel Adams, John Hancock, and Patrick Henry. These were forceful leaders whose opinions carried great weight. Their conclusions respecting the Constitution are therefore quite interesting. For example, when the famous orator, Patrick Henry, read the Constitution, he said that he feared it would enslave them again.[6] Delegate John Lansing of New York described it as a "triple-headed monster, as deep and wicked a conspiracy as ever invented in the darkest ages against the liberties of a free people."[7] These were strong comments made by intelligent and highly re-spected leaders of the day, and they could easily have brought the newly proposed government to an abrupt end.

The State Ratification Process Commences

Given the persuasiveness of the opposition, the odds for ratification by the various state legislatures appeared dismal. Nonetheless, the country faced a pressing problem; the current national government was inept and falling apart. The need for ratification of some alternative to the status quo was desperate. Washington captured the dramatic intensity of their present predicament. In December, 1787, he warned that the "[g]eneral government is now suspended by a thread; I might go further, and say it is really at an end; and what will be the consequence . . . is not in my judgment and the gift of prophecy to predict."[8]

This was the setting as the states, one by one, began to convene their legislative conventions to consider this historic matter. It was only fitting that Pennsylvania, host to the Constitutional Convention in Philadelphia, would be the first to consider ratification. They wasted no time. Their con-vention convened on September 28, the same day Congress voted to send the matter to the states. Yet convening their legislative body was the easy part for the Pennsylvanians. The debate over ratifying the Constitution grew quite rancorous in the city of brotherly love.[9] At one point, filibustering tac-tics kept the Pennsylvania State convention sitting for nearly three weeks, accomplishing nothing. October and November passed with little progress made. Although the first state to convene their legislature, Pennsylvania was about to lose the distinction of being the first state to ratify the Constitution.

Sure enough, while debate raged in the halls of the Pennsylvania state house, news arrived that Delaware had become the first state to ratify the Constitution, on December 6, 1787. They did so in overwhelming style — without a single dissenting vote![10] That news broke the logjam in Philadel-phia. On December 12, 1787, Pennsylvania became the second state to ratify, by a 46 to 23 vote.[11] The momentum continued in New Jersey when its convention ratified on December 18, only one week after assembling their convention.[12] Thus, by Christmas, 1787, one-third of the necessary nine states needed had already ratified the Constitution. This early momentum continued into the new year with Georgia becoming the fourth state to ratify, on January 2, 1788. Their legislative body joined that of Delaware by being the second state to ratify without a dissenting vote.[13] Connecticut was next to ratify one week later, by a vote of 128–40.[14]

As the news of each state delegation's vote was reported, the drama mounted. Everyone knew that the Constitutional Convention had determined the need for nine states to ratify before the new Constitution became effective. Five states had done so thus far, and the subject was no doubt on the lips of many as the people met in the shops, taverns, and various street corners throughout America. Nearly everyone was aware of which delegations had voted, which were meeting, and which were about to meet. The excitement was building.

Up next was Massachusetts, which convened their convention on January 9, 1788. Street corner talk turned to the ratification chances in the state many believed birthed the revolution. However, most people knew the outlook there was not encouraging. Of all the existing thirteen states, none had a greater devotion to states' rights, local control and self-government than Massachusetts. It was there that the town meeting concept flourished, at the heart of the early revolution days. They, perhaps more than most, believed that people should be allowed to manage their own affairs and not have those affairs run by outsiders. They had borne the brunt of government oppression during the years prior to the revolution; they were well aware of the dangers of a strong central government. To many leaders in Massachusetts, the proposed Constitution had given too many powers to a national government far removed from their local concerns. As expected, therefore, the convention debate was thorough and arduous. Chief among the objections was the fact that the proposed Constitution did not contain a Bill of Rights, a concern raised by the anti-federalists and shared by many other states. Clearly, without such a document, Massachusetts was not going to ratify the Constitution; the anti-federalist position was too strong and persuasive on this point. So as a matter of compromise, proponents of the Constitution offered to allow the Massachusetts legislature to propose a Bill of Rights to Congress upon the final presentation of the Constitution after ratification. This compromise worked. Once a Bill of Rights was proposed, support for the Constitution immediately grew. On February 6, 1788, Massachusetts became the sixth state to ratify, by a vote of 187 to 168.[15]

The New Hampshire convention was the next to assemble, but after a brief debate, they decided to adjourn until June to see how the other states would act. With adjournment in New Hampshire, national attention shifted to the state of Maryland, which gathered in April. After a five day convention, the Maryland legislature voted to ratify on April 28, by a vote of 63 to 11.[16] South Carolina was the next state to convene their legislature, and thanks to the slave trade compromise worked out at the Constitutional Convention, the outcome here was not in serious doubt. South Carolina became the eighth state to ratify on May 23, by a vote of 149 to 73.[17]

The stage was now set for the ninth state to have the distinction of making the Constitution official. The spotlight now turned to the state of Virginia, which was next to convene their convention on June 2. Virginia, which played an instrumental, if not leading role in the Constitutional Convention in Philadelphia, now had a chance to make history again. This time, however, it wasn't to be. Largely as a result of the persuasive abilities of such leading anti-federalists as Patrick Henry, George Mason, Benjamin Harrison, and John Tyler, the Virginia convention was stormy and intense. The debate raged for over three weeks, and during that time Virginia lost its opportunity to become the ninth ratifying state. That distinction went to New Hampshire on June 21, 1788, which after only five days in session voted 57 to 46 to ratify the Constitution.[18] Virginia followed shortly thereafter on June 25, but the narrow vote margin of 89 to 79 reveals the struggle that went on in that convention.[19] Turning the tide in Virginia was not easy against the likes of such eloquent men as Patrick Henry and George Mason, but there arose one man who was even more persuasive. At the age of thirty-three, and already the foremost lawyer in Virginia, John Marshall, who would later become Chief Justice of the Supreme Court, was "conspicuous in the ranks of the Federalists, and unsurpassed in debate."[20] The quality and tenacity of debate at Richmond must have been awesome to hear.

In New York, the debate was perhaps as intense, as in Virginia, if not more so. The state convention met on June 17, with over two-thirds of its delegates being avowed anti-federalists! They were led by their Governor, George Clinton, along with Melanchthon Smith, "one of the ablest debaters in the country."[21] On the other side of the issue stood Alexander Hamilton, hardly a light-weight when it came to persuasive political skills. Yet this fight would take every skill and more for Hamilton to succeed.

> When it came to defending the Constitution before the hostile convention at Poughkeepsie, he had before him as arduous a task as ever fell to the lot of a parliamentary debater. It was a case where political management was out of the question. The opposition were too numerous to be silenced, or

cajoled, or bargained with. They must be converted. With an eloquence scarcely equaled before or since in America until Webster's voice was heard, Hamilton argued week after week, till at last Melanchthon Smith, the foremost debater of Clinton's party, broke away, and came to the Federalist side. It was like crushing the center of a hostile army. After this the anti-federalist forces were confused and easily routed.[22]

Nonetheless, on July 26, 1788, New York voted by the thinnest of margins (30 to 27) to ratify. It was a huge victory for the federalists, for which Hamilton deserved most of the credit.

That left only North Carolina and Rhode Island on the national sidelines. Those two states did not join the union until after the first constitutional government was already in operation. North Carolina voted to join on November 21, 1789, and Rhode Island stubbornly waited until May 29, 1790.[23]

The Positive Influence of Religion

The church played a prominent role in the ratification of our Constitution. More than fifty clergy of a variety of denominations were active in the state ratifying conventions. Twenty clergy served as delegates in Massachusetts alone, where the debate was so intense, with one of those urging ratification on the grounds that this "union" was the rock of their national "salvation."[24]

The evidence of religious influence on the outcome of this great act of history was everywhere. From his pulpit in Connecticut, Reverend William Samuel Johnson told his congregation that the system of government designed by the Constitution, which as a delegate in Philadelphia he helped frame, showed the signs of God's intervention. Following the giddy celebration when the vote to ratify was announced in South Carolina, one of their elder statesmen, Christopher Gadsden, declared, "I shall say with good old Simeon [when he saw the Christ child brought into the Temple], 'Lord, now Thou Thy servant depart in peace, for mine eyes have seen the salvation of my country."[25]

Opposition leaders in the major states of New York and Virginia delayed ratification in hopes of killing it, and Rhode Island would have never called a convention if the Senate had not threatened to treat them like a foreign nation two years after the Constitution was in effect. Even then, Rhode Island only passed the resolution to ratify by a vote of 34 to 32; a switch of only one vote would have kept Rhode Island out of the United States! Truly, the effort of ratification had been monumental, but based on some of the eyewitness accounts, it was even more; it was providential.

Reflections

Just prior to the official ratification of the Constitution by the ninth state, New Hampshire, George Washington was overwhelmed by the clarity of God's supernatural intervention in the entire process of our Constitution's birth. He couldn't help summing up the whole process by again referring to the hand of God:

> Should everything proceed as we anticipate, it will be so much beyond anything we had a right to imagine or expect 18 months ago that it will demonstrate the finger of Providence in human affairs greater than any event in history.[26]

As news from New Hampshire's historic June 21, 1788, vote to become the ninth state to ratify the Constitution reached the little towns and villages across America, emotions must have run high. While other states had yet to ratify, the outcome was final, the verdict sure. What started out as a simple meeting to amend the Articles of Confederation had concluded with great fanfare, hopes, and high expectations.

For the participants of that historic Constitutional Convention, the news of what occurred on June 21, 1788, must have brought about a day of thorough reflection on what had transpired. Many of those delegates were well aware that the credit was not theirs to claim, for no group of men on their own could have accomplished so much with so little. The authors of our Constitution knew better than anyone else just how great their own shortcomings were and how close and frequently they came to failure. They recalled all too well the numerous times at which they reached the precipice of collapse, only to experience an unlikely turn of events. They witnessed state delegations arrive at the last minute to change an expected outcome; they witnessed a delegate change his mind at the last minute to alter a vote; and they felt first hand the change in attitude after they commenced their sessions with prayer at the urging of Mr. Franklin. They knew, better than anyone else, that their efforts to find accord on a new Constitution were aided by an invisible hand and force stronger and mightier than they. Is it any wonder that this same Constitution would stand as a model to the world for over 200 years?

As the sun set on that momentous day when they heard the news, as the sounds of celebrants' revelry began to fade in the distance, and as the flickering light of candles began to light up their rooms in the growing darkness of evening, the bright and shining image of God's intervening hand was no doubt burning brightly in their minds.

FOUR

"TRACING THE FINGER OF PROVIDENCE:" Evidence of God's Assistance

When Americans travel overseas, they are constantly reminded of how comparatively young their country is. With a little less than 230 years as a nation, the age of the United States pales in comparison to European and Asian nations of far longer ancestry. Yet despite America's youth among the nations of the world, it is America that has the oldest written constitution still in effect today.[1] It is America's constitution that many other nations look to and seek to emulate.

William Gladstone, one of Britain's great Prime Ministers, described America's Constitution as "the most wonderful work ever struck off at a given time by the brain and purpose of man."[2] William Pitt, the great English Parliamentarian, noted that "[i]t will be the wonder and admiration of all future generations, and the model of all future constitutions."[3] The first Prime Minister of Canada, Sir John A. MacDonald, said, "[I]t is one of the most perfect organizations that ever governed a free people."[4] Noted American historian John Fiske called the Constitution the "Iliad, or Parthenon, or Fifth Symphony of statesmanship."[5] The great scholars and legal minds of the past two centuries have continued to marvel that it is "almost beyond the scope and dimension of human wisdom."[6] America's founders believed human wisdom was not an adequate explanation. Nothing like it has been produced before or since despite the efforts of numerous men of high stature and brilliance. Even as talented a group as that which authored America's Constitution knew that the greatness of their finished product did not stem from their human efforts alone. They had help, and lots of it.

Coincidence or Divine Assistance?

As we read through the historical events which comprised the activity leading up to the Constitutional Convention, the stormy Convention itself, and the subsequent ratification process, we see an amazing number of events that can only be explained in one of two ways: (1) either they were the result of luck or coincidence, or (2) they were divinely directed by a God who is sovereign over all of history. That is a choice that makes many people uncomfortable, especially scholars.

Secular scholars, unwilling to even consider the possibility of a supernatural source for an historical event, traditionally insist on the first explanation. Due to their refusal to accept a supernatural explanation, they automatically exclude such a possibility, without any examination. But for those of us who are willing to pursue the path of truth wherever intellectual probing might lead, luck and coincidence are unsatisfactory explanations. In fact, if scholars were completely honest, they would admit the obvious — that the terms "luck" and "coincidence" are not explanations at all, but mere words of convenience we use as labels when we don't know the cause of an event.

Yet, however inappropriate "luck" and "coincidence" are as legitimate explanatory terms, to the extent we use those terms, we find that they are only adequate to describe something that is both erratic and of a short-term sequence. What happened at Philadelphia in 1787 was neither erratic nor short term. Each amazing "coincidence" built on a prior one, consistently helping to preserve the Convention, preserve the goal of a new Constitution, provide consensus, and ultimately lead to successful ratification. The cumulative nature and consistent direction of these unexplainable circumstances constitute a legitimate and reasonable basis to conclude that each "coincidence" was linked together by an intelligent being directing the process towards a particular result. To America's founders there were simply too many events that fell together in time and manner for them to be attributed to mere luck or coincidence.

Most, if not all, secular scholars will stubbornly insist, despite any amount of evidence to the contrary, that a finding of a supernatural source is never "scholarship," but "faith." Yet those same scholars are willing to conclude that an event was produced by luck or coincidence based upon nothing more than faith themselves — a faith that the supernatural does not exist, or a faith that any supernatural being that does exist, does not intervene in history. Both are conclusions of faith. The key question, then, is whether the faith we exercise is "blind faith" where we refuse to consider any other possibility, or faith based on objective scholarship and reason. Remember, "luck" is a term we use only when we don't know the real explanation. Therefore, saying that luck is responsible for the amazing sequence of events is really an admission that we don't know the explanation. We think it is time to at least be willing to examine the other alternative.

Perhaps it would be more understandable to conclude an event was the product of mere chance or luck if it was an isolated event, or limited to only two or three component events, similar to several rolls of dice coming up the same number on occasion. Yet it defies reason and experience to continue to identify luck as the basis for a large number of consecutive rolls of the dice producing the identical number. A person would be either extremely naïve or outright foolish not to suspect an intervening agent at work that is controlling the rolls of the dice were he or she to roll the identical number more than two or three times in a row. At some point it becomes clear that an explanation other than luck is in order, and an allegation of "loaded" dice is appropriate. Of course, an allegation of "loaded" dice is premised on the belief in an intervening agent at work.

The same concept applies equally to events in history. How many "coincidences" does it take before honest scholarship demands another answer? How many blind chances, all leading to a consistent result, does it take before it becomes clear that an intelligent being is directing the events? The events surrounding America's Constitution point logically and rationally to a cause beyond the luck of the participants.

A Unique Historical Examination

While we certainly do not rule out the existence of prior examinations, we are unaware of any prior efforts to review the various events surrounding the Constitution to determine the extent to which luck or divine providence was involved in producing them. Any such effort is, of course, subjective in nature and cannot provide a definitive answer until such time as God chooses to let us know. Moreover, we certainly do not claim any special insight into this process other than what comes from a careful review of the facts and an application of reason and experience to those facts. But the question of whether the U.S. Constitution is a product of coincidence or divine intervention is critical to a proper understanding of its provisions, its application, and its interpretation. We should therefore be willing to apply common sense reasoning skills, along with our experience, to the events of the Convention and honestly ask ourselves if the events and result seem to be the product of blind chance or if they were more likely directed by an intelligent being for a particular purpose.

Keep in mind, however, that a conclusion either way requires an exercise of faith. Faith, after all, is not limited to a belief in God. It also entails a belief in anything, including faith in one's own human reasoning. Faith, in a nutshell, arises whenever someone puts hope and trust in something. It is the "assent of the mind to the truth of a proposition advanced by another."[7] Atheism requires faith that there is no God and that people are their own gods. Humanism requires faith in the reasoning skills of man. Therefore, secular scholars who conclude that the events of the Constitutional Convention of 1787 were all a product of luck or coincidence are exercising a degree of faith just as much as those who conclude the events were the product of an omnipotent, intelligent creator.

Secular scholars have, for too long, tried to sell us a false "bill of goods"- namely, that the choice is between a secularists' objective view based on facts versus a subjective view based on religious feelings and blind faith. Such a framing of the choice implies that the secularist view is inherently based on "reality" and a religious view of the facts is inherently based in unreality. Secularists have therefore attempted to marginalize the religious perspective based on a false premise that only by eliminating God from the perspective can you find reality. The truth is actually just the opposite. Elimination of God and His principles from one's perspective leads to a false "reality" and, with it, false conclusions. The issue is not whether we are exercising faith in reaching our conclusion, but whether the faith we are exercising is reasonable and based on the facts.

One final note before we start this most unusual review. Each event, if taken out of context and viewed in isolation, could be more easily attributed to luck or coincidence than when the event is kept in the context of all the other events in which it was part. This would be akin to analyzing one roll of the dice in isolation from the 10 rolls that preceded or followed it. The events must be viewed in context, as a whole, the way they occurred. With those words of caution in mind, let's examine the events leading up to and through the Constitutional Convention. See for yourself what we mean by an apparent outside influence seeming to direct the events for a particular result. In doing so, we urge you to be open to a supernatural option if the facts reasonably suggest it.

Coincidence or Supernaturally Directed?

Our analysis will artificially confine itself only to the events surrounding the Constitutional Convention of 1787. However, it should be recognized that in doing so, we are eliminating many other relevant instances of chance or divine intervention that would add further context. The most obvious of these other relevant instances is the very improbable victory of independence the colonies obtained over the world's greatest military power of the day. Before any talk of a Constitutional Convention could occur, the tiny, financially struggling colonies had to figure out how to defeat Great Britain in war. It is hard for people today to understand what a daunting task that was. At the time, Britain was the world's greatest and most formidable military power. The struggle for American independence included numerous instances of either great luck or interventions by God to even continue the fight for as long as it lasted. In the words of Chief Justice John Jay, one of our founding fathers and author of several of *The Federalist Papers*, God's hand was quite clear.

Will it not appear extraordinary that thirteen colonies, the object of their wicked designs, divided by variety of governments and manners, should immediately become one people, and though without funds, without magazines, without disciplined troops, in the face of their enemies, unanimously determine to be free, and, undaunted by the power of Britain, refer their cause to the justice of the Almighty, and resolve to repel force by force, thereby presenting to the world an illustrious example of magnanimity and virtue scarcely to be paralleled? Will it not be a matter of doubt and wonder, that notwithstanding these difficulties, they should raise armies, establish funds, carry on commerce, grow rich by the spoils of their enemies, and bid defiance to the armies of Britain, the mercenaries of Germany, and the savages of the wilderness? But, however incredible these things may in the future appear, we know them to be true; and we should always remember that the many remarkable and unexpected means and events by which our wants have been supplied and our enemies repelled or restrained, are such strong proofs of the interposition of Heaven, that our having been hitherto delivered from the threatened bondage of Britain ought, like the emancipation of the Jews from Egyptian servitude, to be forever ascribed to its true cause; and instead of swelling our breasts with arrogant ideas of our own powers and importance, kindle in them a flame of gratitude and piety which may consume all remains of vice and irreligion.[8]

Many skeptical scholars today like to point to factors that made England's defeat by the American colonists an "expected" outcome having nothing to do with divine intervention. One such factor was England's adversarial relationship with France, which precluded the deployment of sufficient troops to quell the American threat. While such factors should be considered, how many of those scholars would have nonetheless wagered large amounts of cash before the war on an American victory? Of course we will never know, but our suspicion is that, had they had the opportunity, the number of people wagering on an American victory prior to the war would have been very few, if any. Why? Because even despite those factors, final colonial victory over the British was still too improbable to be ascribed to anything other than God's guiding hand of providence.

Now let us consider the events surrounding the Constitutional Convention. The first factor, or roll of the dice to consider in dealing with the Constitutional Convention is the strong lack of agreement, if not outright opposition from the state legislatures for the need to hold such a Convention. Proposals for a convention were not new; they had been made before and all had failed to "break through the crust of a truly English conservatism and dread of centralized power."[9] Indeed, according to historian George Bancroft, between 1643 and 1776, there had been at least fifty separate attempts to unify the colonies under one central government, and every one had failed![10] That they succeeded in assembling together at all was quite remarkable considering that "[a]t no time in this distressed period would a frank and abrupt proposal for a convention to remodel the government have found favour."[11] Add to this attitude the further facts that the state legislatures were disorganized and most had insufficient money to pay to send a delegate to represent them. Delegates who went from many states had to do so in a volunteer capacity, with no hope of financial reimbursement of the substantial expenses of staying in a far off city for months at a time. Therefore, to have brought together a group of any kind to discuss the issue was remarkable. To have brought together delegates from all but one state, considering the lack of agreement on the need and a clear lack of money to fund it, was nothing short of having the roll of the dice come up "snake eyes".

A second factor, or roll of the dice, was the unbelievably high quality of the delegates that did participate in the Constitutional Convention. It is not an easy task to convince the nation's best leaders to gather far from home and for long periods of time. The four- month time frame, during which the Convention met, from mid-May through mid-September, was a considerable portion of the year, covering both planting and harvest time. The selected delegates were busy men with other more needful and likely more lucrative pursuits that demanded their time. Breaking away for months at a time was asking a lot from these men. They were not required to attend the Convention, they did so because they chose to. Therefore, luck might explain the attendance of one or two great leaders, but no more, especially given the lack of financial remuneration they could expect for their sacrifice. Yet, despite all these factors that should have deterred the participation of high quality delegates, the gentlemen who met in Philadelphia in the spring of 1787 were some of the strongest, most experienced leaders this nation had at the time. Indeed, the delegates that attended the Constitutional Convention were arguably of such a high leadership quality that their likes have not been seen in this nation since. The unique qualities of the delegates were instrumental in reaching a successful conclusion to their endeavor. Even today, with our seemingly high educational standards and government experience, it would be difficult, if not impossible absent God's assistance, to assemble a body of delegates with the credentials and abilities to draft such a Constitution as we had in 1787. The delegates of 1787 were far better read on constitutional principles and had far more solid Biblical knowledge than our leaders of today. Was it just good luck that America had so many qualified leaders alive and able to serve at the same time as its nation needed them, or might God have provided this body of great leaders for such a special time? This is the second factor we have considered, yet already it appears that the dice have come up snake eyes again. Reason and experience should tell us that we should be getting suspicious of the dice.

A third factor to consider was the lack of consensus amongst the delegates once they arrived at the Convention as to their objective. There were bitter divisions and rivalries between the states. Most of them came only to revise, not throw out, the Articles of Confederation. Yet on arrival, they were met with the Virginia delegation's radical plan to start from scratch! It was more than good fortune that kept those delegates from leaving and going back home. Even after the Convention chose to proceed with a new constitutional framework, they had difficulty agreeing on the framework. It has been described as the "stormiest convention ever held on American soil."[12] Agreement on a document so significant by such a group at such a time was only possible by the ever-present hand of God Almighty. His fingerprints are all over that convention hall and, likewise, on the document itself.

A fourth factor was the unexpected ten-day delay of the Convention while the arriving delegates awaited a quorum. The Convention was due to begin May 14, 1787, but didn't start until May 25. This was one of those occasions when a delay was clearly beneficial, yet beyond the control of the delegates. The Virginia delegation needed more time to advocate and prepare their plan for an entirely new Constitution, yet had no way of obtaining that extra time, nor control over when the other delegates would arrive. Nonetheless, they received the needed delay. Was that also good luck? Those extra ten days gave the Virginia delegates the necessary time they needed to cultivate friendships and trust they would need to convince the Convention to seek a whole new Constitution. Their grand scheme needed extra time to massage into the hearts of the arriving delegates. Either this was yet another instance of the dice coming up snake eyes, or it was another instance of God directing the events to accomplish His larger purpose.

A fifth factor, separate from convincing so many states to participate in general, was obtaining enough individual delegates to attend for a quorum to exist, allowing the Convention to commence. Recall that the Convention proponents had substantial difficulties convincing the delegates to meet in the first place, let alone in sufficient numbers to reach a quorum. As noted earlier, most of the states were in financial difficulty during this time, so there was insufficient money to send delegates to Philadelphia to represent their interests. Indeed, Rhode Island refused to even send a delegation. The fact that a quorum of Convention delegates arrived at all with sufficient finances for the trip and to stay for its four-month duration was either quite lucky or divinely directed.

A sixth factor, or roll of the dice, was the perfect timing of the Convention for the purposes of fostering success. We previously mentioned that, had the convention tried to meet five years earlier, it would have been premature. The fledgling confederation would not yet have been convinced of their need to have a stronger federal government. Had they met much later than they did, the events of the bloody anarchy of the French Revolution a few years later would have frightened the Americans away from large scale change in their government. The fact the Convention proponents sought to meet in 1787, as opposed to 1782 or 1792, was instrumental to its success. Another lucky roll of the dice?

The seventh factor was the timely absence of the particular delegations known to be opposed to a new Constitution during the key vote to seek a complete revision rather than merely amend the Articles of Confederation. The delegations of Rhode Island, which chose not to come at all, and New Hampshire were both absent when the pivotal vote arose on May 30. The presence of those two delegations, would have prevented any action other than inconsequential changes to the Articles of Confederation. Had that been the case, the Philadelphia Convention of 1787 would have been of no historical significance. Was it luck that kept these two delegations away when the vote was taken? This is the seventh time in a row the dice have come up "snake eyes." Reason and experience should tell us that such an occurrence does not happen by mere "luck."

The eighth factor, or roll of the dice, was the fact that the Delaware delegation completely changed their position for the critical May 30 vote. This unexpected and unexplained reversal of their earlier opposition to a new Constitution brought their vote into the column of the Constitutionalists. No one would have predicted that vote. To have a complete position change by an entire delegation in such a short time was, to this point, unheard. Was this shocking vote change also attributable to luck, or was it ordained by heaven?

A ninth factor was the timely arrival of the Georgia delegation just before the June 19, 1787 vote on the New Jersey plan that helped save the dream of the Constitutionalists. Remember that the New Jersey plan gave the Convention delegates another opportunity to scrap the idea of drafting an entirely new Constitution and provide for amendments to the Articles of Confederation. It was a second bite at the apple for the opponents of a Constitution; it was the easier route to take, and the Continental Congress sanctioned it. The Georgia delegation supported the new Constitution option, but they were very late in arriving at the convention. Their timely arrival for the June 19 vote could be seen by a skeptic as another instance of coincidence or luck, but when combined with all the other apparent instances of luck, it becomes more unreasonable to draw that conclusion. The dice are coming up with the same number too many times.

That June 19 vote also produced a tenth factor to consider in this analysis- a second delegation vote contrary to their stated position. The views of the Connecticut delegation against the new Constitution were strongly held and well-known. Yet, when it came time for Connecticut to cast its vote, another unexpected event occurred. They chose to vote in favor of the new Constitution, and against their stated opposition to it! This was an unbelievable occurrence that no one could have predicted. If all this was merely luck, then luck had a remarkable ability to control itself on a consistent path towards a Constitution!

An eleventh factor was the vote of a convention delegate contrary to his personal viewpoint. During the initial Connecticut Compromise vote, Abraham Baldwin voted contrary to his own position. Knowing that a negative vote by him would likely have terminated the Convention in failure, he chose to vote for the Connecticut Compromise, a compromise he opposed! Again, this was an unexpected occurrence. Was it just another coincidence?

A twelfth factor was the vote switch by the Maryland delegation on the Connecticut Compromise. During the second vote on the Compromise, an opponent of it actually convinced his delegation to vote in favor of the compromise. The effect was to again save the Convention's hope of creating a new Constitution. Despite the known opposition to a new Constitution by the Maryland delegation, one of its delegates, Luther Martin, was able to persuade them to change their vote. That vote switch was the difference in the outcome. Ironically, that vote switch was the work of a delegate who would later refuse to work on or sign the Constitution. Only a few days after persuading Maryland to change its vote, Luther Martin left the Convention for good in disgust at the direction in which it was heading. It is hard to understand how a man so opposed to the idea of the Constitution would play such an instrumental role in ensuring its survival during the tense days of the Convention. Were Luther Martin's efforts and the changed vote of the Maryland delegation another episode in an amazing string of good luck? Reason and experience cry out for another explanation. The only other explanation available is that of divine intervention. Good scholarship demands it be strongly considered at the very least.

A thirteenth factor was how a Convention quorum was maintained through the entire four-month period of the deliberations. Throughout that summer, each day brought greater pressure upon the land owning delegates to leave the Convention to help oversee the harvesting of their crops. Many of the delegates were landowners, and the harvest season was critical to the well-being of their families. Each day the delegates chose to stay in Philadelphia working on the Constitution was another "lucky" day for the Constitutionalists. Perhaps more accurately, it was another instance of divine intervention.

There were at least thirteen factors, or thirteen rolls of the dice, dealing directly with the Constitutional Convention itself that were either attributable to luck or to God's supernatural intervention. To conclude that all these factors were the result of mere coincidence is equivalent to believing that a person could roll the dice thirteen times in a row and have the dice stop on the same number every single time! To believe that it is mere good luck not only requires more faith than to believe the events were directed by the hand of God, it also requires unreasonable faith! Thirteen rolls of the dice coming up the same number does not happen without an intervening cause directing such a result. The cumulative nature and consistent direction of these unexplainable circumstances surrounding the Convention clearly constitute a legitimate and reasonable basis to conclude that each "coincidence" was linked together by an intelligent being directing the process towards a particular result.

The Participants Recognize God's Intervention

Not only does a supernatural explanation for these unexpected events coincide with common experience, it is also consistent with the accounts of the participants themselves. The Framers of the Constitution unabashedly declared that the forming of that document was a miracle of God. Dr. Franklin, the least orthodox of them all, wrote:

> Our General Convention . . . when it formed the new Federal Constitution, [was] . . . influenced, guided, and governed by that omnipotent and beneficent Ruler in whom all . . . live, and move, and have their being.[13]

God's intervention in this historical event was also clear to James Madison. In a letter to Thomas Jefferson just a few weeks after the Convention, he said, "[I]t is impossible to conceive the degree of concord which ultimately prevailed, as less than a miracle."[14] Later Madison would write, "[I]t is impossible for the man of pious reflection not to perceive in it [the Constitutional Convention] a finger of that Almighty hand . . ."[15]

Alexander Hamilton also echoed their opinions when he described, shortly after the Convention, the source of the new frame of government they created in this manner: "For my own part, I sincerely esteem it a system which without the finger of God, never could have been suggested and agreed upon by such a diversity of interests."[16] He too was aware of the great obstacles they overcame just to join together at a Constitutional Convention and the innumerable events that could be reasonably explained no other way.

Perhaps the greatest affirmation of this sentiment, however, came from the most influential of all the framers of the Constitution — George Washington. In a letter to his good friend, Governor Jonathan Trumbull of Connecticut, he wrote that the "adoption of the proposed General Government" disposed him to be of the opinion "that miracles have not ceased." For, he said, one could:

> trace the finger of Providence through those dark and mysterious events, . . . which first induced the States to appoint a general Convention and then led them one after another . . . into an adoption of the system recommended by that general Convention.[17]

Although not a direct eyewitness at the Constitutional Convention, Benjamin Rush, a signer of the Declaration of Independence, and certainly a very interested and close observer of the events at Carpenter Hall in 1787, echoed Washington's sentiments on the miraculous nature of the event.

I do not believe that the Constitution was the offspring of inspiration, but I am as perfectly satisfied that the Union of the States in its form and adoption is as much the work of a Divine Providence as any of the miracles recorded in the Old and New Testament.[18]

We should not lightly consider these opinions of the eyewitness participants in this historic event. Such opinions should always carry greater weight as evidence of what occurred than the opinion of those who were not present at the event. The opinions of Ben Franklin, James Madison, Alexander Hamilton, and George Washington are thus deserving of great weight, especially since they coincide with what reason and experience would conclude. Their rational abilities and opinions on all other issues have been recognized, admired, and given great weight, even by secular scholars. Yet, on no other basis than their own refusal to accept divine intervention as possible, secular scholars dismiss the Founders' opinions as to the Providential interventions in the event they witnessed and participated in.

The Secret to Our Constitution's Success

The secret to the great success of our Constitution is not in ourselves. Man's genius exists throughout the world and has been present at the writing of every national constitution. Yet America's Constitution was different in two respects. First, it was purposefully based upon Biblical principles, not the least of which that it took into account what the Puritans called "the utter depravity of man."[19] But America's Constitution is different for a second reason. It was written by men who earnestly sought God's help, who publicly acknowledged it when it was given, and then gave thanks to God for His blessed intervention. As a result, God chose to bless their efforts over that of all others, and now one of the youngest members in the community of nations, America, possesses the world's oldest continually existing written constitution. In the following chapters, we will explore in greater detail the Biblical and Christian foundation upon which our Constitution rests.

FIVE

"RELIGION...SHALL FOREVER BE ENCOURAGED:" The Indispensable Basis of the Early American Republic

Bells rang from churches throughout the city. They heralded the end of the work of the Constitutional Convention and the beginning of putting the document into action. It was truly an historic moment. The people of New York had gathered in their respective church congregations and began to pray for God to bless this wondrous occasion. Flyers posted on all the major streets and buildings announced the event with a focus peculiar to Americans today.

> . . . On the morning of the day on which our illustrious President will be invested with his office, the bells will ring at nine o'clock, when the people may go up and in a solemn manner commit the new Government, with its important train of consequences, to the holy protection and blessings of the Most High.

Consistent with this announcement, our first president took the oath of office with his hand on a Bible opened to Deuteronomy, chapter 28. That passage of Scripture is particularly appropriate since it promises blessings or curses on a nation according to its faithfulness in keeping God's Word. At the conclusion of his oath, George Washington added the words, "So help me God" and leaned over and kissed the Bible. Since that day, every president thereafter has repeated this same appeal to God,[1] but our first president was not finished appealing to God on this momentous day in our nation's history. His inaugural address to Congress reflects this man's deep faith and integrity:

> It would be peculiarly improper to omit, in this first official act, my fervent supplications to that Almighty Being who rules over the universe, [and]

who presides in the councils of nations . . . . No people can be bound to acknowledge and adore the Invisible Hand which conducts the affairs of men more than the people of the United States. Every step by which they have advanced to the character of an independent nation seems to have been distinguished by some token of providential agency . . . . We ought to be no less persuaded that the propitious smiles of Heaven can never be expected on a nation that disregards the eternal rules of order and right which Heaven itself has ordained.[2]

The great day was concluded with one final act. According to the congressional resolution of April 29, following the oath of office, the president, the speaker, and the members of the House of Representatives accompanied Washington to St. Paul's Chapel to hear divine service performed by the Reverend Provost.[3]

Public acknowledgment and adoration of God was universally affirmed and practiced by every aspect of our government in its early years. Our Founders considered it to be an indispensable element to the success of our form of government. All three branches of government emphasized its importance to the health and well being of our nation.

America's Early Government Publicly Acknowledged God

On September 25, 1789, the same day the first Congress proposed the Bill of Rights, they also passed the Northwest Ordinance, which emphasized that "religious liberty . . . [is] the basis whereon these republics, their laws and constitutions are erected" and that, being necessary to good government, "religion, morality and knowledge . . . shall forever be encouraged" through the public schools. Such public acknowledgment of the importance of religion in school is rarely heard from our leaders today.

On that same day, Congress also passed a resolution for a National Day of Prayer. The Journals of Congress record the following:

> Mr. Sherman justified the practice of thanksgiving on any signal event, not only as a laudable one in itself, but as warranted by precedents in Holy Writ: for instance, the solemn thanksgiving and rejoicing which took place in the time of Solomon after the building of the temple was a case in point. This example he thought worthy of imitation on the present occasion.[4]

This resolution by Congress was unanimously adopted, and President Washington issued a proclamation for the people of the United States to thank "the great Lord and Ruler of Nations" for enabling us "to establish constitutions of governments for our safety and happiness, and particularly the national one now lately instituted."[5] He went on to say that it is "the duty of all nations to acknowledge the providence of Almighty God, to obey his will, to be grateful for his benefits, and humbly to implore his protection and favor."[6]

Our Congress and presidents have fulfilled this "duty of all nations" for nearly 210 years in our nation's history under our present Constitution, yet it was only a continuation of what the Continental Congress had already done before. They had established official Days of Fasting and Prayer on the national level beginning in 1775. Moreover, in 1777, a special committee of Congress reported "that the use of the Bible is so universal and its importance so great" that it resolved "to import 20,000 copies of the Bible." Four years later, the need for Bibles arose again, and so Congress approved the printing of the "Bible of the Revolution," a translation prepared by Robert Aitken in 1781.[7]

There are numerous examples of America's early government publicly acknowledging reliance on and trust in God and His principles, but that trust in God did not end with our early leaders. In May, 1854, the House of Representatives passed a resolution proclaiming that "the great vital and conservative element in our system is the belief of our people in the pure doctrines and divine truths of the gospel of Jesus Christ. . ."[8] Abraham Lincoln frequently acknowledged both his personal dependence on God as well as the nation's dependence. For instance, when calling for a National Day of Fasting on March 30, 1863, President Lincoln reminded Americans "that those nations only are blessed whose God is the Lord."[9] President Eisenhower gave his support to the Congressional Act in 1954 which added the phrase "under God" to the Pledge of Allegiance.[10] President Kennedy, in his Inaugural Address on January 20, 1961, recognized that the rights of man do "not come from the generosity of the state but from the hand of God."[11] Even more recently, Congress and President Reagan proclaimed 1983 as the "Year of the Bible." There are an abundance of other similar examples.

Both the Congress and the Supreme Court begin each business day with prayer. Many are not aware of the prayer that starts each session of the Supreme Court, yet a prayer it is when the crier proclaims "Oyez, Oyez, Oyez, God save the United States and his honorable court!" Over the head of the Chief Justice hang the Ten Commandments, and over the head of the Speaker of the House is found our official national motto: "In God We Trust."

The Supreme Court had recognized the importance of Christianity to America's heritage and its basis for our form of government as early as 1799. In 1892, in *Church of the Holy Trinity v. The United States*,[12] the Court declared the following:

Our laws and institutions must necessarily be based upon the teachings of the Redeemer of mankind. It is impossible that it should be otherwise; and in this sense and to this extent our civilization and our institutions are emphatically Christian. . . . This is historically true. From the discovery of this continent to the present hour, there is a single voice making this affirmation. . . that this is a Christian nation. We are founded to legislate, propagate, and secure Christianity.[13]

Again, in 1947, the Court recognized that "we are a religious people and our laws presuppose" the existence of God. In 1979, the Supreme Court upheld our national motto, "In God We Trust," as constitutional, and in 1983 it upheld the long-standing practice of paying chaplains for Congress.

Three Indispensable Elements of a Christian Nation

The state governments, as well, called numerous days of prayer and thanksgiving. The proclamations on both the state and national levels consistently emphasize three indispensable elements in a Christian nation. Here is a typical example found in a "Proclamation for a National Thanksgiving," in 1787:

that it may please him . . . to raise up from among our youth, men eminent for *virtue, learning, and piety*, to his service in Church and State . . . and to fill the world with his glory.

Virtue, learning and piety are the three elements found emphasized throughout our official documents and the statements of our Founders. Sometimes they are called "morality," "knowledge," and "religion," such as in the Northwest Ordinance. References to "religion" in that era were references to Christianity; "morality" meant Christian character; and "knowledge" meant a Biblical world view. These were consistently emphasized by our Founders as the indispensable foundations or supports of our system of government. Hence, if they are ever completely lost, our nation will eventually collapse.

Christianity is Government's Best Support

John Adams expanded on the need for a religious and moral foundation in 1798, when he said, "Our Constitution was made only for a moral and religious people. It is wholly inadequate for the government of any other."[14] Thomas Jefferson said that religion is "deemed in other countries incompatible with good government and yet proved by our experience to be its best support."[15]

The Father of the Constitution, James Madison, said in his *Memorial and Remonstrance* of 1785 that "religion . . . [is] the basis and foundation of government. . . . Before any man can be considered as a member of civil society, he must be considered as a subject of the Governor of the Universe."[16]

George Washington, President of the Constitutional Convention, said in 1783 that "without an humble imitation" of the "characteristics of the Divine Author of our blessed religion . . .we can never hope to be a happy nation."[17] Later, in his Farewell Address in 1796, he continued that same theme: "Of all the dispositions and habits which lead to a political prosperity, religion and morality are indispensable supports." He called them "the essential pillars of society" in 1797.[18]

The Father of the American Revolution was Samuel Adams, who said that to change any age in which we live we must simply "study and practice the exalted virtues of the Christian system." "While the people are virtuous," he said, "they cannot be subdued; but when once they lose their virtue they will be ready to surrender their liberties to the first external or internal invader. . . . If virtue and knowledge are diffused among the people, they will never be enslaved. This will be their great Security."[19] Perhaps no one said it more clearly than Noah Webster, who wrote, "No truth is more evident to my mind than that the Christian religion must be the basis of any government intended to secure the rights and privileges of a free people."[20]

Jefferson, Madison, and the Christian "Coalition" in Virginia to Separate Church and State

Although the Founders believed religion was the essential basis of their Constitutional form of government, and that it should "forever be encouraged," they still wanted to prevent the possibility of a national church from being established here as it was in Britain. Many of the states had their own state-established denominations at the time of the writing of the Constitution, but there began to emerge movements in early America to do away with an official favored denomination on the state level. The movement in Virginia led by Thomas Jefferson and James Madison has received an inordinate amount of attention from the modern Supreme Court.[21] This focus on the efforts in Virginia has led many to believe that they exemplified the efforts across the rest of America. Such was not the case, each state was unique in its effort. Nevertheless, to better understand the movement for separating the church and the state in America, we will begin where the Supreme Court did in *Engel v. Vitale*,[22] in Virginia, with the efforts of Jefferson and Madison.

Putting the Movement in Perspective

When America boldly declared her independence from England in 1776, she also officially severed her ties to the Anglican Church, the established church of England. Recall that both the Pilgrims and Puritans had chosen to pull away from that established church to form their own. They came to America not only to spread the light and truth of God's word, but also to worship God as they pleased. Thus, during the early development of our nation, many colonies set up their own churches that received the encouragement and benefits of that particular community. By 1776, nine of the thirteen colonies had established churches, in which the local governments were financially supporting a particular denomination.[23] The colonists did not see any contradiction between their opposition to an established national church and their approval of an established church in their own chosen colonies. In the former situation, no one had a choice if he or she wanted to stay in that country. In the latter, if a person did not choose to support the established colony's church, he or she could move a few miles down the road to another colony with a different church.

In Virginia, the Church of England was the established church,[24] although Baptists, Presbyterians, Lutherans, and other denominations also existed in Virginia and actually outnumbered the Anglicans.

Jefferson's Involvement in Church and State Issues[25]

In the fall of 1776, Jefferson was named chairman of the General Assembly's Committee on Religion, and he also served on a special committee to revise all of Virginia's laws. He had already become interested in issues of church and state as early as 1771, when he was asked by the Anglican vestry in Nansemond County, Virginia to help them sue and get rid of their troublesome minister, Rev. Patrick Lunen, who was charged with drunkenness, quarrelling, and profane language.[26] At least one biographer believes that this was the case that "clearly aroused" Jefferson's "keen interest in the relation of church and state."[27] Some commentators wrongly characterize his agreement to take this case as evidence of Jefferson's anti-clericalism; but, being an Anglican vestryman himself, he was an attorney that other vestries felt comfortable in hiring to represent their interests. In other words, he was a defender of the church, not an opponent.

Between 1771 and 1773, Jefferson also gave his support to Rev. Samuel Henley in Williamsburg who, as an Anglican, spoke out against the persecution of dissenters.[28]

Meanwhile, the dissenting churches in Virginia were letting their views be known to Jefferson and the committee to revise the laws. Rev. John Todd, Moderator of the Hanover Presbytery in Louisa County, and Rev. Caleb Wallace, pastor of Cub Creek Church and a helper in the founding of Hampden-Sidney College, personally presented one of nine religious petitions to the Virginia legislature. The essence of this Presbyterian petition can be captured by the following excerpt:

> when our blessed Savior declares his kingdom is not of this world, he renounces all dependence upon state power, . . . and the duty which we owe to our Creator and the manner of discharging it, can only be directed by reason and conviction; . . . Therefore, we ask no ecclesiastical establishments for ourselves; neither can we approve them when granted to others.[29]

Note that the gist of this concern by Rev. Todd and Rev. Wallace was not based upon any animosity towards religion, nor a desire to see religious influence removed from the public arena. They were concerned that the church would become dependent upon the state, which, in turn, would compromise the duties and convictions they owed their blessed Savior. Both of these pastors became allies of Jefferson in the fight for religious freedom.

Another Jefferson ally was Rev. William Irvin, pastor of the D.S. Presbyterian Church in Jefferson's home county. Rev. Irvin drafted a *Petition of Dissenters in Albemarle and Amherst Counties*, and obtained the signatures of almost 200 of the leading families (including both Anglicans and dissenters) to put pressure on the legislature to "put every religious denomination on an equal footing, to be supported by themselves independent one of another." It further stated ". . . their sense of the great iniquity, contained in the Establishing of any one religious denomination of people . . . in preference to all others."[30] Like his cohorts, Todd and Wallace, Rev. Irvin was not attempting to thwart religious influence upon political issues or governmental bodies. He was concerned about an equal playing field, that no particular denomination would be favored over another.

The Presbyterians were not the only religious group making their opinions known to Jefferson and his committee; so were the Baptist ministers. They began meeting with Jefferson to give him their petitions in the fall of 1776, and Jefferson had some of them published in the Williamsburg newspaper so that people would understand their views on religious freedom.

At this time in Virginia, the Anglican or Episcopal Church, to the exclusion of all other denominations, was receiving tax money for its support. In December of 1776, the Rev. John Leland of Louisa became the leader of the General Association of Baptists. In that capacity, he drafted a declaration urging the disestablishment of the Episcopal Church. He wrote: "It is contrary to the principles of reason and justice that any should be compelled to contribute to the maintenance of a church with which their consciences will not permit them to join."[31] Notice his concern about government interference with the church:

> We believe that Preachers should be supported only by voluntary Contributions from the People, and that a general Assessment (however harmless, yea useful some may conceive it to be) is pregnant with various evils destructive to the rights and privileges of religious society. . . . The consequence of this is, that those whom the State employs in its Service, it has a right to regulate and dictate to: it may judge and determine who shall preach; when and where they shall preach; and what they must preach. . . . Sorry should we be to see the seeds of oppression sown by the hand of power amongst us, and we think it our duty, to [do] our utmost in a legal way, to retard, or if possible, to prevent [it].[32]

Rev. Leland feared that government interference would rise to the point of dictating federal regulations on whom the church could hire or invite to preach, and even the content of what they should preach.

The Baptists wanted the freedom to preach what they believed were the truths of the Bible, to follow the dictates of their own conscience, without the government telling them what they could or could not preach. Their concern had nothing to do with wanting to silence the voice of morality by the church in public affairs and issues. In October, 1778, Rev. Elijah Craig of Orange County was sent by the Baptist churches to lobby the Virginia General Assembly on the bill establishing religious freedom. The message he conveyed from the Baptists was that they supported the bill since it "prescribes the just limits of the power of the State with regard to religion, and properly guards against partiality towards any religious denomination."[33]

Even those in the area who remained loyal to their Anglican church, such as devoted Fredericksville vestryman and prominent revolutionary leader, Dr. George Gilmer, spoke out in favor of religious freedom. Gilmer's refusal to join the brand new independent Calvinistical Reformed Church in Charlottesville apparently caused some to think that he was *opposed* to Dissenting churches. Gilmer sent a *Circular Address to the People of Albemarle County* on October 17, 1777, that was intended to counteract such a false report.

> Nor do I think that any individual or collective body, Legislative or Executive, have any right to interfere with any such [religious] society. . . nor can they. . . give preeminence to any one religious Society over any other, or . . . compell the one Society to contribute to the support and maintainance of

any other, but each Society be supported . . . by free and voluntary Contributions. . . . Let us aim at following the Apostles and Evangelists as our guides, who, tho' they differed in opinion, quarrelled not.[34]

James Madison's Presbyterian friend Rev. Samuel Stanhope Smith, the new President of Hampden-Sydney college in Prince Edward County, began to rise in political influence in 1777. Two years later, he wrote letters to Jefferson in which he proposed "a coalition of the principal religious sects."[35] The purpose of his proposal? To provide nonsectarian religious instruction in the public schools! Many today would label such a proposal a blatant violation of the principle of separation of church and state. However, Rev. Smith felt his proposal was quite consistent with his opposition against a "legal establishment" or a "public religion."

Jefferson's Public Church - State Actions

Thomas Jefferson is well known for his authorship of the *Virginia Statute for Religious Freedom,* yet a review of all his legislative efforts demonstrates a significant interest in religious liberty that revealed his opinion on church-state relations. While serving on a committee for a general revision of the Virginia laws in 1777, Thomas Jefferson actually drafted and submitted a group of five bills that were all religious in nature. One of those bills, never formally enacted, was entitled a *Bill Annulling Marriages Prohibited by the Levitical Law.* In this marriage bill, which ostensibly would have enacted Biblical law by reference, Jefferson wrote that "[m]arriages prohibited by the Levitical law shall be null; and persons marrying contrary to that prohibition and cohabitating as man and wife. . . shall be [fined] from time to time until they separate."[36] If Jefferson is the champion of those who wish to remove religious influence from the public square, then they have the wrong man. Jefferson clearly advocated a Biblical basis for America's laws in a direct and express way! He obviously believed that God's laws were not old fashioned, out of date, or no longer applicable to his society. He was reasoning from a standpoint of Biblical absolutes.

Another bill Jefferson submitted was enacted on November 27, 1786. It was called the *Bill for Punishing Disturbers of Religious Worship and Sabbath Breakers.* In it, Jefferson proposed the following: "If any person on Sunday shall himself be found labouring at his own or any other trade or calling. . . he shall forfeit the sum of ten shillings for every such offense."[37] This law was not based upon any type of Enlightenment or deistic thinking to which so many historians have claimed he adhered. Instead, the law Jefferson proposed was derived from the Bible and God's fourth Commandment to respect the Sabbath and keep it holy. It was another example of Jefferson's support for a Biblical basis of law.

Yet another bill by Jefferson, the *Bill for Appointing Days of Public Fasting and Thanksgiving*, said that "the power of appointing Days of Public Fasting and Thanksgiving may be exercised by the Governor, . . . every minister of the gospel shall on each day so to be appointed, attend and perform divine service and preach a sermon, or discourse, suited to the occasion, in his church, on pain of forfeiting fifty pounds (in silver) for every failure, not having a reasonable excuse."[38] This shows his agreement with the public acknowledgement of God by the highest elected state official, and his belief in the importance of giving thanks to God in a public way.

While Jefferson was serving as Virginia's Governor in November, 1779, he endorsed a "day of publick and solemn Thanksgiving and prayer to Almighty God," which was published in the *Virginia Gazette*. The proclamation included the one made on October 20, 1779, by the Continental Congress and had introductory and concluding paragraphs by Jefferson. Governor Jefferson reminded the citizens of Virginia of how "Almighty God" had blessed them, and then he included some prayer requests of an overtly, Christian nature, such as the following:

> That He would grant to his church, the plentiful effusions of divine grace, and pour out his holy spirit on all Ministers of the Gospel; that He would bless and prosper the means of education, and spread the light of christian knowledge through the remotest corners of the earth. . . [and t]hat **He would establish the independence of these United States upon the basis of religion and virtue**.[39] [emphasis added]

Notice that as the state's highest elected official, Thomas Jefferson had no problem publicly advocating religion, and not just any religion, but specifically Christianity. He asked for public prayer for "all Ministers of the Gospel," which excludes all religions other than Christianity, and he asked for public prayer to spread the light of "christian knowledge," and no other. He even attributed the need for our nation to rest upon the pillars of religion and virtue. This proclamation made it abundantly clear that Jefferson was not a complete secularist, as we see often asserted today. He felt strongly that government, at least at the state and local level, should be influenced by Christianity. His public endorsement and encouragement of a public religious event can lead to no other conclusion.

Jefferson also believed that witnesses in a court of law could only be competent to testify if they took an oath sworn on the Bible and subscribed the oath, "So help you God." This was the exact legislative requirement he proposed in his *Bill for Establishing General Courts* in Virginia.

As for Jefferson's most famous work, the *Virginia Statute for Religious Freedom*, although originally drafted in 1777 and presented to the legislature in 1779, it only found success when Madison proposed it again in late 1785. It is worth noting the highly religious language of the text itself:

> Almighty God hath created the mind free; that all attempts to influence it by temporal punishments or burdens, or by civil incapacitations, tend only to beget habits of hypocrisy and meanness, and are a departure from the plan of the Holy author of our religion, who being Lord both of body and mind, yet chose not to propagate it by coercions on either; . . . that to compel a man to furnish contributions of money for the propagations of opinions which he disbelieves, is sinful and tyrannical; . . . that it tends only to corrupt the principles of that religion it is meant to encourage; . . . that to allow the civil magistrate to intrude his powers into the field of opinion.. . is a dangerous fallacy, which at once destroys all religious liberty: [Therefore] Be it enacted by the General Assembly, That no man shall be compelled to frequent or support any religious worship, . . . but that all men shall be free to profess, and by argument to maintain, their opinion in matters of religion, and that the same shall in no way diminish, enlarge, or affect their civil capacities.[40]

Jefferson's World View

Today's staunch proponents of separation of church and state would be disappointed to realize what a strong religious world view Jefferson maintained throughout his life. He would not support the devout secularism so many propose today. Indeed, Thomas Jefferson would have very little in common with the Carl Sagans and Norman Lears of today. While Jefferson clearly was one of the stronger advocates in his day for disestablishing the church, he would still be considered a "right wing religious conservative" compared to today's far reaching secularism. That realization alone should be a wake up call to all of us as to how far our nation has drifted away from the Biblical world view that was so much a part of America's culture and history.

Moreover, given his strong awareness that the nation's strength stemmed from her strong Biblical foundations and beliefs, it is unlikely that Thomas Jefferson would ever have condoned the intolerant secularism within our country today.

Look afresh at the language contained in Jefferson's *Virginia Statute for Religious Freedom* cited above. The world view presented by Jefferson in that statute was not of the Enlightenment nor of evolution. Neither Rousseau nor Darwin used such religious ideas and concepts in their writings. In stark contrast to such non-Biblical philosophers, Jefferson made many critical philosophical assumptions based upon the Bible.

Consider just a few of the more obviously Biblical assumptions made by Jefferson. First, he accepted the premise that God is sovereign over all of creation, and that He created us, as well as our minds. He never hesitated to put God in His rightful place as sovereign over mankind. Second, Jefferson's characterization of God was always positive and reverent, referring to God as being "Holy" and "Almighty." Third, he supposed that God has a plan ("the plan of the Holy author") and that we are obligated to obey God's plan. We, as God's created beings, are subject to the will and direction of our Creator and His laws. Each of these premises of Jefferson have been long since rejected by today's secularists, secularists who attempt to justify their philosophy by invoking Jefferson. When they do so, they are not being honest. Again, if they are going to use Jefferson as the champion of secularism in society and government, they have the wrong man. The evidence shows quite clearly that Thomas Jefferson held a Biblical world view and saw nothing wrong with state government authorities relying upon and encouraging its citizens in that world view.

In referring to Jefferson's *Virginia Statute for Religious Freedom*, Thomas Buckley wrote that "[t]he God described here is not deistical. . . rather Jefferson posited a creator who is personally involved. . . . The Statute is not neutral toward religion."[41] Therein lies another critical difference, often ignored, between Jefferson's beliefs on the subject of church-state relations and today's proponents of strict separation between church and state. Jefferson was not neutral toward religion, even in his capacity as Virginia's Governor! The moral authority for this legislative act was cited as "Almighty God," "the Lord," and "our religion," meaning Christianity in the general sense. The state statute labeled certain actions, such as coercion, as being "sinful," and affirmed that the state was "meant to encourage" the "principles of that religion."

Where have you read in today's censored version of our history that Jefferson stood for state and local government encouragement of the principles of religion? Where have you read in today's censored version of our history that Jefferson held a Biblical world view? Where have you read in today's censored version of our history that Jefferson did not support government neutrality toward religion, as those that cite him so often advocate?

It is important that we view history in its proper context. Remember that Virginia at this time had an established state church, the Anglican church. Certain rights and privileges of Virginia citizens were determined based upon whether or not the citizen was affiliated with the Anglican Church. According to Jefferson's statute on religious freedom, being a member of a particular church would no longer be used to "enlarge" the "civil capacities" of a citizen, but neither would it be used to force a person's political activity to "diminish", as many strident advocates of separation now urge.

Another fact is often forgotten about Jefferson's statute. Remember who proposed it and was ultimately responsible for getting it passed? It was James Madison. We can safely assume that he would not have taken such actions on a proposal he disagreed with. So to that extent, we can assume that Madison, too, held a Biblical world view; Madison, too, felt it was proper for state and local governments to encourage religion, and Madison also opposed the idea of government neutrality toward religion.

When we consider all of Jefferson's bills on religion and the state, including the *Virginia Statute for Religious Freedom*, we can see that Jefferson's "ultimate aim was not separation of church and state but the fullest possible freedom of religious belief and opinion."[42]

Jefferson's Views on Religion in Education

Jefferson's legislative efforts also included education. In 1779, he drafted a proposal for a complete and universal school system. In that same year, Governor Jefferson also worked with Rev. James Madison, president of the College of William and Mary, to do away with a Professor of Divinity in the school. His purpose in doing so was not to secularize the school, but to create a more non-denominational environment. Jefferson clearly believed that Christian principles were appropriate to be taught in the educational environment. Commenting upon his hopes for the Indian school at the College, Jefferson said that one of the "purposes of the . . . institution would be . . . instructing them in the principles of Christianity. . . ."[43] That comment is contrary to the neutrality and strict separation concepts articulated by so many people today.

At this time in our history, the Bible was the primary reading textbook of the schools. Rhys Isaac pointed out that "any child . . . who had instruction in reading, had the Bible for his reader."[44] There is no evidence that this literary use of the Bible was discontinued with Jefferson's bill for public schools. It was only the Bible's use in association with *sectarian* teaching that he wanted to end. Jefferson's *Bill for Establishing Elementary Schools* said that "no religious reading, instruction, or exercise, shall be prescribed or practiced inconsistent with the tenets of any religious sect or denomination." As explained by historian Robert M. Healey, "[t]o Jefferson the elimination of whatever was inconsistent with the tenets of any particular sect did not mean that religion itself was to be outlawed in public education. . . . Rather, the purpose of this provision was to guarantee and encourage religious freedom. This meant that those areas of religion upon which all sects agreed were certainly to be included within the framework of public education."[45]

It is also illuminating to see that in 1780, while still Governor of Virginia, Jefferson approved of two government acts favorable to religion. First, he signed legislation, enacted largely through the efforts of Rev. John Todd, that chartered a state college in Lexington, Kentucky, and granted it 8,000 acres through the Virginia Assembly.[46] This school, later named Transylvania Seminary in 1783, was not to favor any one denomination according to its charter, but it was run by a Presbyterian-dominated board of trustees, and it had organized religious preaching, prayer, and worship services. Second, Jefferson directed that an official state medal be struck with his favorite religious motto inscribed on it: "Rebellion to Tyrants is Obedience to God." This was the same motto he had proposed for the national seal four years earlier.[47]

In 1783, Jefferson continued to mix government and religion in his public acts. He proposed a new constitution for Virginia which contained a reference to "the Sovereign Disposer of all human events."[48] While serving a term in the Continental Congress, he drafted the *Reply of Congress to General Washington on Resigning His Commission*. In it, he wrote these words:

> We join you in commending the interests of our dearest country to the protection of Almighty God, beseeching Him to dispose the hearts and minds of its citizens to improve the opportunity afforded them of becoming a happy and respectable nation. And for you we address to Him our earnest prayers, that a life so beloved may be fostered with all His care; that your days may be happy as they have been illustrious; and that He will finally give you that reward which this world cannot give.[49]

These public declarations, in the context of an official government action, again reveal a man who held a Biblical world view, who had no interest in religious neutrality, and who found no contradiction in mixing religious expressions with public life.

The positive influence of Christianity upon our nation was an idea Jefferson vibrantly supported. Lest we forget, after designing the University of Virginia, he designated a room on the middle floor of the Rotunda for chapel services.[50] He invited various religious schools to locate on or near the University property;[51] "he praised the use of the Charlottesville courthouse for religious services;[52] and he stated that religion is 'deemed in other countries incompatible with good government and yet proved by our experience to be its best support.'"[53]

True Motivations for the Early Movements to Separate Church and State

To summarize, our Founders strongly believed in the positive influence Christian principles had upon our nation's governmental structure and institutions, and the overwhelming majority of them held a world view based on the Bible. Yet they realized that for the church to be most effective in the culture, it had to be free from the constraints and limitations of government. Recall the fears of Reverend Leland, who felt that government interference could one day lead to federal regulations dictating whom churches could hire or the content of what they preached. While the Founders clearly wanted the church to be influential in government ideas and policies, they wanted all the Christian churches to have an equal opportunity to influence society, rather than one denomination exercising greater power. Instead of endorsing the particular creed of any one church, and thereby limiting religious freedom, the Founders envisioned a government that would unite its people by recognizing the basic Biblical truths they held in common.

Even Jefferson made public endorsements of religious events and encouraged participation in his official capacity as governor. Even Jefferson sought legislation that reflected a Biblical basis. Even he recognized the importance of Biblical teaching in the schools, and even Jefferson approved the federal appropriation of money to spread Christianity to the Indians. Seeking equal freedoms of the churches and protecting the churches' voices from the interference of the government were the true motivations of Jefferson and others in the movements for separation of church and state, both in Virginia and in the other states.

In the movements to separate church and state in America, they were overwhelmingly seeking to provide for equality amongst the Christian churches; not the removal of their societal influence we see today. The Founders consistently gave credit for the principles of freedom and liberty that formed America to the influence of Christianity, not other non-Christian religions. Therefore, they saw that the best hope for those liberties and freedoms to continue in the future, would be to encourage and protect the influence of the Christian church, yet still protecting the freedoms of all other beliefs and non-beliefs.

PART II

THE BIBLICAL PRINCIPLES THAT UNDERGIRD AMERICA'S CONSTITUTION

"STEPPING STONES:" Significant Events in World History Prior to America's Constitution

The United States Constitution was the culmination of ideas and efforts at political reform that go back to the earliest American colonists. They brought to the New World ideas that originated many centuries before in Europe and Asia.

Our forefathers, who landed at Plymouth in 1620, endured the storm-tossed waves of a dangerous ocean crossing, the frigid cold of New England's winter, and even the hardship of death itself. Why? Because they had a vision of God's liberty that burned in their souls, inspiring them to risk everything in order to plant God's truth on American soil. One of those participants, Captain Weymouth, reported "that the main end of all these undertakings, was to plant the gospel in these dark regions of America."[1] That goal was amplified by Cotton Mather, a contemporary historian of that period, who asserted that planting the gospel in America "was not only a *main end*, but the *sole end* upon which it was erected."[2]

Fulfillment of their Godly quest meant more to our forefathers than their physical comfort or safety. Despite losing nearly half their original number that first winter in New England, including 13 out of the 18 wives,[3] when the Mayflower sailed back to England the next spring, not one of them chose to leave. Theirs was a heroic act of faith to establish a "single covenanted body of Christians, united for civil as well as spiritual purposes."[4] For the Pilgrims who landed on the shores of Plymouth and gave us the Mayflower Compact, the first example of self-government, their noble undertaking was to be "for the glory of God and for the advancement of the Christian faith."[5]

Their Governor William Bradford wrote that: "A great hope and inward zeal they had of laying some good foundation, or at least to make some way thereunto, for the propagating and advancing the gospel of the kingdom of Christ in those remote parts of the world — yea, though they should be but even **stepping stones** unto others for the performing of so great a work." He added that "as one small candle may light a thousand, so the light here kindled hath shone unto many, yea in some sort to our whole nation; let the glorious name of Jehovah have all the praise."

Many individuals and nations were stepping stones before them who passed on the light of Biblical truth regarding government and liberty over centuries of providentially guided history. They carried the torch light of God's truth from the shores of Europe to ignite a new flame on distant shores to the west, where new beginnings were possible. But before we examine the historical journey of the flame of liberty, let us first consider some of the primary combustible elements that ignited the flame and kept it burning.

Contributions of the Hebrew Republic

The primary element of the flame of liberty is God Himself, for God is the author of life, and hence, liberty is not possible without God's initial hand of creation. Government itself was an institution that began by God's decree in the post-flood world, when in Genesis chapter nine, He told Noah to establish a system of capital punishment for those guilty of murder. It was a decentralized, family-based government where elders or patriarchs of family groups or clans handled civil matters at the gates of each city. Eventually God gave us a more complete system of laws and government that was recorded in the books of Moses. These Old Testament scriptures set forth an historical example of godly government through His chosen people, the Israelites.

Largely overlooked by modern scholars, the influence upon America and its constitutional structure of the ancient Hebrew nation of Israel is nothing short of profound. Consider the words of one of our founders, John Adams, from 1809:

> I will insist that the Hebrews have done more to civilize men than any other nation . . . If I were an atheist, and believed in blind eternal fate, I should still believe that fate had ordained the Jews to be the most essential instrument for civilizing the nations. If I were an atheist of the other sect, who believe or pretend to believe that all is ordered by chance, I should believe that chance had ordered the Jews to preserve and propagate to all mankind the doctrine of a supreme, intelligent, wise, almighty sovereign of the universe, which I believe to be the great essential principle of all morality, and consequently of all civilization.[6]

As John Adams makes clear, without an understanding of the Bible and its description of the Hebrew republic, it is difficult, if not impossible, to understand America's legal and constitutional foundations. Historian Russell Kirk, although differing some from Adams, said that:

> In colonial America, everyone with the rudiments of schooling knew one book thoroughly: the Bible. And the Old Testament mattered as much as the New, for the American colonies were founded in a time of renewed Hebrew scholarship, and the Calvinistic character of Christian faith in early America emphasized the legacy of Israel.[7]

On a larger scale, Moses and the Israelites made known to the world that there exists but one true living God, that God made a covenant with His people, and that He gave them laws by which they must live. Although this Biblical law handed down to Moses was not the first code of laws, it has survived the test of time and still influences American society today.[8]

> The other creeds of the ancient world are dust and ashes now, but the Decalogue of Moses and the understanding of man's existence under God which Moses communicated to the people remain a living power, the source of order.[9]

Thus, while other scholars prefer to focus on the Code of Hammarabi or the laws of ancient Greece or Rome to find the primary influence upon America's governmental foundations, the most influential source cannot be found outside the framework of ancient Israel. Indeed, it only stands to reason that God would want the world to turn to His chosen people for the best example of government and principles of liberty. In fact, the Israelites illustrated several principles that caught the imagination of America's founders.

The Concept of Covenant or Constitutionalism

While there was more than one covenant made by God with His people, the Sinai Covenant had special significance to the Hebrew Republic since it also established the pattern of democratic consent in covenants. Exodus 18 and 19 show that a democratic element of elected rulers called judges was first set up before God gave to Moses the Book of the Covenant, i.e. a written constitution. When this constitution-like document was submitted to the Hebrews, through their elected representatives, they ratified the document and thus gave their official consent. Then, and only then, did this covenant or constitution, if you will, go into effect. True, the source of this higher law was God, but it was recognized and consented to by the people. It was a democratic constitutional ratification process. All subsequent renewals or amendments to this first covenant were also done in this democratic pattern that God established.

According to the historical philosopher Russell Kirk, this theory of covenant which provided the foundation for liberty greatly influenced America's founders. Here is what he observed:

> Throughout western civilization, and indeed in some degree through the later world, the Hebraic understanding of Covenant and Law would spread, in forms both religious and secular. The idea of an enduring Covenant, or compact, whether between God and people or merely between man and man, took various styles in various lands and ages; it passed into medieval society through Christian teaching, and became essential to the social order of Britain, from which society most settlers in North America came. . . .
>
> And from Israel, even more than from the Roman juris-consults, America inherited an understanding of the sanctity of law. Certain root principles of justice exist, arising from the nature which God has conferred upon man; law is a means for realizing those principles, so far as we can. **That assumption was in the minds of the men who wrote the Declaration of Independence and the Constitution of the United States.**[10] [emphasis added]

This moral aspect of the Ten Commandments and the other laws conveyed by Moses, having their source in God Himself, brought a sense of justice and stability to the law that enables liberty to flourish. It applied to everyone equally, regardless of one's position or power in society, and it recognized that man's nature, when in rebellion from God, required restraint, but only to the degree man failed to restrain himself in accordance with God's laws.

Democratic Elections of Representatives

Another principle that caught the attention and admiration of America's founders was that of the democratic form of government practiced by the Hebrew republic, along with its necessary companion, local self-government; that is, the people voluntarily choosing their leaders and representatives. Israel was organized into tribes, each with their own tribal leaders or elders. These leaders were not chosen democratically, but the people began to have democratic choice of their leaders when, through the advice of Jethro in Exodus 18 and Deut 1:13, it is clear that judges were elected by the people according to the size of each local community (tens, fifties, hundreds, or thousands of families). It should be noted that Jethro was a priest of both Ethiopian and Hebrew descent. Thus it should be remembered that the world-changing idea of a democratic republic with free elections was largely due to the leadership of a clergyman who was a man of color.

Two hundred years later in their history, when Israel had lost much of its virtue, the elders of Israel came to Samuel, who was the current judge over Israel, and demanded to have a king instead.[11] Although Samuel, at God's instruction, tried to warn the people of the dangers of such pagan models of centralized power, the people chose to disregard the warnings. As a result of the people's will, their constitution was amended to establish a constitutional monarchy. Though this development led the Israelites away from liberty, it is crucial to note that this change was a direct result of free civic choice.

These same principles of local self-government upon which the republican form of government is based would continue to be a part of the teachings of Jesus Christ and the early Christian church.

Attempts at Democracy Without Biblical Concepts

Prior to the coming of Christ, there were attempts made by pagan nations, such as Greece and Rome, at more democratic forms of government. Yet, without the inclusion of the Higher Law of God, they were short-lived and disappointing.

The Framers of our Constitution were masters of the Greek and Roman periods because they were full of useful lessons in civil government. Where those lessons were successful and Biblical, they were praised, but the failures of the Greek and Roman periods were very well known by our Founders. James Madison wrote that the Greek and Roman history of democracy has "always been spectacles of turbulence and contention . . . incompatible with personal security or the rights of property."[12] Equipped with the knowledge of Biblical principles, our Founders carefully avoided pure democracy and an absolute majority rule system.

As commendable as they were, the pagan ideas of man and of government, at their best, could never go beyond the following basic assumptions:

• They believed in the natural inequality of men;

• They believed that man's value was determined by his contribution to the State;

• They believed the state was paramount over the individual man; and

- They believed that the State is controlled by and exists for the good of an elite class.

The wisest of their philosophers and statesmen could never rise above this basic non-Biblical world view. The principles of the Old Testament and the teachings of Jesus Christ would bring a worldview that produced liberty for all.

The Political Teachings of Jesus Christ and the Apostles

Jesus Christ sacrificed His own life to conquer sin, the ultimate source of problems in society, but He did not stop there, he also taught a few world changing matters about government and liberty. When He commissioned His disciples (Matthew 28:18-20) to go out and disciple the nations, He told them to do so by teaching all that He taught, including these five main concepts:
- The supreme value of all persons (over the state).

This also implies the principles of equality and individuality before the law. (Matthew 10:30,31)

- Sovereign jurisdictions and separation of institutions.

Jurisdiction of government is limited and does not extend to the sphere of the mind and soul. This means that government is not supposed to control religion, education, the press, or any institution that deals in the realm of faith or knowledge. (Luke 20:22-25)

- Citizens are obligated to support and submit to government that limits itself to its proper areas of jurisdiction. (Luke 20:22-25)

- Government leaders are to be public servants; i.e. the state exists for the individual, not vice-versa. (Luke 22:25,26)

- The duty of citizens to oppose unlimited, i.e. tyrannical government through successive stages of peaceful protest and legal appeals, flight or emigration, and the use of defensive force. (Luke 10:10; Luke 22:36)

The Apostles and early Christians were faithful to teach these principles as is evident from the following Biblical accounts:

- AD 51, Paul went westward into Europe (Greece) and there protested injustice. (Acts 16:6-10; 35-39)

- AD 56, Paul's *Epistle to Corinthians* urged Greek believers to elect Christians as more competent rulers, just as Jethro did in the Hebrew republic. (1 Cor 6:1-5)

- AD 56-57, Erastus, a fellow-minister (Acts 19:22) with Paul, went into politics in Corinth. (Rom 16:23)

- AD 57, Paul wrote the *Epistle to Romans* (from Corinth) and told Italian believers that government is a ministry of God established to help them love their neighbor, overcome evil, and protect the innocent. He also said to obey and serve rulers who do this, but to resist those that rebel against this higher law. (Rom 12:19, 21-13:7)

- AD 58-63, Paul was arrested wrongfully, and instead of taking an easy release when he had a chance, kept appealing for his rights to be addressed as a Roman citizen. (Acts 24, 25)

- AD 64, The *First Epistle of Peter* affirmed submission to government as a divine institution, but insisted that it must punish evil and protect the innocent. (1 Peter 2:13,14)

Hence, another combustible element of liberty's flame, the teachings of Jesus Christ and the early church, shook the Middle East and the Roman Empire to their knees.

Christian Influence Spreads West

For whatever reason, God clearly intended that His message be directed toward the West. In the book of Acts, chapter 16, verses 6-10, the apostle Paul kept seeking to take the message of Christ to the East into Asia, but he was forbidden to do so by the Holy Spirit. Instead, Paul received a vision in which he was led to understand that God's purpose was for Paul to go west into Europe.[13] Paul's first convert was a prominent, leading woman named Lydia.[14] This is significant because Christianity would gradually elevate the status of women in Europe. From this point forward, the Gospel would make an external impact on societies that lay toward the West. Paul made plans to go to Italy and then on to Spain in obedience to this westward calling of

God.[15] As a result, the flame of liberty would spread west to many locations in Europe, before it would be carried across the Atlantic to America.

Irish Celtic and Anglo-Saxon Influence[16]

Historians continue to debate whether medieval England owed most of this credit for its laws to the influence of the Romans, the Normans, or the Celtic-Anglo-Saxons. While there is evidence to support each of these sources, the most convincing, and the understanding adopted by most of America's founders, was to acknowledge the importance of the Celtic-Anglo-Saxons.

Of the three potential influences, the Romans arrived first. Julius Caesar twice invaded Britain, but was unable to maintain a Roman foothold there. It would take the invaders over 130 years during the first century A.D. before the Romans could bring the resistant locals under their control.[17] While the Romans would occupy Britain for almost 500 years,[18] by the year 407, the overextended Roman empire withdrew its hold over England.[19] Since they had never truly "Romanized" the local citizens or prepared the British population for a transfer of Roman jurisprudence, once the Romans withdrew from England, the continuation in England of their legal institutions quickly ceased, as did its influence.

The indigenous form of Christianity in Britain was Celtic. Churches of this tradition were established in the British Isles long before the coming of Roman Catholic missionaries at the end of the third century. Celtic Christianity was Bible-centered and decentralized, much like that of the Early Church. In 432 a Celtic missionary named Patrick was sent over to Ireland, where even Roman soldiers had never reached. He converted this pagan land and went a step further, discipling their nation by teaching them the laws of Moses and other Biblical principles of liberty. Patrick selected 35 Old Testament passages and printed them in his *Liber Ex Lege Moisi* that was given to civil leaders that he discipled. Ireland eventually became the most advanced Christian nation in all of Europe, and when the Germanic tribes attacked Rome in 476 and plunged the European mainland into a time of chaos and darkness, many leaders and sons of European nobility came to Ireland and studied in her schools. From there, Irish Celtic missionaries were sent to the rest of western Europe beginning in the middle of the sixth century, and brought Biblical liberty, law, and light to many cities. Seeking to reclaim Britain after the Germanic tribes had conquered it a century earlier, an Irish Celtic missionary named Columba went to Scotland in 563, and his disciples began to spread southward into England.

In 596 A.D., Pope Gregory of the Roman Catholic Church commissioned St. Augustine of Rome to "preach the word of God to the English nation."[20] St. Augustine arrived on his mission to southern England in 597 A.D. in Kent, which just happened to be the most powerful and influential of the numerous Anglo-Saxon kingdoms on the island.[21] The kingdom of Kent was ruled at the time by King Aethelbert. Once the King heard Augustine preach, he allowed the Christian missionary to proselytize to all the people of his kingdom, and in the process, King Aethelbert himself converted to Christianity.[22] After his conversion, King Aethelbert was the first Anglo-Saxon king to reduce the customary law of his people to writing, in what was called "The Dooms" or decrees of the realm.[23] While we can only speculate as to his reasons for codifying the laws, we do know he did so only after he had been exhorted by both Augustine and Pope Gregory to "edify the manners of [his] subjects by much cleanness of life, exhorting, terrifying, soothing, correcting, and giving examples of good works [so] that [he might] find [in] Him [a] rewarder in heaven, whose name and knowledge you shall spread abroad upon earth."[24] While the Dooms of Aethelbert were not blatantly Christian, they contained many Christian principles and influences. For example, the entire code was an elaborate system that remedied "wrongs" by means of restitution by the wrongdoer to the victim, a principle seen throughout the Bible. It also included the Biblical concept of personal responsibility and accountability for wrongdoing by insisting that only the perpetrator could pay the restitution amount. Unlike other legal systems of that era, the Dooms of Aethelbert provided for the Biblical concept of equality under the law by setting a fixed amount of restitution based upon the degree of injury inflicted, regardless of the social status of the wrongdoer.[25] Since the Dooms fixed the amount of restitution for each type of injury, they eliminated the arbitrary nature of the law, providing the Biblical concept of legal order and predictability. Moreover, in setting the hierarchy of victims, the first order of deference, and thus greatest protection under the law, was given to the clergy. Thus, King Aethelbert ensured that the "church stood preeminent" in his Doom, affording it and the clergy even greater protection than that given to the King and the royal family![26]

Shortly after this success of the Catholic Church in the south of England, the Celtic Church began to convert northern England in 634. King Oswald of Northumbria was converted and traveled and interpreted for the Celtic missionary Aiden. By 664, English allegiance began to shift to the Roman Catholic Church, but Celtic Church ways remained dominant in more Christian practice and thinking. In 693, Ina (Ine), king of the West Saxons in Wessex, framed laws for England, drawing specifically on Celtic laws shaped by Patrick. After another 200 years, another Saxon king arose who was also greatly influenced by Irish Celtic ways, having studied in Ireland; he became England's beloved king known as Alfred the Great. Alfred was truly concerned for the people and made his government serve the public. He established the Ten Commandments as the basis of law and adopted many other patterns of government from the old Hebrew republic described in the Bible.[27] His government was organized into units of tens, fifties, hundreds, and thousands, and they had an elected assembly known as the Witen. These representatives were respectively called a tithingman (over ten families), a vilman (over fifty), a hundredman, and an earl. The earl's territory, which he oversaw, was called a "shire," and his assistant was called the "shire-reef," the source of our word "sheriff" today. The Witen also had an unelected House made up of the noblemen, but the king was elected, not hereditary. Their laws were established by the consent of the people. They were the originators of the common law, trial by jury, and habeas corpus, enduring legal principles that have since become an influential part of the heritage in America.

It was only later, when the Normans, led by William the Conqueror, invaded England in 1066, that a pagan monarchy was re-established.[28] The Normans have been described as a "group of avaricious marauders...wholly without learning, literature, or written law," and thus "found they had no readily transplantable system of legal adminstration with which to govern the indigenous Anglo-Saxon populace."[29] Therefore, the Normans adopted the Anglo-Saxon structures already in place without fundamentally changing those structures. Those structures were in place largely due to ancient Christian Celtic ideas of law and liberty, and they survived much historical turmoil to ulitmately serve as a model for the young American nation.

The Saxon influence was well understood by our Founders. Thomas Jefferson said that the Anglo-Saxon laws were ". . . the sources of the Common Law . . . [and] the wisest and most perfect ever yet devised by the wit of man, as it stood before the eighth century . . ."[30] Thomas Jefferson was so convinced that these principles clearly stemmed from Biblical roots and the faith of Christian men, that the National Seal he proposed for our country in 1776 combined devotion to God with a tribute to Anglo-Saxon government. The seal was so overtly Christian as to be shocking to today's revisionist historians. On one side of the proposed seal was a picture of the children of Israel on their knees in the wilderness before God's pillar of fire, to represent them being led by God with "a cloud by day, and a pillar of fire by the night." This side was inscribed with the words, "Israel Led by God's Pillar of Fire," with a sub-title below that read, "Liberty under God's law – Man's Inalienable

Birthright of Freedom." On the other side of that seal, Jefferson proposed the images of "Hergist and Horsa, the Saxon chiefs . . . whose political principles and form of government we have assumed."[31] This side was inscribed with the words; "Anglo-Saxon Common Law – Guardian of Freedom."

The Basis for the Magna Carta

The seeds sown by the Celtic Church and Catholic Saxon leaders like Alfred the Great eventually leavened the land so much for liberty that, by 1215, King John was forced to recognize individual rights in a document known as the Magna Carta. This document was the result of a horrible series of tyrannical acts by King John, in which he seized the property of his subjects at will and threw many of them into prison. In response, the English barons organized themselves into an army that they called "the Army of God."[32] When King John learned that "the Army of God" was marching to seize him, he became fearful and sent word for them to meet him at Runnymede, where he would accede to their demands. The barons, therefore, wrote out those demands in the Magna Carta, a document that the King signed. Fittingly, it is believed that the chief architect of that document written for "the Army of God" was a clergyman named Stephen Langton.[33] On June 15, 1215, King John signed his name to their document, sealed it with his sovereign seal, and rode back to his castle in defeat, swearing his revenge.

The Christian nature of this document is clearly evident. In its first line, the Magna Carta states that John is the King of England "by the grace of God." Thus they recognized an important Biblical principle: that earthly authorities derive their power and authority to rule by the allowance of the one and only King of Kings. God alone is sovereign. As such, according to its purpose statement, the Magna Carta sought to bring honor to God and exalt the church.

> Know that before God, for the health of our soul and those of our ancestors and heirs, to the honour of God, the exaltation of the holy Church, and the better ordering of our kingdom.[34]

Having rightfully established the authority of God upon matters of liberty, civil authority and earthly rule, the barons set about listing the rights of freedom to which all people are entitled. The priority of liberties they listed commenced with the English Church itself, committing that the church shall be free and its rights "undiminished." They also finished the listing of rights in the Magna Carta with paragraph 63, where they reiterated that the "English Church shall be free."[35] Church freedoms were of great importance to

"The Army of God" who drafted the great provisions of liberty contained in the Magna Carta.

The Magna Carta also set forth a list of liberties to be afforded to "all free men of our kingdom." Some of the more important of those are as follows.

In paragraph 20, there is a protection against excessive fines for offenses, to ensure that "a free man shall be fined only in proportion to the degree of his offense." Paragraph 27 sets up a system of intestate succession that is similar to current laws. Accordingly, if a free man dies intestate (without a will), his property is to be distributed by his next-of-kin and friends. To protect the process, the distribution was to be made under the supervision of the Church. Additionally, the process protected the rights of debtors. The Magna Carta recognized the right of property as a liberty to be protected. Authorities could not take corn or other moveable goods from any man without paying for them (paragraph 28), nor could they take horses or carts from any free man without his consent (paragraph 30). In paragraph 35, provision was made for standard weights and measures throughout the kingdom, similar to the Biblical commands set forth in Leviticus 19:35-36 and Deuteronomy 25:15. This provision alone fulfilled the barons' desire to honor God, since Proverbs 11:1 says that a false balance is an abomination to the Lord, but a just weight is his delight.

Biblical principles of justice were also incorporated. The requirement to have "credible witnesses" before any man could be taken to trial is made in paragraph 38, and no man could be seized or imprisoned, stripped of his rights or possessions, or deprived of his standing in any way except by the lawful judgment of his equals in a way consistent with the law of the land (paragraph 39). Thus, the charter provided for fundamental due process, recognized universally today. Freedom of movement was provided in paragraphs 41 and 42, and restoration provisions were included for any man who had previously been deprived or dispossessed of his lands, liberties or rights "without the lawful judgment of his equals" (paragraph 52).

As these examples indicate, within the clauses of the Magna Carta, we find the basis for such fundamental privileges and rights as trial by jury, Habeas Corpus, equality before the law, freedom from arbitrary arrest, and fundamental due process of law. These principles that are such an important part of liberty, as set forth in the Magna Carta, clearly had a strong Christian influence and a Biblical basis.

Translation of the Bible into English

Although the New Testament canon had been established for centuries, and the gospel had spread westward to Europe by the 13th century, God's "textbook of liberty"[36] was still largely unavailable to the masses. Only elite classes of society were educated to read Latin, the language of the scriptures at that time. It wasn't until more than 150 years after the Magna Carta, in 1382, that the Bible was translated into English for the first time. An English clergyman named John Wycliffe completed this mammoth undertaking.

The efforts of such Christian men as Wycliffe also helped spread the gospel in England during this time. Referred to as the "Morningstar of the Reformation," John Wycliffe, along with the "Lollard" preachers he trained, worked hard to prepare the English nation for spiritual revival. He and the Lollards distributed hand-written copies of the Bible throughout England and taught the people how to read so that the gospel message would be available to all people. As the masses began to read the scriptures for themselves, it began to create great upheaval within the Roman Catholic church, which had tried to retain its power to interpret scripture by limiting those who had access to it.

Wycliffe knew that as people gained access to the Bible and could read it for themselves, social and political change was inevitable. Upon completion of his English translation, he made a comment that most Americans have long attributed to Abraham Lincoln from his Gettysburg Address, yet it was Wycliffe who first used the phrase in the context of the Bible: "This Bible is for a government of the people, by the people and for the people."[37] This great statement of liberty thus had a Christian origin, and indeed, the history of the Bible itself is closely tied to the history of civil liberty. The great charters of freedom that suddenly were born from 1600-1800 cannot be explained apart from the dispersion of the Bible in the two centuries preceding it. Its availability to the masses certainly did result in significant social and political changes.

Years later, those who resented the changes and recognized that it all began with Wycliff's translated Bibles were so incensed that they dug up his grave, burned his bones, and threw the ashes into the river. Ironically, what happened to Wycliff's ashes represents what happened to his ideas: as the waters of the river poured into the ocean, and those waters in turn spread around the globe, so, too, did Wycliff's ideas of freedom of internal and external freedom for the common people.[38]

Other Stops in the Flame's Journey

While we wish to introduce the reader to some of the other more interesting stops in this journey that preserved the principles for later impact in America's development, we do not attempt to address them all. There are simply too many for our purposes, and previous authors have already treated this subject well.

Nonetheless, there are some other aspects of this journey we do want to mention. For example,within the next century, around the year 1455, Johann Guttenberg would invent the printing press, which would lead to the dissemination of the Bible even further.[39] Later still, a whole new world, from the perspective of Biblical truth, would be discovered by Christopher Columbus. That man, although much maligned by some people today, was prompted by God to go west and open the gospel to yet another group of people, to whom Columbus referred as Indians.[40]

The land that is presently the United States, however, would be providentially preserved from being successfully colonized until later, after the 16th century, when God's Biblical principles of liberty would be better ingrained in the hearts of a people He would prepare to carry His truth. While many earlier colonies flourished in Canada to the north and other nations to the south, God preserved the colonization of America for a later, more opportune time. Gold and the greed it spawned had been too much a part of other colonization efforts. If the flame of civil liberty based on Biblical precepts was to continue burning, it had to be preserved by a people more committed to following the will of God than the lure of material gain. Godly talk would not be enough for this task. God would need a people softened by heartache and difficult sacrifice, a people united and strengthened by a common love for His truths, and a people willing to sacrifice their own selfish desires for a bigger plan. So God had to prepare a people, both spiritually and mentally, by means of the Reformation. Historian B.F. Morris wrote of the providential nature of this period as follows:

> Meantime, God held this vast land in reserve, as the great field on which the experiment was to be made in favor of a civil and religious liberty. He suffered not the foot of Spaniard, or Portuguese, or Frenchman, or Englishman to come upon it until the changes had been wrought in Europe which would make it certain that it would always be a land of religious freedom.[41]

While the colonies to the north and south of what would become America were colonized by Roman Catholic explorers who were largely godly men, they knew not how to govern according to Christ's Biblical pattern.

The Reformation played a crucial role in educating believers about this pattern.

The Reformation Transformation

The 16th and early 17th centuries were quite significant to the progress of Biblically based liberty. Europe was transformed by the protests of such men as Martin Luther in Germany, William Tyndale in England, and John Calvin in Switzerland and France. Martin Luther's emphasis on the priesthood of the believer, elaborated by John Calvin, further elevated the Biblical principle that man is superior to the state, not the other way around. That concept alone contributed mightily to the emphasis on individual rights that became so firmly rooted in America's early history. Historian George Bancroft[42] recognized the clarity of his Christian influence upon America so much that he called Calvin "the father of America" and said, "he who will not honor the memory and respect the influence of Calvin knows but little of the origin of American independence."[43]

Calvin not only helped establish a new form of church government known as Presbyterianism, but his *Institutes of the Christian Religion* (1536) were also influential in restoring the concept of the dominion mandate to the church, and providing guidelines for Christian resistance to tyranny. He especially influenced the Reformation in France and Switzerland as a result of the training center he established in Geneva for French Protestants, who became known as "Huguenots."[44] The teachings of Calvin about government in particular would later provide the moral foundation for America's independence efforts against a tyrannical English king.

The 16th century Reformation was a time when Christians were reasoning from the Bible as to the correct forms of church government. After England's King Henry VIII broke off from the Catholic Church, in an effort to destroy the papal system, he authorized and encouraged the sale and reading of the Bible. As only God could orchestrate, the Bible version the King had unknowingly distributed (it had been published under the name of the Matthew Bible) was that of William Tyndale, the man he had earlier burned at the stake as a heretic.[45] With the wide distribution and reading of William Tyndale's Bibles, the Reformation spawned a whole new movement in England — the Puritan movement. The Puritans pushed for more and more reform, but when persecuted, many began to separate out and establish independent congregations beginning in the 1570s.

God's Flame of Liberty Prepares for an Atlantic Crossing

God was clearly preparing the stage for His word to be planted on America's shores through a group of committed but persecuted Christians who felt the need to break away from the impurities of the Anglican Church. These Christians, known as "Separatists," began to establish a congregational form of church government led by Robert Browne. He defined a church as "a company or number of Christians or believers, which by a willing covenant made with their God, are under the government of God and Christ, and keep His laws in one holy communion."[46] That covenant concept would prove instrumental in the Pilgrim settlement at Plymouth and the historic drafting of the Mayflower Compact, designed as their first instrument of self-government in America. When Browne formed a congregation at Norwich, England, he had this to say about what is meant by a covenant:

> A covenant was made and then mutual consent was given to hold together. There were certain points proved unto them by the scriptures, all which being particularly rehearsed unto them with exhortation, they agreed upon them and pronounced their agreement to each thing particularly, saying, "to this we give our consent."[47]

Dr. McLaughlin elaborated upon this idea in his book, *Foundations of Constitutionalism*, stating that, "[w]here Congregationalism or Separatism or Independence went, there also went the theory and fact of compact and covenant."[48]

One of the reformers in England, Rev. William Perkins, championed the idea of freedom of conscience, and had a profound influence on Rev. William Ames and Rev. John Robinson, the pastor of the Pilgrims. Ames wrote a catechism called *The Marrow of Theology,* which was used by all three streams of the Puritan movement: Episcopalians, Presbyterians and Congregationalists. In it he asserted that civil government is part of divinity, and that God governs the world mainly by teaching, that is, by first forming internal character in each person, not by forming external laws.

The historical stage was now ready. God had sovereignly prepared a special group of people, inculcated with His principles of Godly liberty, to bring them forth in a new land uncorrupted by the long since corrupted church of the Old World. Thus, when the persecution in England became too intense, the Christians of these various movements fled to an isolated wilderness thousands of miles west, known as America, "for the glory of God and advancement of the Christian faith."[49] They carried with them the torch light of Christian liberty. That light would later illuminate the minds and inspire the dreams of liberty that would become a prime motivating force within our Founding Fathers who were not yet born.

SEVEN

"WE COVENANT AND COMBINE OURSELVES:" American Colonists Practice Christian Self-Government and Voluntary Union

The Christian worldview of man and government that shaped our Declaration of Independence and Constitution was so much a part of American colonial life, that historian Dr. Lutz wrote in his publication, "Publius," the following observation:

> If we are ever to produce a complete and accurate American constitutional history, we must recognize that without the state constitutions in force in 1789, the national Constitution is an incomplete text. They must be read together. The state constitutions themselves did not simply spring into being, but were the culmination of a long development, . . [beginning with] those documents establishing local self-government on American shores during the early 17th century.

Indeed, in the first one hundred years of American history, at least 86 separate colonial documents were written. They reflected the Christian idea of covenant and consent of the governed that was common in the colonies. Dr. Lutz says that "[o]f the 86 constitution-like documents written by American colonists before 1722, . . . the word covenant is rarely used to describe a document, even though a number of them were in fact understood to be covenants." The first of the documents establishing local self-government originated in Jamestown, the first successful permanent English colony in America. Puritan Episcopalians settled it in 1607. They wrote the very first civil compact or constitution-like document in history in 1610, entitled Articles, laws and orders, divine, politic and Martial for the Colony of Virginia.

The more historically well known occurrence in Jamestown, however, was in 1619, when the colonists organized the first General Assembly of freemen in the New World and enacted their own laws. This Assembly was based on the Christian principles that man has unique value and worth and that all men stand equal before God. They also publicly acknowledged God as the source of their blessings when they celebrated the first Thanksgiving Day in America that same year, although these events never became as well known as what occurred farther north just a scant two years later.

The Mayflower Compact of Massachusetts

In 1620, a congregation of Separatists who had fled to Holland for 12 years determined now to settle in the northern parts of this same Virginia Colony. They set sail on the Mayflower with 102 passengers living for 66 days' duration in a space no larger than a volleyball court. During their voyage, they ran into a violent storm that blew them far off course, causing them to land at Cape Cod, well outside the jurisdiction of the Virginia Charter they had sailed under. Being without laws to govern them, they drew up a document originally called the Plymouth Combination, but better known to us as the Mayflower Compact (a name it did not acquire until 1793). As Verna Hall described the event:

> Each religion has a form of government, and Christianity astounded the world by establishing self-government. With the landing of the Pilgrims in 1620, Christian self-government became the foundation stone of the United States of America.

On November 11, 1620, while still on board the Mayflower, America became forever covenanted "for the glory of God and the advancement of the Christian faith." This covenant or compact contains many Biblical principles we have previously identified, such as the consent of the governed ("We whose names are underwritten"), the principle that government exists for the common good ("for the general good of the Colony"), and the principle that the people must combine themselves together to form a government ("We . . . do . . . covenant and combine ourselves into a civil body politic").

A covenant or compact creates a community and defines its common values and goals in a sort of "Bill of Rights." The community subsequently establishes a "Constitution" or body of laws for itself. The Mayflower Compact created and defined the Plymouth community and its goals, and the Plymouth Code of Law of 1636 was its constitution or legal system.

Colonies of New England and Pennsylvania

One year later, in 1637, a Separatist clergyman named Roger Williams founded the new colony of Providence, Rhode Island. It was significant for its example of toleration of diverse Christian persuasions. Williams championed the causes of liberty of conscience and pluralism, but not as they are held today. Instead, he spoke in terms of Christian pluralism in a Christian state, not a secular one.[1]

Another clergyman, Rev. Thomas Hooker, founded the colony of Connecticut the following year. In 1639, he wrote the Fundamental Orders of Connecticut, which many consider to be the first full-fledged written constitution in history.[2] Whereas other documents in the colonies were later modified or replaced, the Connecticut Constitution remained intact up to, and well beyond the adoption of the national Constitution. Historian John Fiske said, therefore, that our national Constitution is "in lineal descent more nearly related to that of Connecticut than to any of the other 13 colonies."[3] Rev. Hooker preached and reasoned from Deuteronomy 1:13, that the people should freely elect their civil rulers and make their laws.[4] Notice the close association he saw between government and God's word:

> Well knowing where a people are gathered together the word of God requires that to maintain the peace and union of such a people there should be an orderly and decent government established according to God . . . [W]e do therefore . . . enter into combination and confederation together to maintain and preserve the liberty and purity of the gospel of our Lord Jesus Christ.

Yet another clergyman was used by God to spread the flame of Christian liberty through the Massachusetts Body of Liberties. In 1641, Rev. Nathaniel Ward wrote what became the first "Bill of Rights" in history to guarantee individual liberties that "humanity, civility, and Christianity call for as due to every man . . . without impeachment and infringement."[5]

Rev. William Penn, a devout Quaker, founded Pennsylvania in 1682 and wrote the Frame of Government, which established laws "as shall best preserve true Christian and civil liberty in opposition to all unchristian licentious and unjust practices, whereby God may have his due, Caesar his due, and the people their due,"[6]

He firmly believed that good government depended upon Christian character and reliance upon God. Among the many things Penn had to say about government are these two gems: to the Russian Czar, Peter the Great he advised that "if thou wouldst rule well, thou must rule for God, and to do that, thou must be ruled by him." Later he said, "[T]hose who refuse to be governed by God will be ruled by tyrants."[7] This colony, like Rhode Island, became a model of true religious liberty for all sects of Christians.

The Influence of Colonial Clergy

Williams, Hooker, Ward and Penn are only a few examples of why the colonial clergy as a whole must be considered as a vital part of our constitutional foundation. Historian Alice Baldwin wrote that "the Convention and the written Constitution were the children of the pulpit."[8] In 1983, the American Political Science Review documented that over 10% of all colonial political writings were sermons by the clergy.[9] In 1633, Rev. John Cotton helped initiate the annual Election Sermon in Massachusetts, as well as a weekday lecture in the Old South Meeting House (Church) on topics relating to government. These practices were adopted by the clergy and legislatures of most of the colonies and endured for over two hundred years, into the mid-1800's.

The clergy would also preach what were called "artillery sermons," Fast Day sermons, and other commemorative sermons dealing with public policy. The clergy also started the first common schools, and founded the first universities in America, such as Harvard, Princeton and others, that the seeds of liberty might be sown continually. But they did not stop there. They also actively took the lead in political and government affairs. Lists of clergymen on Town Committees, in Provincial Congresses and Conventions evidence their active role in government matters.

Perhaps the most famous example of colonial clergy taking part in government was that of Dr. John Witherspoon. Dr Witherspoon was a member of the Continental Congress who signed the Declaration of Independence in 1776. That same year he preached a Fast Day sermon entitled The Government of God, in which he stated that:

> it is in the man of piety and inward principle that we may expect to find the uncorrupted patriot, the useful citizen, and the invincible soldier, — God grant that in America true religion and civil liberty may be inseparable, and the unjust attempts to destroy the one, may in the issue tend to the support and establishment of both.[10]

Without a doubt, the colonial clergy played a vital role in the chain of liberty. Today, some of these men are honored with statues in the U.S. Capitol Building.

The American Christian Revolution and Declaration

When conflict between England and its American colonies came to a head in the 1770s, Samuel Adams, the "Father of the Revolution," organized committees of correspondence to help citizens discuss the principles at stake. An essay of his in 1773 was typical of the way that the American colonists approached the issues:

> The Rights of the Colonists as Christians' [sic] . . . may be best understood by reading and carefully studying the institutes of the great Law Giver . . . which are to be found clearly written and promulgated in the New Testament.[11]

In the summer of 1776, following the outbreak of armed conflict in the colonies, delegates from all 13 American colonies gathered in Philadelphia. They agreed to propose a Declaration of Independence that would become the compact and covenant of a whole new nation. It would clearly reflect their Christian and Biblical worldview. After each delegate signed that document on July 4, Samuel Adams declared what was obvious to them all:

> This day we have restored the Sovereign to whom alone all men ought to be obedient. He reigns in Heaven, and from the rising to the setting of the sun, may His kingdom come.[12]

The Words of the Declaration Conveyed a Biblical Foundation.

The most significant additions to Thomas Jefferson's original draft of the Declaration by Congress were the insertion of phrases that asserted the unapologetic Christian faith of our Founders. In those phrases they appealed "to the Supreme Judge of the World" and they expressed a "firm reliance on the protection of Divine Providence." This country was truly declaring itself "Under God."

The Founders stated in the Declaration of Independence that they all held certain self-evident "truths" in common that united them. The truths they listed were as follows:

- "All men are created equal"
- "All men are endowed by their Creator with unalienable rights"
- These include "life, liberty and the pursuit of happiness"
- To "secure rights, governments are instituted"
- Governments derive "their just powers from the consent of the governed"

- When government destroys these rights "it is the right of the people to alter or to abolish it"
- Laws should serve the common or "public good"
- "The right of Representation"

Each of these truths is based on Christian principles that were first enunciated in the Bible.

The Declaration was the first national covenant in history that created a community and defined its values and goals solidly on the Christian ideas of man and government. It was followed by new constitutions in every state, as well as by a "national" constitution of sorts in the Articles of Confederation in 1777.

Those Declaration principles and truths are still "self-evident" in our modern era. Justice Douglas, in the U.S. Supreme Court case of *McGowan v. Maryland*, decided in 1961, included this statement in his court opinion:

> The institutions of our society are founded on the belief that there is an authority higher than the authority of the State; that there is a moral law which the state is powerless to alter; that the individual possesses rights, conferred by the Creator, which government must respect. The Declaration of Independence stated the now familiar theme: "We hold these Truths to be self-evident, that all Men are created equal, that they are endowed by their Creator with certain unalienable Rights, that among these are Life, Liberty, and the Pursuit of Happiness." And the body of the Constitution as well as the Bill of Rights enshrined those principles.[13]

The principles of liberty preserved from Jerusalem, into Europe, across the great expanse of the Atlantic, to the shores of America were captured forever in the bold words of the Declaration.

The Declaration Set Forth America's Legal Standard for a Nation.

In August, 1775, the English King declared the American colonies to be in rebellion and the colonists no longer were entitled to any of their rights as Englishmen. Thus, by the time the Declaration was proposed on July 4, 1776, English law no longer applied to the colonists. Had America held a secular worldview at this time in history, losing her rights as Englishmen would have posed a significant problem, as they would have had no other basis to seek redress. But the colonists' Biblical worldview enabled America to base her entitlement to independence upon a higher law which governed all nations at all times and which took precedence over any law contrary to it.

The founders appealed "to the Supreme Judge of the world" and based America's legal system upon "the laws of nature and of nature's God."

According to the foremost legal scholar recognized in America at the time, Sir William Blackstone, in his Commentaries on the Laws of England, the phrase, "the laws of nature and of nature's God" contained two components: (1) "Of nature's God" referred to the revealed law of Scripture itself, while (2) "the laws of nature" referred to the law of God written on the heart of man which must be consistent with Scripture. Blackstone noted that all law must be based upon those two components: God's law written on man's heart as best that man understands that law, and the revealed law as found in the Scriptures.[14]

Since all true, legitimate law is based on God's laws, no human laws can be valid if they contradict this higher law. Sir William Blackstone was emphatic about this point of legal supremacy of God's laws over man-made law.

> Nay, if any human law should allow or enjoin us to commit it, we are bound to transgress that human law, or else we must offend both the natural and the divine.[15]

There are four Biblical principles of law that were derived from the phrase, "the laws of nature and of nature's God" that also formed the basis for America's legal system set forth in the Declaration of Independence:

- God is the ultimate source of law;
- God's law is universal and unchanging;
- Only laws and judicial decisions consistent with God's laws are legitimate; and
- Any law contrary to God's law is considered void or invalid.

This idea of the law of nature, written upon our hearts, is consistent with Scripture. In the book of Romans, chapter 1, verses 19-20, it says that His laws have been made known to each of His creations.

This idea of the law of nature, consistent with Scripture, was not only held by most Americans at the time, it was specifically held by most of the Founding Fathers at the time. Notice the words of one of the signers of our Constitution, Rufus King:

> The . . . law established by the Creator, which has existed from the beginning, extends over the whole globe, is everywhere and at all times binding upon mankind. . . . [This] is the law of God by which he makes his way known to man and is paramount to all human control.[16]

In a speech before the U.S. Senate, after the Constitution was enacted, he made this comment about the need for our laws to be consistent with the laws of God.

> I hold that all laws or compacts imposing any such condition [as involuntary servitude] upon any human being are absolutely void because contrary to the law of nature, which is the law of God.

James Wilson, another signer of our Constitution, and later a U.S. Supreme Court Justice, emphatically stated that "God . . . is the promulgator as well as the author of natural law."[17]

Thus, when Jefferson and the other Founding Fathers cited to the "laws of nature and of nature's God" in the Declaration of Independence, they were creating a legal heritage for America based upon the Bible! That heritage was consistent with the principles upon which America was founded and the beliefs of its citizens.

The Declaration Based American's Rights on God.

One of the greatest contributions to liberty set forth in the Declaration of Independence is its reference to the concept of rights that were "inalienable." Because their source was God and they were not provided or created by any government, these inalienable rights could never be taken away legally and justly by any government. The Declaration's reference to "inalienable" rights was unique to the world and critical to the true value of liberty.

The rights of Americans are given to us by God through the "laws of nature and nature's God." Thus what God gives, man cannot take away at any time, in any place, or under any conditions other than those which God determines. By using the term "inalienable" to describe our rights, the Founders were emphasizing that the Bible would be the basis for what rights were held by the citizens of America. Moreover, the obvious implication is that rights that God gives can only be defined consistent with God's standards. Hence, our legal system as enunciated by the phrase, "the laws of nature and nature's God," and our rights that were described as "inalienable" recognized that our rights had to be interpreted and defined consistently with Scripture, where they were set forth.

This idea that our rights do not derive from the Constitution or from government, but were already existing and God-given, is novel to the modern mind, but it was not novel to the Founders or the legal scholars of that time. One of the signers of the Constitution, John Dickinson, clearly stated this belief as follows:

[T]he rights essential to happiness. . . . We claim them from a higher source – from the King of kings and Lord of all the earth.[18]

Samuel Adams echoed this idea when he expressed that:

[T]he only true basis of all government [is] the laws of God and nature. For government is an ordinance of Heaven, designed by the all benevolent Creator.[19]

There are numerous other quotations of the Founders that have a similar sentiment to those noted above. The ideas expressed by John Dickinson and Samuel Adams were not radical for their day, but rather were quite mainstream.

By so interpreting our rights, our Founders anchored them to an unchanging standard that was predictable, knowable, and understood by all.

The development of Biblical ideas of civil liberty over thousands of years had finally culminated, by the establishment of America, in the world's first Christian republic.

The Founders Biblical natural law philosophy remained the unquestioned standard for law and government until the turn of this century." It was certainly the legal standard in place when the Founders drafted our Constitution, and based on writings of the signers, it accurately represented their worldview.

Those Biblical precepts are what America's founders used to form our nation. President George Washington during his first Inaugural Address, emphasized that :

[The] propitious [favorable] smiles of Heaven can never be expected on a nation that disregards the eternal rules of order and right which Heaven itself has ordained.[20]

As such, the American government and Constitution were clearly a political expression of Christian ideas.[21] Our Founders were universally convinced of this truth, for they reasoned from the Bible far more than any other source.

Historian C. Gregg Singer, in his book, *A Theological Interpretation of American History*, summarizes this strong, Biblical worldview commonly held by Americans during the Constitutional period.

A Christian world and life view furnished the basis for this early political thought which guided the American people for nearly two centuries and whose crowning lay in the writing of the Constitution of 1787. This Christian theism had so permeated the colonial mind that it continued to guide even those who had come to regard the Gospel with indifference or even hostility. The currents of this orthodoxy were too strong to be easily set aside by those who in their own thinking had come to a different conception of religion and hence of government also.

Even to an outsider, this strong mix of Biblical thinking was seen as being thoroughly interwoven into American's ideas of liberty. The famous French historian and social philosopher, Alexis de Tocqueville, who provided one of the most penetrating assessments of America during the early1800s, observed that:

> The Americans combine the notions of Christianity and of liberty so intimately in their minds, that it is impossible to make them conceive the one without the other. [22]

The Constitution Continues What the Declaration Started

Nothing changed between the writing of the Declaration in 1776 and the Constitution eleven years later. Indeed, the Constitution was intended to build upon the foundation already established by the Declaration. As such, the authors of our Constitution adhered to the same legal standard as did the authors of the Declaration. The governmental framework outlined in the Constitution would be built upon the same foundation, that of Biblical Christianity.

Indeed, without Christianity, there never would have been a Constitution. As Noah Webster, the father of the dictionary and a key Federalist in the passage of the Constitution, said: "The religion which has introduced civil liberty, is the religion of Christ and his apostles, which enjoins humility, piety, and benevolence; which acknowledges in every person a brother, or a sister, and a citizen with equal rights. This is genuine Christianity, and to this we owe our free constitutions of government."[23]

Consistent with this view, twelve years following the Declaration, the Constitution stated as one of its purposes to "secure" those God-given liberties. It is interesting to observe that the original constitutional text, which did not include a Bill of Rights, did not define or delineate which rights were to be "secured" by the Constitution. That is because it was understood that those rights were the same inalienable rights referred to in the Declaration, those given by God and which man brought with him into civil society. It was further understood that the civil society was bound by the laws of nature and of nature's God, in order to protect those rights. Hence, one of the purposes of America's government, as noted in the Preamble, was to protect the rights given to its citizens by God.

According to constitutional scholar and former law professor, Herbert W. Titus, the "blessings of liberty referred to in the Preamble were recognized by the Declaration as having been given by God; the Constitution provided an organizational structure of diffused and disparate powers, in part, to secure those God-given rights."[24] There is another important hint given in the Preamble that our liberties come from God and not government. Recall the modifier the Founders used in describing the "liberties" which our Constitution was "to secure;" they were called "blessings." There is only one entity that can bestow blessings, and that entity is neither man nor government. Blessings can only come from God, our divine Creator. The authors of our Constitution recognized the same dependence of government upon God as did the signers of the Declaration of Independence.

The very fact that the drafters of the Constitution did not seek to create rights in the text of the Constitution is strong evidence that they incorporated the Biblical worldview that such rights already existed. Even later, when several leaders asserted the need for a Bill of Rights to specify which rights the Constitution embraced, they did not abandon the Biblical view. It was precisely the Biblical view that motivated their belief that future government leaders, given the sinful nature of all mankind, might later seek to deprive the citizens of their God given rights. Therefore, they sought to specify some, though not all of the more important rights.

This was an idea that naturally found its way into the early judicial decisions of the Supreme Court. An excellent example of this recognition comes from a dissent by Chief Justice John Marshall in the case of *Ogden v. Saunders*.[25] The issue of the case was the Constitution's prohibition of any state law impairing the obligation of contracts. Chief Justice Marshall sought to explain the guarantee "secured" by the Constitution by referring to rights that already existed apart from the Constitution.

> ...[I]ndividuals do not derive from government their right to contract, but bring that right with them into society; that obligation is not conferred on contracts by positive law, but is intrinsic, and is conferred by the act of the parties. This results from the right which every man retains to acquire property, to dispose of that property according to his judgment, and to pledge himself to a future act. Those rights are not given by society, but are brought into it.[26]

Chief Justice Marshall recognized that the right to hold another party to his contractual obligations is not created by the Constitution; it can't be because it already existed. The Constitution could only "secure" that right since God had created it and given it to man as an unalienable right.

The Constitution Was Intended to be Interpreted Consistent with the Declaration

The Declaration of Independence was the charter for our nation, setting forth the general principles upon which it would be based, and the Constitution was intended as the bylaws for that charter, providing greater detail consistent with the previously established framework. The Declaration provided our Constitution with its "core" values, philosophies, principles and worldview. Therefore, to properly interpret the provisions in the Constitution, they must be read in conjunction with the provisions in the Declaration.

Our Founders certainly understood the Constitution as a further development of the principles set forth in the Declaration. John Quincy Adams described this connection as follows:

> [T]he virtue which had been infused into the Constitution of the United States . . . was no other than the concretion of those abstract principles which had been first proclaimed in the Declaration of Independence. . . . This was the platform upon which the Constitution of the United States had been erected. Its virtues, its republican character, consisted in its conformity to the principles proclaimed in the Declaration of Independence and as its administration . . . was to depend upon the . . . virtue, or in other words, of those principles proclaimed in the Declaration of Independence and embodied in the Constitution of the United States.[27]

To John Quincy Adams, our Constitution was "the complement to the Declaration of Independence; founded upon the same principles, carrying them out into practical execution, and forming with it, one entire system of national government." It is a mistake, therefore, to read the Constitution as a stand-alone document. It is inexplicably tied to its charter, the Declaration, and the principles it established.

This interconnection between these two historic documents was well recognized by many authorities in the history of this nation, not the least of whom was the U.S. Supreme Court. In the case of *Gulf, Colorado and Santa Fe Railway Company v. Ellis*, the Court noted:

> [The Constitution] is but the body and the letter of which the former [the Declaration of Independence] is the thought and the spirit, and it is always safe to read the letter of the Constitution in the spirit of the Declaration of Independence.[28]

During the Pennsylvania Ratifying Convention, on December 4, 1787, James Wilson, one of the delegates at the Constitutional Convention, made clear his view that the Constitution was based on the principles of the Declaration. Referring to the second paragraph of the Declaration, Mr. Wilson noted that "[t]his is the broad basis on which our independence was placed; and on the same certain and solid foundation this system [the Constitution] is erected. James Madison, another delegate to the Constitutional Convention, declared unequivocally that the Declaration of Independence was the "best guide" to interpretation of the Constitution.

Senator Charles Sumner was even more emphatic. On the Senate floor on January 31, 1872, Senator Sumner made this impassioned appeal:

> Sir, I insist that the Constitution must be interpreted by the Declaration. I insist that the Declaration is of equal and coordinate authority with the Constitution itself. I know, sir, the ground on which I stand. I need no volume of law, no dog eared book, no cases to sustain me . . . And now sir, I am prepared to insist that, whenever you are considering the Constitution, so far as it concerns human rights, you must bring it always to that great touch-stone; the two must go together, and the Constitution can never be interpreted in any way inconsistent with the Declaration.

There is an abundance of evidence for the proposition that the Constitution is to be interpreted consistent with the principles of the Declaration of Independence.

The Important Link Between the Declaration and the Constitution.

The fact our Constitution was not written for the purpose of creating a new nation, but instead to build upon that prior foundation, is just another confirmation that the Constitution was intended to be read in conjunction with the founding document, the Declaration of Independence. Such a distinction is important because it clarifies the roles of our two founding documents.

This linkage between these two great documents of freedom is critical to a true understanding of the purpose and meaning of our Constitution, as well as for a proper judicial interpretation.

The documents throughout America's early history were consistently convenental in nature, emphasized Christian self-government and union, and sprang from a Biblical worldview. Many historians who claim that the Constitution is a secular document, void of any Biblical principles, have reached such a conclusion, at least in part, by ignoring these key factors as well as the interrelationship between our Constitution and the Declaration of Independence. Such a disconnection has led to a great distortion of the spirit behind the Constitution and such an ignoring of the Biblical worldview they were based upon has led to an erosion of the "blessings" they were meant to "secure."

EIGHT

"WE HOLD THESE TRUTHS:" Christian Ideas of Man and Government in the Constitution

Many of the general principles and specific ideas contained in America's Constitution, and previously set forth in the Declaration, come directly from the Bible. In this chapter, we will discuss some of the internal principles that are implicit in the Constitution and America's frame of government. Biblical principles that influenced the external form of our Constitution will be discussed in the next chapter.

Importance of the Internal Basis of Government

Unlike today's one-dimensional focus upon government's external form, a Christian structure based upon God's Biblical principles is always more concerned about the internal basis of government. The spirit of the law, as opposed to merely the letter of the law, is what transforms a government structure into either a liberty enhancing body or a liberty confining body.

The Bible contains numerous passages that focus on this internal dimension or inward character of government. For example, Isaiah 10:1-2 gives this admonition:

> Woe to those who enact evil statutes, and to those who constantly record unjust decisions, so as to deprive the needed of justice, and rob the poor of My people of their rights, in order that widows may be their spoil, and that they may plunder the orphans.

Leviticus 19:15, instructs leaders as follows:

> You shall do no injustice in judgment; you shall not be partial to the poor nor defer to the great, but you are to judge your neighbor fairly.

Because such internal character of leaders and government was so important from a Biblical perspective, the Bible also carefully stipulates that the character of the people we place in authority must be Godly. Contrary to the assertions of some people in recent national elections, character is very important, far more important than the economy or other external circumstances. Notice the words contained in Exodus 18:21:

> You shall select out of all the people able men who fear God, men of truth, those who hate dishonest gain; and you shall place these over them, as leaders of thousands, of hundreds, of fifties and of tens.

Internal Basis of America's Constitution

Our Founding Fathers were greatly concerned about the need to retain the internal basis of our Constitution — Biblical and Christian principles with God as the ultimate authority. The often repeated words in the Founders' writings that referred to this essential basis were "religion (or piety), morality (or virtue) and knowledge (or learning)," by which they meant the Christian religion, Christian character, and a Biblical world view. Without this Christian basis, they knew our Constitution would be only a "hollow shell."[1] Indeed, early Americans, in general, believed that good government was a logical extension of the exercise of inward Christian character.[2] Daniel Webster, one of our early leaders, perhaps captured the thoughts of most Americans during this period when he observed the causal connection between the inward qualities of our citizens as produced by the Bible and the success of our nation.

> If we abide by the principles taught in the Bible, our country will go on prospering; but if we and our posterity neglect its instructions and authority, no man can tell how sudden a catastrophe may overwhelm us and bury all our glory in profound obscurity.[3]

This connection noted by Webster certainly applied to the thinking of our early leaders. James Madison, on June 20, 1785, wrote that "religion [is] the basis and Foundation of Government."[4]

George Washington repeatedly emphasized the foundation of religion in our nation. These are not the statements of men who intended to separate government and religion or even to make government neutral toward religion. Religion, at least that based on the Bible, was too important to the success of government for government to take a neutral stance toward the matter.

These men were not saying anything new or unusual. They were simply echoing a Biblical truth: "[w]here the spirit of the Lord is, there is liberty" (2 Corinthians 3:17). This is one of those universal truths that will stand the test of time. It holds true regardless of time in history or place on earth. Even a cursory glance at recent history confirms this truth. Behind the veil of the former "iron curtain" nations where communism ruled, government was based on a man-centered philosophy that excluded God's principles from the public square. Those nations were characterized by a complete absence of liberty, and a great presence of oppression. The nation best known for liberty and freedom in the world, America, was the one that initially sought a Biblical basis for its government. The connection was not coincidental.

With that background in mind, let us now review specific internal Biblical principles that are implicit in America's Constitution.

Internal Principle No. 1: Man is of Divine Origin

Beliefs about man's origin lie at the heart of the difference in much of our current debates on governmental issues and solutions. If you believe, as the public schools now teach and liberal scholars insist is rational, that man is here through an evolutionary process devoid of a Creator, then you must conclude that individual man has no intrinsic value. Man is only a biological coincidence or accident. As such, man has no purpose, no standards, no lofty goals. Man is no different than a rock, or a slug crawling on the ground. This is the ultimate conclusion you must draw if you insist that man was not God created, but created by an evolutionary process from matter that has always existed. Lofty ideas of liberty or freedom could not exist if man had no intrinsic value. Liberals who decry apartheid and racism have no basis for declaring such social acts morally wrong if they do not accept the truth that man was created by God, because man would have no value.

It is only through the acceptance of our divine origin that man has intrinsic value that demands liberty and freedom for all. Only through the Christian world view, that man is created, that he is made in the image of God and has greater value than a rock or a slug, can we decry apartheid or racism or other social ills. "And God created man in His own image, in the image of God He created him; male and female He created them." Thus this principle of man's divine origin, and hence our individual worth, upon which America's Constitution is based, stems from the Bible.

Jesus taught that all persons are created by God with dignity and inherent value, *independent of what they may contribute to society*.[5] The four Gospel accounts repeatedly show Jesus affirming the value of people *who were out-*

cast by their society: women, children, lepers, tax collectors, and Gentiles. He alone noticed the poor widow's mite over and above the more ostentatious offerings of the rich. Jesus affirmed people, not their position in society.

A non-Biblical, pagan view asserts that man's value is based upon what he can contribute to society. Therefore, if a baby is born mentally or physically handicapped, his value is seen as greatly diminished and he can be extinguished through abortion or infanticide. The same is said for the non-contributing elderly by those who support euthanasia or so-called "mercy killing." This pagan, or secular view connects decisions about whether a person should live or die to their likely "quality of life." But this view focuses completely on the physical part of life and ignores the spiritual. We were not created to have a good time and pursue our selfish interests, although God allows us to if we choose. We were created to honor God. How Christians respond to poor "quality of life" situations is often the best way of honoring God and demonstrating His spiritual truths. To encourage a person to take his or her life because he or she will likely have a poor "quality of life" may be taking away their opportunity to honor God. More important, it may take away their chance to accept Jesus Christ as their savior, thereby gaining the best "quality of life" for all eternity. Therefore, to tie life to its physical "quality" is contrary to what God intends for us. Over the last few years, this pagan view of man's worth has gained influence in America over the Christian world view, but it wasn't a part of the beliefs of our Founding Fathers.

Only as an intentionally and purposefully created being, made in the image of God, can man have any value. The evolutionary teaching, if based on the idea that there is no God, leads to only one conclusion about man; an accidentally created being with no purpose can have no real value over anything else. The Biblical idea of man's divine origin is the cornerstone of our Constitution, for absent that view, man is not deserving of "domestic tranquility" or any of the other lofty purposes for which the Constitution was written.

Internal Principle No. 2: Man Has Individual Value

Not only does the Bible provide us with the basis for man's value in a general sense since we have a divine source, it also gives us the basis for believing that each individual is important. In 1 Corinthians 12:14-18, God tells us the following:

> For the body is not one member, but many. If the foot should say, "Because I am not a hand, I am not a part of the body," it is not for this reason any the less a part of the body. And if the ear should say, "Because I am not an eye, I am not a part of the body," it is not for this reason any the less a part of the body. If the whole body were an eye, where would the hearing be? If the whole were hearing, where would the sense of smell be? But now God has placed the members, each one of them, in the body, just as He desired.

This passage demonstrates that each person has a unique purpose and that God gives us our purpose. Thus, whatever talents you have, they are important because they are God-given.

Indeed, in all of God's creation, we can see God's desire for individuality. With the rare exception of identical twins, no two people look alike and no two personalities are the same, each snowflake is unique, the multitude of types of animals, plants, and topography all scream loud and clear of the principle of individuality. All are described in the Bible. Thus, the world, and all it consists of, reflects the nature of its source, Almighty God. Moreover, the world, and all it consists of, contradicts the idea that we arrived here by evolutionary accident.

Recognizing that man has value as an individual is one of the reasons why individual liberties were so important to the authors of the Declaration and our Constitution. This recognition was contrary to what the Greeks and Romans taught. Their ideas of democracy and freedom extended only to a select class of people, while the lower classes were denied basic individual rights.[6] This was consistent with the pagan world view which dominated the world at that time. Historian Richard Frothingham's comment is illustrative:

> At that time, social order rested on the assumed natural inequality of men. The individual was regarded as of value only as he formed a part of the political fabric, and was able to contribute to its uses, as though it were the end of his being to aggrandize the State. This was the pagan idea of man. The wisest philosophers of antiquity could not rise above it.[7]

Certainly the wise philosophers Aristotle and Plato couldn't rise above it. Neither man attributed the source of rights to God, the Creator, nor did they believe that men were created equal. In fact, not only did Greek polytheism declare that all men are inherently unequal, but Aristotle believed that some men should be slaves.[8] The principle that each person has value apart from what he or she contributes to the State cannot be found in either Greek or Roman history.

Internal Principle No. 3: Government Exists to Serve the People

This Biblical principle of individuality and worth affects our view of the purpose of government. Government in America was established to be an aid and assistance to individual citizens, not a ruler over them. Government was set up *for the people*, not the people for the government.

In the book of Romans, chapter 13, God reminds us that there is no power on earth that is not from God. Thus, "the powers that be (including government) are ordained of God."[9] It then goes on to set forth man's duty to obey the rulers or government leaders. Why? Because they are "the minister of God *to you* for good."[10] Hence, according to a Biblical view of government, government leaders are considered "ministers" or public servants of the people **for the people.** While we have largely tossed away this Biblical basis for our law and government, some vestiges still remain. Today, we often hear politicians, when they decide to run for public office, describe their decision as a desire to go into "public service." It has become common for Western nations to call their chief rulers "ministers" or "prime ministers," or even "public servants." Each of these terms, and the governmental principle behind them, reflect the teachings of Jesus Christ.

Along this same line of thought, Christ taught that man is superior to the government and that government exists to serve the public, not the other way around. Paganism teaches just the opposite — that the State is paramount to the individual. This third principle is set forth in Matthew 20: 25-27, where Jesus called his disciples to Himself and said:

> You know that the *rulers of the Gentiles* lord it over them, and their great men exercise authority over them. It is not so among you, but whoever wishes to become great among you shall be your servant, and whoever wishes to be first among you shall be your slave . . . .

Jesus was telling his disciples that the ungodly civil rulers they knew did not use their offices properly. Jesus wanted Christians to know that when the day came when they were able to rule, they were to see themselves as public servants. This teaching was revolutionary. Caesar and practically every other monarch in history never saw themselves as servants of the people. In both ancient Egypt and the Mesopotamian civilizations, individuals were considered the servant of government.[11] They existed to serve their government, not the other way around. A person's individual importance was directly linked to the perceived significance of his contribution to his local government.[12] It clearly was not inherently tied to man's being created by God and in His image . The theories advanced by Plato and Aristotle and the practice of Greece and Rome were therefore nothing to admire. This direct correlation between individual worth and contribution to the State[13] would have been repugnant to the authors of our Constitution. Rome also treated the government as the grantor of rights instead of God, whereas America treated government as the securer of those rights. Thus, in Rome, what the government grants, government can deny. These philosophies were diametrically opposed to the principles the authors of our Constitution worked hard to protect.

Internal Principle No. 4: The Source of Individual Rights is God, Not Government

This principle was also contrary to the prevailing, non-Biblical world view. Going back to the Greeks, law did not have its source in God, but in man.[14] Thus whatever rights man had were determined by the state. Both Socrates and Plato believed the source of rights was the state.[15] By removing God as the source of law, a society automatically removes the unalienable characteristic of that law. Since all Greek and Roman laws were seen as derived from government, they were alienable, and could be taken away by government.

The Founders believed that individual rights derived from God, not man. Hence, in the Declaration of Independence, they declared that we had certain "inalienable" rights, and that God was their source. God-given rights are much more secure than government granted rights, for what is granted by God, no man or government can lawfully deny. The Declaration also stated that since man was created, in the image of God (Genesis 1:26-27; 9:6), man had value. As a creature with God-given value, he was entitled to the inalienable rights of life, liberty, and the pursuit of happiness. Thus, human rights have their origin in the Bible.

The specific rights listed in the Declaration are also Biblically based. The Biblical command "Thou shalt not kill," found in Exodus 20:13, signifies a right to life. The command not to kidnap or enslave others, found in Exodus 21:16 and Deuteronomy 24:7, signifies a right to liberty. Finally, the commands "Thou shalt not steal" and "Thou shalt not covet," found in Exodus 20:15 and 20:17, signify a right to be secure in the ownership of property. Life, liberty, and property rights, all cornerstones in our Constitutional framework, are derived from the Bible.

There can be no basis for believing in human rights absent the Biblical view that demonstrates the worth of individual man and the source of our rights. Thomas Jefferson echoed this thought with these words:

God who gave us life, gave us liberty. And can the liberties of a nation be thought secure when we have removed their only firm basis, a conviction in the minds of the people that these liberties are the gift of God?[16]

Thus, the Founders understood, far better than we do today, that individual rights are God-given. Governments do not give rights, nor do they have the authority. Governments can only "secure" rights that have already been given by God.

Our Constitution recognized this Biblical distinction. In the Preamble, it declares that government is designed to *"secure* the Blessings of Liberty to ourselves and our Posterity." If the writers of our Constitution did not recognize that our rights had already been given to us by God, they would have had to create, not secure, those rights in our Constitution. Inalienable rights do not come from an evolutionary, atheistic world view. The true author's style and characteristics are evident. Moreover, the use of the term "blessings" is another indication that the Founders were extending their belief that our rights come from God, a belief they publicly announced in the Declaration of Independence only twelve years earlier.

Not only does our Constitution place a general emphasis on individual rights consistent with the Bible, it also contains many specific protections of liberty and property. For instance, Article I, section 9 establishes protections of individual rights through the right to petition for writ of habeas corpus and the right not to be prosecuted by bills of attainder or ex post facto laws. Article III, section 2, paragraph 3 ensures that people shall have a right to trial by jury for all crimes other than impeachment proceedings; Article IV, section 2 provides for the privileges and immunities of persons to be protected; and of course, the Bill of Rights is filled with protections for individual rights. All of these protections are a direct extension of that Biblically-based idea that man has intrinsic value as a created being made in the image of God, and that our rights are God given and can only be "secured," not "created," by government.

Internal Principle No. 5: God is Sovereign Over Government

A further principle of godly self-government taught by Jesus was that God is sovereign over government and that God delegates His power to men.[17] Pontius Pilate did not understand this truth when he asked if Jesus realized that he had the power to crucify him. Jesus' response must have been startling to the Roman leader, for Jesus answered him thus: "Thou couldest have no power at all against me, except it were given thee from above."[18] Neither Pilate, nor any other ruler would even hold their government office or any political authority had it not been granted to him by God. Thus government structures exist at the will of God and operate under His authority.

Historical scholars have concluded that "the founders specifically designed a government that would be accountable to higher sovereignties."[19] Under the American system, the people are the "proximate sovereign," while the people "affirm the higher sovereignty of God."[20] This is the fundamental reason why our Founders required public officials to swear a religious oath before taking office. They had to acknowledge a supreme power above themselves.

Internal Principle No. 6: All Men Are Created Equal

This idea, too, originated with the Bible. In the Book of Acts 10:34, scripture tells us that "God is no respecter of persons." In Galatians 3:28, it says that in Christ, "there is neither Jew nor Greek." In fact, the entire legal code in the Bible demonstrates equal justice under law.

When Jesus said that government exists to serve the public, he implied that it exists for the *common good of all men*; not just a special or select class of men. As we have discussed, in Greece and Rome, under a pagan view of government, only the upper classes were granted all the privileges of free men; they never became available to all men. According to Dr. Gary Amos, *"[t]he Greeks, and later the Romans, believed that some men by nature were superior to others and had an inherent right to rule others."*[21] But the view of government taught by Jesus brought liberty to all and removed all class distinctions.[22] The teachings of Christ and the Bible were unique to the principles of liberty, such as this basic concept of equality we all take for granted today. Perhaps this is why Benjamin Franklin, who was not a Christian, declared, *"He who shall introduce into public affairs the principles of primitive Christianity will change the face of the world."*[23]

The ancient Greeks have been given far more credit than they deserve in terms of their great thinkers and philosophies of man and government. Greek ideas could never have provided a government structure that recognizes that all men are created equal. For example, "[n]either Aristotle nor Plato believed that all men were created, or that they were created equal, or that they were endowed by a Creator with rights, or that such rights were inalienable."[24] Greek philosophy, based on polytheism, declared that all men are unequal and that such an unequal state was inherent.[25]

Nor does a system of government based on evolution lead to the concept of equality for all people. Darwin's evolutionary theory is coupled with the "survival of the fittest" mentality, which concludes that the stronger species are superior, while the weaker are less deserving. Recall that Hitler espoused the evolutionary idea that the Aryan race was superior to that of Jews or other mixed races. His belief system was not Bible-based, and as a result, millions of Jews lost their lives. Only the absolute standards of the Bible guarantee equality for mankind.

This does not mean that all people are entitled to the same economic standards of living. Policies for redistributing wealth, for instance, would have been shocking to the Founders' Biblical view of equality. They realized that people who work harder or take greater risks and responsibilities are entitled to greater material rewards as the natural fruit of their labors. Equal treatment under the law was the goal, not equal rewards.

The Founders incorporated this Biblical view of man's equality into our Constitution. For instance, our Constitution prohibits the government from granting titles of nobility in Article I, section 9, paragraph 8. This provision is contrary to the practice of numerous other nations which were not organized under a Biblical view.

Internal Principle No. 7: Civil Government is Dependent Upon Successful Self-Government

Self-government is "the ability to restrain oneself and follow a right course without someone else always overseeing and directing one's life."[26] It is the goal every parent has for his or her children. Simply put, it is maturity under the authority of God's morality. Throughout the Bible, it teaches that man must learn to govern himself according to God's law before he is ready to govern others. Only then can society flourish in peace and happiness.

In Scripture, this principle is seen in many places. For instance, in a text which deals with leadership, 1 Timothy chapter 3, verses 2-5 set forth the principle as follows:

> An overseer, then, must be above reproach, the husband of one wife, temperate, prudent, respectable, hospitable, able to teach, not addicted to wine or pugnacious, but gentle, uncontentious, free from the love of money. He must be one who manages his own household well, keeping his children under control with all dignity (but if a man does not know how to manage his own household, how will he take care of the church of God?).

Therefore, if the individual is out of control, it will affect his ability to govern in all other spheres. In his work *The Law of War and Peace*, Hugo Grotius echoed this Biblical sentiment.

He knows not how to rule a kingdom, that cannot manage a province; nor can he wield a province, that cannot order a city; nor he order a city, that knows not how to regulate a village; nor he a village, that cannot guide a family; nor can that man govern well a family that knows not how to govern himself; neither can any govern himself unless his reason be lord, will and appetite her vassals; nor can reason rule unless herself be ruled by God, and be obedient to Him.[27]

Each person must learn to rule himself first, in obedience to God and His laws. Ruling ourselves by our own laws is not self-government, but licentiousness, just doing what we please. Proverbs 16:32 gives similar instruction: "He who is slow to anger is better than the mighty, and he who rules his spirit, (who is self-governed) than he who captures a city." This principle is clearly a Biblical one.

Self-government, or self-control, must begin with the mind and the control of our thoughts. In II Corinthians 10:5, the apostle Paul admonishes us that we must take "every thought captive to the obedience of Christ." For "as a man thinketh in his heart, so is he."[28]

The early founders of America took these Biblical principles and applied them to their form of self-governing bodies in the New World. For example, when William Penn established the Quaker colony of Pennsylvania, he had no desire to be an autocratic ruler. Instead he assured the people that they "shall be governed by laws of your own making, and live a free and, if you will, a sober and industrious people."[29] Our Founders recognized that self-governing bodies are the best means of assuring liberty. As noted by Robert C. Winthrop in 1852:

> Men, in a word, must necessarily be controlled either by a power within them, or by a power without them; either by the word of God, or by the strong arm of man, either by the Bible, or by the bayonet.[30]

Internal Principle No. 8: Government and Law Are Based Upon Moral Absolutes

There are only two choices we have when we contemplate the nature of morality. Either morality is absolute, as stated in the Bible, or it is relative, as stated by current liberal scholars. There is no middle ground, unless you deny that there is a morality at all. So, let's examine these two choices to determine which one was the principle incorporated into our Constitution.

Like a religious mantra thoughtlessly repeated ad nauseum, today's liberal scholars claim that there are no moral absolutes and that all truth is relative. The ultimate conclusion of their claim is that we have no right to say that anyone is right or wrong about anything. Just because you think an activity is wrong does not mean it is. Evil, like beauty, is therefore strictly a subjective concept, limited to "the eye of the beholder." There is no objective basis to claim that anyone or any activity is "wrong." That kind of moral judgment is not absolute, but relative. This was the philosophy of John Dewey, who is called "the father of modern education." He claimed that there are no eternal truths or moral absolutes (except of course for his own absolute statement). He built modern education on this statement:

> Faith in the prayer-hearing God is an unproved and outmoded faith. There is no God and there is no soul. Hence there are no needs for the props of traditional religion. With dogma and creed excluded, then immutable truth is also dead and buried. There is no room for fixed, natural law or moral absolutes.[31]

Notice how many moral absolutes Dewey includes in his own belief statement that there are no absolutes! As a result of his philosophy, values clarification courses were introduced into public schools throughout America, and all public school children were indoctrinated with Dewey's belief that there are no moral absolutes and all right and wrong is relative. If the words of today's liberal censors were applied to Dewey, he was "forcing his beliefs" upon malleable young minds.

Aside from the obviously contradictory nature of a belief (which is absolute) that there are no moral absolutes, there is a more dangerous ultimate consequence: society loses its ability to claim that any activity is wrong. In preparation for the Nazi war crime trials at Nuremberg, Germany, prosecutors faced a perplexing defense which was the natural result of Dewey's philosophy of moral relativism. The Nazis accused of war crimes claimed that they had done nothing wrong in murdering six million Jews. They claimed they acted in conformity with their own moral culture, the dictates of their own consciences. Since morality is relative, who are you, they challenged, to place your morals on us?[32] The only way the prosecutors were able to avoid this defense was to rid themselves of the nonsense that morals are relative. They had to claim that morals were indeed absolute, although they never mentioned the source of those absolute morals!

Ted Bundy was executed in Florida for committing a series of heinous crimes in the late 70's and early 80's. He raped, then killed and mutilated several young women, all who had many hopes and dreams for the future which he destroyed through terror and violence. Was he wrong? He couldn't be if morals are only relative. Who are we to place our moral judgments upon him? Sound ludicrous? Of course it is, yet that is what Ted Bundy claimed.

According to him, "[W]hat you call wrong, I call attempts to limit my freedom."[33] That is exactly the end result of the moral relativist argument. During his terrorizing of one of his victims, he tape recorded the event. Here is part of what he told his victim before he raped and killed her:

> Surely, you would not, in this age of scientific enlightenment, declare that God or nature has marked some pleasures as 'moral' or 'bad.' Let me assure you, my dear young lady, that there is absolutely no comparison between the pleasure I might take in eating ham, and the pleasure I anticipate in raping and murdering you. That is the honest conclusion to which my education has led me — after the most conscientious examination of my spontaneous and uninhibited self.[34]

Is this the moral foundation upon which our Founders set our Constitution? The answer is obvious. They rested the Constitution upon the Biblical view that morals are absolute and universal, as affirmed by the Declaration of Independence. How else could our Founders claim that the laws of nature and nature's God were superior to the laws of England and the King? The principles of liberty and justice were absolute and universal. Likewise, murder, rape, racism, and other moral standards are wrong absolutely and universally, in Germany and America, in Laos and Russia. The same moral standards given to us by our Creator apply to all of His creation everywhere on earth. By tying the Constitution to our common law heritage, the Founders intended for the people to look to God as the supreme source of all law. Moreover, they recognized that good government could not be separated from Christian character based on those moral absolutes taught in the Bible.[35] Certainly our second President, John Adams, recognized this truth when he made the following observation:

> We have no government armed with power capable of contending with human passions unbridled by morality and religion. Avarice, ambition, revenge, or gallantry, would break the strongest cords of our Constitution as a whale goes through a net. *Our Constitution was made only for a moral and religious people. It is wholly inadequate for the government of any other.*[36]

Internal Principle No. 9: Man's Nature is Sinful

In contrast to the French philosopher Jean Jacques Rousseau and other Enlightenment thinkers who viewed man as naturally good, the Bible teaches that all men are sinners and tend toward disobedience to God. In Jeremiah 17:9, it says that "(t)he heart is deceitful above all things, and desperately wicked; who can know it?" Thus, placing government in the hands of the general will without checks and balances could be dangerous since the general will could be wrong. Moreover, placing great amounts of power in the hands of a few would be dangerous, for those few men are sinful in nature and thus cannot be trusted to always act in the best interest of their constituents.

Governmental philosophies such as socialism or communism ignore this absolute truth. Thus, neither system could work in America, and as history has demonstrated, neither system works well anywhere else.

In contrast, the Founders accepted the Biblical view of man, succinctly stated in Romans 3:23; "All have sinned, and come short of the glory of God." This "Biblical view of man drove them to develop a form of government that would neither depend blindly upon the will of the masses nor give absolute power to one man."[37] Thus, they sought to form their government based upon their belief in the sinful nature of man. This struggle and intent is described in *The Federalist No. 51* wherein James Madison stated the following:

> But what is government itself but the greatest of all reflections on human nature? If men were angels, no government would be necessary. If angels were to govern men, neither external nor internal controls on government would be necessary. In framing a government which is to be administered by men over men, the great difficulty lies in this: You must first enable the government to control the governed; and in the next place, oblige it to control itself.[38]

Constitutional provisions such as separation of powers and checks and balances are all rooted in the Biblical idea that man is not to be trusted. Limits on government authority likewise recognize this truth.

Internal Principle No. 10: External Forms are a Result of Internal Power

Following His resurrection from the dead, Jesus was with His disciples for forty days, instructing them and emphasizing "the things concerning the kingdom of God."[39] This emphasis, along with the undeniable proof that He was the Messiah spoken of by the Prophets, led the disciples to anticipate that the prophecies of external liberty were ready to be fulfilled at once, for they asked: "Lord, is it at this time You are restoring the kingdom to Israel?"[40] For years we read the Lord's response to their question in an incorrect manner. We, and many others, had always thought that Christ looked upon their "carnal" question with an attitude of disdain and simply avoided addressing their desire for external liberty. But in reality, He did address their concern. He did not rebuke them or tell them never to expect external liberty; He simply said that the "time or epoch" for that event was not to be their concern. External liberty would come in the timing of God, not only to Israel, but "to the remotest parts of the earth,"[41] but it must first arise through, and be a consequence of, Christ's internal liberty.

Jesus Christ did not ignore external liberty. He merely focused the disciples' attention upon the proper method by which God would bring about external liberty — it would involve a progression from *internal change to external change*. This is God's principle of power and form. External forms are only a result of internal power.

> But you shall receive power *(internal)* when the Holy Spirit has come upon you, and you shall be My witnesses. . ."[42]

Under God's plan, the only way to attain external liberty is to first allow the Holy Spirit to bring people internal liberty from sin and selfishness. Only then are people released to attain external liberty through self-government and Christian character.[43] This process eventually creates a people who are capable of exercising externally free government, but they must have their minds renewed with the Biblical principles of liberty we see in this chapter. If we teach "all" that Jesus commanded, the nations will be discipled and transformed.[44]

NINE

"IN THE SACRED WRITINGS:" Biblical Roots of American Constitutional Government

The ideas embodied in our Constitution stem primarily from the Bible or, as Ben Franklin described them, the "Sacred Writings." In the Constitutional Convention this least-orthodox Founding Father made a speech in which he said:

> We have been assured, Sir, in the Sacred Writings that 'except the Lord build the house, they labor in vain that build it" [Psalm 127:1]. I firmly believe this, and I also believe that without His concurring aid we shall succeed in this political building no better than the builders of Babel [Genesis 11].[1]

The only proper way to determine whether a nation is Christian or not is to look to the principles upon which its form of government is based. If the form of a nation's government is shaped by Biblical ideas of man and government, in contrast to secular or man-centered ideas, then that nation is a Christian nation. In the previous chapter, we discussed the internal Biblical principles inherent to our Constitution. They were deeply rooted in America's founding, they were deeply part of America's world view, and they were naturally reflected in America's form of government. In this chapter, we wish to examine the Biblical principles reflected in the external framework of our Constitution, starting with the Preamble. We will see that the structures of government established by our Founders also have their sources in Scripture.

Look in the corner of any famous painting and you will likely see the name of the painter who created that work of art. Often we must look at that corner to know its creator, but with the more famous artists, we can recognize the work merely by its style and characteristics; we don't need to see the author's name painted in the corner. So it is that we are able to recognize the author of the universe. God does not write His name in the lower corner of the sky or on a rock to the side of a great majestic mountain; He expects us to look at the style and characteristics of His work and know immediately who its author is.

Herein lies the misunderstanding with another masterpiece: the American Constitution. The skeptic looks for the author's name written in the corner, yet he sees no words that mention God, the Bible, Jesus, or Christianity, and thus boldly claims that the Constitution is not founded on Biblical or Christian principles. Since it does not overtly declare itself to be a Christian document, it must not be so. The skeptic has forgotten that you don't need the author's name written in the corner to know who was responsible for that work of art. There is only the slight reference to "Our Lord" Jesus Christ in the final date of the Constitution, yet it is clear the founders who wrote it built it upon the "truths" they held about man and government from the Bible.

For people who are willing to look a little closer before drawing their conclusions, there is a lot of evidence that our Constitution is not a secular document.

The Preamble Lists Biblical Functions of Government

Having determined that the Articles of Confederation provided a faulty structure for national government, our Founders ultimately drafted the Constitution "in order to form a more perfect Union" built upon the Christian ideas of man and government. The Preamble of that Constitution lists five basic government functions. It is not coincidence or mere happenstance that every government function listed is also revealed in Scripture.

The first function listed in the Preamble is "to establish justice," a mandate readily found in the Bible. 1 Peter 2:14, states that civil rulers exist "for the punishment of evildoers and the praise of those who do right." Additionally, in the first book of the Bible, God told Noah that "Whoever sheds man's blood, by man his blood shall be shed" (Genesis 9:6). This is an example of justice. Thus, the first purpose of civil government listed in the Preamble was a Biblical concept.

The second purpose in the Preamble is "to insure domestic tranquility." This, too, is found in Scripture, in 1 Timothy 2:1-2, where Paul urges Christians to pray for civil rulers "in order that we may lead a tranquil and quiet life in all godliness and dignity."

The third listed purpose of civil government is "to provide for the common defense." Protection of innocent human life is at the root of this governmental purpose. Thus militaries are to protect the citizens of a nation against external threats. Romans 13:4 affirms that civil government "does not bear the sword for nothing." Jesus Christ even taught His disciples the legitimacy of being armed militarily, instructing in Luke 22:36, "[n]ow . . . let him who has no sword sell his robe and buy one." The "sword" in Scripture is equivalent to any military weapon used today for the purpose of protection.

The fourth purpose is for government to "promote the general welfare." Romans 13:4 states that civil rulers are servants "to you for good." The common good of all classes of citizens must be promoted by the passage of laws guaranteeing equal opportunity. Our Framers carefully chose their words here to reflect a Biblical perspective. Government was to promote the general welfare, not to provide it. It clarifies that God, not government, is to be the provider to the people. Thus, those in need of various assistance programs are to be cared for through private acts of charity, voluntarily provided. A Biblical economic system should promote compassionate use of wealth on a voluntary basis, and not through coerced taxes. To look to government as our provider instead of God is a form of idolatry.

The fifth stated purpose of civil government is to "secure the blessings of liberty." Blessings can only come from God. Governments don't "grant" blessings, they can only "secure" them. That Biblical perspective is reflected in this governmental purpose.

The most basic of these Creator-endowed blessings were defined in the Fifth Amendment of the Constitution that mentions "life, liberty and . . . property." Scripture defines God as the source of life in Genesis 1:27, "And God created man in His own image." He is the author of liberty as well: 2 Corinthians 3:17 - "Where the Spirit of the Lord is, there is liberty," and Leviticus 25:10 states, "Proclaim liberty throughout the land to all its inhabitants." Scripture also states that God is the source of private property and "the pursuit of happiness" as expressed in the Declaration of Independence. According to Ecclesiastes 5:19, "For every man to whom God has given riches and wealth, He has also empowered him to eat from them . . . and rejoice in his labor; this is the gift of God."[2]

Thus, as aptly distinguished in the Preamble to the Constitution, America's national government has been formed to "secure" that which God has already provided.

Our External Form of Government Stems From a Biblical Basis

The form of government a nation establishes depends greatly on whether or not the people believe mankind has an inherent sin nature. James Madison said, in *The Federalist No. 51*, "What is government itself but the greatest of all reflections on human nature?" One's world view is directly tied to one's view of government.

A secular view of government has a natural tendency to establish too much centralized power in the hands of men. That is the natural result of a world view that believes man is inherently good and can be trusted with power. Both history and the Bible have demonstrated the foolishness of such an idea.

Our Founders, while not all Christian, firmly believed in the Biblical ideas of man and government implicit in a Christian union. They believed man's sinful nature meant that he should not be entrusted with too much power, even if he was regenerated through the blood of Jesus Christ.

Therefore, the government established in our Constitution contains at least four structural mechanisms that reflect a Biblical basis: (1) representative government; (2) separation of powers; (3) federalism; (4) prohibition of government involvement in religion, education, & media; and (5) permanent union.

Structural Framework Principle No. 1: Elected Representative Government

Both the Old and New Testaments provide a basis for representative government. In Exodus 18:13-21, Moses is encouraged by his father-in-law to choose judges and representatives to help him lead Israel. His advice entailed the use of group representatives. The focus was on strong local self-government with problems being solved, as much as possible, at the lowest level, nearest where they originated. If the leader of that group could not solve the problem, he could take it to the leader of the next larger group. In Deuteronomy 1:12-18, the Bible speaks of choosing wise and understanding men to make them heads; captains over thousands, and captains over hundreds, and captains over fifties, and captains over tens, and officers among the tribes.

Likewise, the New Testament describes the governmental structure of the first century church as an example of representative government. In I Timothy 3 and Titus 1:6-9, the churches were advised to choose elders and deacons (representatives) and to do so applying qualifications God gave them. Also, in Acts 6, the whole congregation chose seven men to represent them as deacons. The Bible describes a representative system grounded firmly in God's morality. It was an external form set upon an internal foundation of godly principles.

Since the Founding Fathers held to a Biblical view of government, they created a republic through the Constitution. In so doing, they lodged power in representatives elected by the people. This was not by accident or coincidence, but an intentional decision.

Specifically, Article IV, section 4 of the U.S. Constitution states that the federal government "shall guarantee" to every state in the country "a republican form of government." In this modern era, many Americans are no longer sure what a republican form of government is. The original American Dictionary of the English Language of 1828, produced by Noah Webster, a peer of the Founders, captured the meaning clearly. It is that form of government that pertains to a republic, in which the "exercise of sovereign power is lodged in representatives elected by the people." One of the responsibilities of the federal government, then, is to ensure and protect the concept of representative government throughout all the states.

This external structure of our government system is firmly reflective of Biblical principles.

Structural Framework Principle No. 2: Separation of Powers

In the Constitution, our Founders sought to disperse power and check it, for they knew from Scripture that sinful man could not be trusted to always be virtuous and public minded. They therefore chose to divide the government structure into three branches to match the Biblical formula. According to the book of Isaiah 33:22,

> "the Lord is *our judge*; the Lord is *our lawgiver*; the Lord is *our King.*

Isaiah set up the model for judicial, legislative, and executive branches that coincided with the three roles of our Lord. However, while God, who is perfect and infallible, can possess all three powers and still be just, sinful man cannot. Hence, the Founders followed that Biblical model of government roles, but separated them from each other. As a result of their Biblical perspective, the Founders were very much aware of the dangers of power, and they made a conscious effort to thwart those dangers through the government structure that they established in the Constitution.

Included within this idea of separate powers, the Framers added the unique concept of checks and balances, by which one branch of government can prevent or check the improper exercise of power by another branch.

Thus the president can veto acts of Congress, but Congress can override his veto by a two-thirds vote of each house (Art. I, Section 7). The Supreme Court can declare acts of Congress unconstitutional, but the president appoints the court, and those appointments are subject to the advice and consent of the Senate (Art. II, Section 2). Moreover, provisions exist for the removal from office of the president, vice-president, and all civil officers on conviction under impeachment for treason, bribery, or "other high crimes and misdemeanors" (Art. II, Section 4).

The checks and balances concept is consistent with the Biblical view of man's sinful nature.

Structural Framework Principle No. 3: Federalism

While both the principles of a representative government and separation of powers reflected our Founders' Biblical view of the sinfulness of man, the greatest indication of their fear of centralized government was their formation of a national union based upon the principle of federalism. Such a form of government, created by the Constitution in 1787, was unique to the world at that time.

Federalism is the principle that disperses government power to different levels of government. It was not enough to set up separate branches of government at the federal level with checks and balances within that structure. The authors of our Constitution also wanted to divide up the powers of government between the federal government and the various state governments. Often referred to as a dual form of government, our founders intentionally sought to divide government authority between two different levels, national and more local.

As originally divided, the vast majority of government power was left with the state and local governments. Only a few carefully delineated powers were *delegated* to the federal government.[3] This was expressly established in Article I, section 8, where the federal government is specifically granted only eighteen powers. To emphasize this limited delegation of power to the federal government, the Founders further reinforced this idea in the 10th Amendment. That amendment reserves every other non-delegated power to the states. Thus, the states permanently surrendered eighteen distinct governmental powers to the federal legislative branch and some additional foreign policy related powers to the executive branch, but retained virtually all others.

According to this original design, the federal government could only make laws that dealt with such specified powers as the regulation of interstate or foreign commerce, coining money, operating postal services, granting copyright protection, regulating the laws for citizenship, and maintaining the armed forces. While the state governments had no authority to interfere with these distinct federal government powers, all other government functions were retained at the state and local levels. Thus, state governments were left with the authority to make laws dealing with such issues as public education, marriage and divorce, housing, pension plans, voting procedures, and traffic regulations. Neither federal nor state authorities could legislate in the area assigned to the other without violating their constitutionally limited authority.

Through this carefully crafted form of federalism, each level of government was held in check from encroaching upon the other by the higher law of the Constitution, declared to be the supreme law of the land in Article 6, paragraph 2. State governments were far more than powerless administrative arms of an imposing national government. Through this dual form of government, both the national and state governments had supreme authority over their defined areas of jurisdiction.

Like the concepts of separation of powers and representative government, federalism was based on the Founders' recognition of the sinfulness of man. Jefferson noted that "the way to have good and safe government, is not to trust it all to one, [e.g., the federal branch] but to divide it among the many."[4] Thus, the Biblical view of man's inherent nature guided their selection of a federalist form of government.

The Bible not only provided a basis for the need to disperse power by means of a federalist system, it also provided a model for federalism in its description of church government. The Bible was the only model in history to which our Founders could refer, since no civil government to that point in history had ever attempted such a scheme. But with the Bible's description of the New Testament church, our Founders saw evidence of dual government. The great bulk of power in church government resided at the local level, in each congregation's local presbytery of elders (1 Timothy 3:1-5, 4:14; 5:17). Yet there was also a limited measure of authority exercised by the apostles and prophets in the mother church at Jerusalem, which was binding on the local churches (Acts 15:2, 4,6; and 16:4).[5] This relationship between the mother church in Jerusalem and the other outlying churches was the first example of a federalist form of government where authority was divided between two separate levels.[6] The dual government arrangement of the New Testament church was also reflected in the denominational structures of the Colonial churches of the day. For example, a Presbyterian in Virginia was loyal to his local church leadership, but he was also subject to the Presbyterian denominational leadership at large.

Structural Framework Principle No. 4: Prohibition of Federal Government Involvement in Religion, Education, & Media

Thus it was, under a carefully designed plan to limit the power of the federal government, that our founders provided it with only eighteen specifically delineated powers. These eighteen powers were permanently surrendered to the national government by the states when they ratified the Constitution.

The concept of limited government also echoed the Declaration of Independence, which asserted that "just powers" are derived from "the consent of the governed." Thus, the Constitution recognized that it is the people who must delegate certain powers to the government, and that government has no power other than what was delegated.[7]

The principle of delegated powers means that government power is inherently limited, operating properly only when confined to specifically delegated activities. This idea that government should be limited is also a Biblical concept. For example, in Deuteronomy 17:14-20, the Bible describes the limits upon Israel's government structure at that time. From these verses, clearly, there were certain activities that government had no legal authority to engage in such as making money, redefining marriage, etc.

Structural Framework Principle No. 5: Permanent Union with Amendment Process

The only way to expand the powers given to Congress or allow Federal government to regulate religion or speech or education would be through amendments to the Constitution. This made the federation a permanent union, unlike the uncertainty of a confederation that they initially suffered under the Articles of Confederation.

The distinction is critical to understanding our constitutional system. The Constitution did not form thirteen independent states connected only by a voluntary agreement. Such an arrangement is a temporary unity, but it is not a true union. According to Webster's Dictionary, a union is "the act of joining two or more things into one, and thus forming a compound body."[8] It is the difference between living together and marriage. The former is meant to be a temporary arrangement that can be voluntarily dissolved when the parties wish; the latter is meant to be a permanent arrangement.

That is why the secession of the Confederate states prior to the Civil War was an unconstitutional act. Our Founders had established a permanent union of states by a national covenant — the Constitution. The significance of any covenant, whether in marriage, in church, or in civil government, is that when both parties are acting as they should, there is no divorce. All problems and conflicts must be patiently discussed and debated until they are resolved. This requires nothing less than Christian character, virtue, and reliance on God to work. Unfortunately, due to the sinfulness of man, God made provision for divorce when one of the parties materially violates its obligations and duties. It was on this basis that America was forced to split from Great Britain and declare herself an independent nation.

However, in order to form an external union, there must first exist an internal unity, or voluntary agreement.[9] In terms of our constitutional structure, this internal unity or agreement was initially achieved through the ratification process. But for internal unity to continue over the long term, there must also be a common foundation of beliefs, convictions, and purposes. That common basis existed in 1787. While individuals were diverse and religious beliefs differed, the general populace held to the same set of Biblical principles. According to historian K. Alan Snyder:

> . . . a Christian consensus dominated the era. They were generally united on certain self-evident truths: that there was a creator God who gave them their rights; that He had absolute standards of right and wrong; that someday every person would have to stand before this God and give an account of his actions; and that heaven and hell were actual places where people would spend eternity.[10]

Thus a Ben Franklin, who described himself earlier in life as a deist, and the non-denominational Thomas Jefferson could still have a common basis of belief with a traditional Christian, George Washington, in recognizing that "God governs in the affairs of men." They respected diversity without throwing away our common set of beliefs in God and His Biblical principles.

Other Biblical Principles Incorporated into our Constitution

In Article I, section 8, the Constitution set up a monetary system based on gold and silver coins and gave Congress the power to fix a standard of weights and measures. This conformed to the Biblical example of having honest weights and measures, found in Deuteronomy 25:13-15.

In Article I, section 7, paragraph 2, the Constitution sets forth the president's veto power and declares that "If any bill shall not be returned by the President within ten days (Sundays excepted) after it shall have been presented to him, the same shall be a law . . . ." This clearly was in response to the Framers view of the Fourth Commandment taken from Exodus 20:8-10, which states in verse 10: "but the seventh day is the Sabbath of the Lord thy God: in it thou shalt not do any work."

In scripture it says that at least two witnesses are required before a person could be put to death.[11] The Constitution provides a similar protection in Article III, section 3, paragraph 1, where it states that "no person shall be convicted of Treason unless on the testimony of two witnesses to the same cover act, or on confession in open court." Similarly, protection against self-incrimination was provided for in the Fifth Amendment.

The entire code of justice set up in our Constitution modeled that found in the Bible. For instance, evidence was required before a person could be convicted of a crime, innocence was presumed, and witnesses were required.[12] All these ideas stem from principles outlined in the book of Deuteronomy.[13]

Final Observations

Certainly the delegates to our Constitutional Convention held to a common core of beliefs, evident in the government structure they designed. Their general adherence to the Biblical principle of man's inherently sinful nature is obvious in their overwhelming efforts to design a government that attempted to check the power of evil men.

America's national seal can be found on the back of every dollar bill. The significance of the pyramid located in its center is unknown to many Americans today, but it was hardly a mystery to our Founding Fathers. One of the Founders who understood it best was James Wilson. Mr. Wilson had the distinction of being one of only six Founding Fathers who signed both the Declaration of Independence and the Constitution. He was appointed by President Washington as a Supreme Court Justice in 1789. James Wilson described the republican form of government which he helped design in the Constitution as being "best symbolized by a pyramid," where the large majority of powers are decentralized among the people at the base and only a few powers are granted to the national government at the top. It is the perfect symbol of the federalist form of government.[14] But there is another part of that pyramid that is even more significant. On the uppermost stone which caps the pyramid is an eye surrounded by rays protruding outward. Notice the description of this unusual symbol recorded in the Journals of Congress:

> A pyramid unfinished — of 13 layers of stone. In the zenith, an eye of
> Divine Providence, surrounded with a glory proper. Over the eye these

words, "Annuit Coeptis" [Latin words that mean "He [God] has blessed our undertakings."][15]

Thus, our national seal is itself evidence for the overwhelming conviction on the part of our Founders and our early citizens that God was the true source of our freedoms and that our government structure should reflect His Biblical principles. The basis of our constitutional form of government, including representative government, separation of powers at the federal level, a dual form of government called federalism, limited government, and the principle of permanent union, reflects what current historians deny. America's external form of government, written on pages of parchment, is founded upon internal Biblical principles, written upon the hearts of its citizens.

PART III

UNDERMINING AMERICA'S GODLY FOUNDATION

"JUDGES AS THE ULTIMATE ARBITERS OF ALL CONSTITUTIONAL QUESTIONS IS A VERY DANGEROUS DOCTRINE": An Unconstitutional Judicial System

Unbeknownst to many Americans, a crime of monumental proportions has been committed. This travesty took place without the suddenness that would wake us from our stupor, yet it was nonetheless systematic and thorough. Like a thief prowling quietly in the shadows of darkness, this crime was initially carried out surreptitiously, later, more boldly. Now that the crime is complete, most of America's soul has been lost. Its religious underpinnings, which Alexis de Tocqueville believed set America apart from other nations, which he wrote had made America so great, are now gone. The crime of which we speak is that of robbery. It was not a fair and transparent taking based on informed consent; instead, it was based on fraud, underhandedness, and guile. America was systematically robbed of her legal heritage, a heritage that was the basis for our Constitution and a heritage that provided our ship of state with the only true anchor it had to the great principle of liberty which birthed our country.

The weapon used to secure the theft was a battle of ideas and worldviews that successfully supplanted the ideas and worldview that motivated our Founding Fathers. It is time for citizens to reclaim that treasure that is rightfully ours as Americans, by engaging in a similar battle. It won't be easy. It will take much time, toil, and effort in a cause where the odds are stacked against us. But then, our Founding Fathers knew a lot about such challenges, for in their great struggle for liberty from Britain, they showed us that some things are worth the fight.

The writers of the Constitution intended the judicial role to be a limited one. Their documents reflect their intent, even in the amount of attention they gave to each branch. Consider that the Constitution devotes 255 lines of copy to the powers of Congress, 114 lines of copy to the powers of the President, and only 44 lines to the courts. The Founders did not envision a powerful judicial branch and thus did not feel the need to place extensive restraints on it. One of the few to anticipate future problems was Thomas Jefferson, although he was not a participant at the Constitutional Convention. His words of warning are quite accurate considering what has occurred:

> The germ of dissolution of our federal government is in the constitution of the federal judiciary; an irresponsible body working like gravity by night and by day, gaining a little today and a little tomorrow, and advancing its noiseless step like a thief, over the field of jurisdiction, until all shall be usurped from the states, and the judges as the ultimate arbiters of all constitutional questions is a very dangerous doctrine indeed, and one which would place us under the despotism of an oligarchy...The Constitution has erected no such tribunal.[1]

A Reminder of What We Once Possessed

What our Founders worked so diligently to protect and guard, we have left unprotected and exposed. We failed to understand the value of what we had. Our Founders gave us a precious treasure in our legal heritage, yet we were blind to the gift.

We discussed earlier that America's legal system was based on the phrase "the law of nature and of nature's God" set forth in the Declaration of Independence. This "law of nature and of nature's God" standard provided the Founders and our nation with a legal heritage that was anchored to God's word. It was predictable, unchanging, and secure for all people at all times. This anchor is the only sure means of "securing the blessings of liberty," for it is the Bible that expressly ties God to liberty when it states, ". . . where the Spirit of the Lord is, there is liberty" (2 Corinthians 3:17). Our heritage stemmed from a commonly held Biblical worldview.

Without God's word as our anchor for law, we are ultimately governed by activist judges and their judicial whims. Under that standard, law is manipulated to correspond, regardless of the constitutional text, to what the judges think it should say rather than what it actually says. Such judicial activism allows a small, often unelected minority to hijack the law that was intended to be developed by legislatures accountable to the people. Law becomes whatever a few elitist judges say it is, even if that ruling is contrary to will of the majority. Such a conclusion was drawn by Charles Evans Hughes, the Supreme Court's Chief Justice from 1930-1941, when he said, "We are under a Constitution, but the Constitution is what the judges say it is." The ultimate arbiter of what is constitutional or not should never be left to a group of judges, nor should it be determined even by a majority of legislators. It should go back to the legal standard of our nation set forth in the Declaration, "the laws of nature and nature's God." All our elected officials and judges have a responsibility to secure the blessings of liberty by interpreting the Constitution in terms consistent with the Bible it is based on. Rights come from God, not man, so it should be God and His standard that defines those rights.

Without the Bible as our ultimate basis for law, our legal system has no anchor and the nation will drift ultimately into anarchy as small, yet powerful and active minority groups insist on their own way with their own interpretation of what the law is. Law needs an unchanging standard. Without it, America is at the mercy of whatever radical element is able to take over and convince a court of its point of view.

That is exactly what happened on February 3, 2004, when the Massachusetts Supreme Court, in a 4-3 decision in *Goodridge v. Dept. of Public Health*, ignored hundreds of years of legal precedent that had been clearly founded on God's higher law in the Bible, to rule for the first time in Massachusetts history that homosexuals have a right to marry. That decision will now affect the entire nation as homosexual couples married pursuant to that Massachusetts ruling go to other states to have their marriages validated and obtain other rights and privileges of their marital status. According to the Constitution, each state is required to recognize as valid marriages performed according to law in other states. Therefore, only four activist judges, who chose to ignore the law and create what they thought should be the law, have effectively impacted the laws of the entire nation.

Is that all there is to law? Whatever four judges say it is, regardless of legal precedent to the contrary, regardless of long-standing social institutions to the contrary, and regardless of the will of the people to the contrary? To conclude that that is enough for law to be enacted in this nation goes against every principle of liberty and justice upon which it was founded. Such a decision is not law, but rather judicial anarchy. Once we determine that we can make laws contrary to the Biblical standard and the legal standard set forth in prior judicial rulings, then our liberties will be lost. Those rights given by God and defined by God can become manipulated and perverted to whatever man thinks is right at the time. If all we need to do is convince a few judges to overturn the will of large majorities and hundreds of years of legal precedent, then anything is possible in the law. Suddenly apartheid can be lawful, so long as someone can convince a few judges to so rule. It does not matter if that is consistent with prior precedent or higher law. Under today's perverted basis for law, the law is whatever has been imposed on the people by a court, regardless of whether that court followed the law or applied the correct law.

Example of Judicial Tyranny

The U.S. Supreme Court decision in *Lawrence v. Texas* illustrates today's judicial activism run amok. The issue before the Court in *Lawrence* was the validity of a Texas statute making it a crime for two persons of the same sex to engage in acts of sodomy.Both men were convicted and fined under the state criminal statute, but they appealed their convictions, asserting that their rights under the Equal Protection and Due Process Clauses of the Fourteenth Amendment had been violated. The *Lawrence* Court found in favor of the petitioners, but in doing so it had to (1) overturn a prior Supreme Court decision in *Bowers v. Hardwick,* rendered only 17 years prior, which found a similar statute constitutional; (2) ignore countless prior judicial decisions and legislative enactments that held that a state is constitutionally justified in regulating certain deviant sexual behavior as "immoral and unacceptable," and (3) seek refuge in similar rulings by the European Court of Human Rights and the views of "other nations!" Indeed, the Court also had to ignore another one of its decisions in *Barnes v. Glen Theatre, Inc*, which upheld Indiana's public indecency statute as furthering "a substantial government interest in protecting order and morality."

What is significant about the *Lawrence* decision is that the legal standard of proof necessary to uphold a state criminal statute when no fundamental right is involved that is "deeply rooted" in the nation's history and tradition (which the Court admitted did not exist in this case) is extremely minimal, yet the Court did not find that even that low standard had been met. Under traditional substantive due process analysis, all that is required to uphold a state criminal statute is a "rational basis" for the law. It has been an "ancient proposition" that the safeguarding of public morality "indisputably is a legitimate government interest under rational basis scrutiny." Yet even though those same "safeguarding of public morality" justifications were present in the *Lawrence* case, the Court dismissed them. It did so, incredibly enough, by noting the reasonings in "other nations" and the European Court of Human Rights, concluding, "[T]here has been no showing that in this country the governmental interest in circumscribing personal choice (as opposed to "deviant sexual behavior") is somehow more legitimate or urgent." Justice Scalia, in his dissenting opinion, also found it hard to believe that the statute did not meet the "rational basis" test. According to Justice Scalia, "[T]his proposition is so out of accord with our jurisprudence — indeed, with the jurisprudence of any society we know — that it requires little discussion." Justice Scalia provided a dire warning of the consequences of the Court ignoring the longstanding moral basis of a statute:

> The Texas statute undeniably seeks to further the belief of its citizens that certain forms of sexual behavior are "immoral and unacceptable," (citation) — the same interest furthered by criminal laws against fornication, bigamy, adultery, adult incest, bestiality, and obscenity." *Bowers* held that this was a legitimate state interest. The Court today reaches the opposite conclusion. The Texas statute, it says, "furthers *no legitimate state interest which can justify its intrusion into the personal and private life of the individual.*" [emphasis added] The Court embraces instead Justice Stevens' declaration in his *Bowers* dissent, that "the fact that the governing majority in a State has traditionally viewed a particular practice as immoral is not a sufficient reason for upholding a law prohibiting the practice." This effectively decrees the end of all morals legislation. If, as the Court asserts, the promotion of majoritarian sexual morality is not even a *legitimate* state interest, none of the above-mentioned laws can survive rational-basis review."

Justice Scalia's dissent includes his opinion that the *Lawrence* decision is a clear case of judicial activism. He notes that "[i]t is clear from this that the Court has taken sides in the culture war, departing from its role of assuring, as neutral observer, that the democratic rules of engagement are observed." An objective reading of the case shows the bias of the Court even in their framing of the issues. Rather than referring to the language in the criminal complaint describing the behavior at issue as "deviate sexual intercourse," the Court chose to legitimize the activity by referring to it as merely "private conduct." When you couple the way the Court characterized the behavior with the need to overturn its own decision in *Bowers* and ignore its own decision in *Barnes*, as well as to substitute hundreds of years of American judicial and legislative history for that of the "other nations" and the European Court of Human Rights, it is abundantly clear that in *Lawrence* the Supreme Court, sought to foster a pro-homosexual agenda and was determined to do so whatever the law might say to the contrary.

The *Lawrence* decision demonstrates the lengths to which activist judges will go to establish the law as they want it, regardless of precedent or societal sanction. If necessary, they will even ignore or actually overturn prior decisions contrary to their personal agendas. Hence the danger to judicial stability and predictability crucial to order in a society. What is lawful today may be unlawful tomorrow. What was unlawful yesterday can become lawful today. The language of the Constitution becomes irrelevant. If it includes language contrary to the judge's agenda, the judge can simply ignore it. If it fails to include language consistent with the judge's agenda, the judge simply creates the desired right by asserting it is in there somewhere, as with the right to privacy mysteriously found in *Cantwell v. Connecticut* and used in *Roe v. Wade* (1973). There is no anchor to our law when it has no basis other than our ability to convince a few activist judges to accept it.

Conflicting Worldviews

What has happened to change our view of law? Many fancy, complex theories exist, but they all come down to a single reason. Simply put, our worldview has changed. We have discarded the Biblical worldview which our Founders maintained and which De Tocqueville recognized as making America great.

Little by little, our nation has consistently moved away from a recognition that God is its source of law to embrace a counterfeit idea that law is evolutionary and based in the people or in the state itself. This different legal philosophy has carried various labels — "relativism," "pragmatism," and "legal positivism"— but the idea is the same. It was introduced in the 1870s when Christopher Langdell, then Dean of Harvard Law School, introduced Darwin's ideas of evolution to the field of jurisprudence. Soon, our nation's law schools ignored Blackstone, Coke, and our Declaration principles in which America's law was rooted, and began to teach this new legal philosophy rooted in evolution. British scientist A. E. Wilder-Smith commented on this change of legal philosophy in his forward to *The Creation of Life*:

> Why have law and order deteriorated so rapidly in the United States? Simply because for many years it has been commonly taught that life is a random, accidental phenomenon with no meaning except the purely materialistic one. Laws are merely a matter of human expediency. Since humans are allegedly accidents, so are their laws. No wonder that the result of such teaching is a contempt for the courts and for all due order. The older supernatural views taught that life was a plan or code, which needed for its government a plan of supernaturally given codes or laws.

When the worldview in America changed in regard to the source of our laws, the theft of our legal heritage commenced. Since ideas have consequences, and the Biblical and evolutionary worldviews lead in opposite directions, we cannot sit on the fence and hope for some compromise to resolve the problem. The Biblical worldview that was responsible for America's liberty and freedom also enabled espousal of the evolutionary worldview which now seeks to destroy it.

The latter is now consuming the former, and evolution has proven to be a very intolerant worldview, allowing for no other competing voice on its public stage. Scientists who dare claim that evolutionary ideas are counterfeit and who propose a creation-science perspective are quickly ridiculed and ostracized rather than respectfully debated in the marketplace of ideas. Through the subtleties of denying tenure or generating negative peer reviews of such professors, the evolutionists and secularists are able to chase out of the university arena anyone who challenges their orthodoxy. There is little tolerance for those holding a Biblical worldview. Public school teachers who desire to teach our children that we did not come from apes, but instead were created by a Supreme Being, are not given an equal opportunity to debate and discuss these ideas in the marketplace of free speech; instead they face lawsuits or loss of their jobs. We quickly hear the secularists cry how wrong it is to teach "religious" views to "impressionable young minds," yet those same secularists have no qualms about teaching the religious view of evolution to those same "impressionable young minds." The evolutionist worldview now dominates our culture, and it is a jealous god, proclaiming its tolerance, yet demonstrating just the opposite. Now the evolutionists and secularists have the stage, and America is suffering the consequences of its stolen heritage in a moral base that is rotting right before our eyes.

Many people argue that America has retained many of the blessings of liberty since becoming a nation dominated by the secular view. While that is true, the credit for those continuing liberties is not due to this secularism. For a time, our nation has been able to retain some of the blessings of our Biblical heritage, as we have maintained a remnant of that Biblical worldview. But as that worldview diminishes with each successive generation of Americans, so too does its influence on our nation and the liberties upon which they were founded. Our nation has lived off the liberties our religious heritage has brought us for several generations, but the more we remove the source of our liberties, the more intolerant and repressive our nation becomes toward people of religious faith. Surely if one were truly objective, he or she would recognize that had our nation been formed solely on secular principles, America would never have become the beacon of liberty it once was.

We should heed the warning of Thomas Jefferson, whose words have become hauntingly prophetic: "the liberties of a nation [cannot] be thought secure when we have removed their only firm basis, a conviction in the minds of the people that their liberties are the gift of God." Today we are suffering from laws that are without an anchor, ever changing, and completely disconnected from any universal, unchanging principle of justice or liberty. Law's noble character has been destroyed by a legal system that bases its arguments on whatever it takes to convince the authorities to pass a law by a majority of lawmakers. There is no transcendent basis for justice and law anymore because our true legal heritage has been stolen. There isn't even a requirement that the laws be made in accordance with the consent of the governed, although that alone would not ensure that law be just and in conformance with the laws of God.

Selective Acceptance of the "law of nature and of nature's God"

Under the standard of the "law of nature and of nature's God," American law had to be consistent with Scripture. That alone ensured stability in the law. If a person could get a law passed that made it lawful to kill people over the age of 80 because they are an unnecessary burden on our economy, that law would be invalid under this standard since it is contrary to God's law, which places a supreme value on all human life, without qualification. It wouldn't matter if the legislature passed it, the media adored it, and the Supreme Court affirmed it; the law would be invalid and Americans would not be obligated to obey it. Indeed, they would have a duty to disobey it under America's legal heritage of Biblically based law. This is exactly the justification Martin Luther King Jr. and his followers invoked when they refused to obey segregation laws in the early 1960's. As he noted in his famous *Letter from the Birmingham Jail*, laws contrary to higher law, or the laws of nature, should not be obeyed.

In reality, we all subscribe to this theory of a higher law that must be followed, regardless of our political persuasions or religious beliefs. We all accept the idea that if a law is "wrong," it is unjust and we must not obey it. It's the last vestige of God's law of nature written on our hearts. Who can doubt that if someone could get the legislature and the states to pass a Constitutional Amendment that said African-Americans or Jews or any other group of people were not real people and thus have no rights or liberties, that such a law would be invalid? Even if the Supreme Court were to uphold the law, in our hearts and minds we would know that such a law would be wrong absolutely. But why? It is because of the law of nature written on our hearts. Our conscience knows there is a higher law — the law of our Creator.

The abortion issue reflects this recognition of a higher law by both supporters and opponents of the practice. Abortion opponents have asserted a higher law in the value and protection of human life over that of personal choice by picketing against abortion clinics. They recognize, as did our Founding Fathers, that laws contrary to God's revealed law as reflected in the Scriptures, are not valid law. On the other hand, the former President of the National Organization for Women, declared that should the Supreme Court some day rule that abortion is unconstitutional, she would continue to advocate abortion and persuade others to violate the law. Why? Because she believes that there is a higher law that must be obeyed. Obviously, the two sides do not agree on the source of higher law, but nonetheless, they share the idea of the existence of a higher law. When college campuses were aflame in the 1970's with protests urging American corporations to stop doing business with South Africa because of its practice of apartheid, they, too, were appealing to a higher source of law that transcended the actual laws of South Africa. While they likely did not share the same idea of the source of that higher law either, they believed there existed some higher concept of justice than the law in South Africa. They had to, for otherwise they would have had no basis for their appeal. For an evolutionist worldview, it is intellectually difficult to accept the existence of a higher law, but they do so nonetheless, because God has written His law upon their hearts, even though they have chosen to disregard its source.

Court Interpretations Are No Longer Biblically Based

Our Founders believed strongly that legitimate law starts with God and His word spoken through the Bible. Such law was unchanging, absolute, and universal in nature. Hence, when the colonists declared their independence from England in the Declaration of Independence, they did so based expressly upon the power which "the laws of nature and of nature's God entitle them." They further relied on "self-evident" truths, truths that are universally accepted as true, among which are that we are endowed by our Creator with certain inalienable rights, which cannot be taken from us because they are given to us by God. Unlike man's laws, which change with the political whims of the times, God's laws and rights remain constant and absolute.

The Seventh Amendment, firmly rooted our Constitution in these unchanging absolutes by establishing our legal basis upon the early common law. Common law began around 1100 A.D. with the Anglo-Saxons, who established the right of "trial by jury," which was set forth in the Bible in Deuteronomy 19:15-19 and is now found in the Sixth and Seventh Amendments and Article III, Section 2, Paragraph 3 of our Constitution. The right to a jury trial is a good example of a common law principle with a Biblical basis.

Over the course of hundreds of years, judicial decisions were made from the absolutes found in the Bible and from the moral base rooted in Christianity. These decisions became the common law, precedents for justice in future cases where the facts were substantially the same.

An early basis for our common law arose out of the Magna Carta in 1215. That English document recognized and established the rights of trail by jury and the principle of "habeas corpus," now found in our Constitution at Article I, Section 9, Paragraph 2. The habeas corpus provision of the Magna Carta, that "no man can be confined without inquiry," as well as the entire "due process" concept of which it is a part, were revolutionary thoughts at that time.

Common law principles were continued with the Englishman Sir Edward Coke, who emphasized them in his works, which were studied by such early American jurists as Chancellor Kent, John Marshall, and Joseph Story. Common Law and constitutional law were therefore both originally based upon what the Declaration of Independence defined as "the Laws of Nature and Nature's God."

The Judicial Tendency to Legislate

Moral and legal absolutes have taken a beating in recent years by judicial activists, but the truth is that law not founded upon absolutes is very dangerous to society. Consider that without absolutes, the Supreme Court has reversed itself over 100 separate times! Absent absolutes, the Court also has a tendency to expand its authority beyond well-defined legal limits.

For instance, in 1973, the Court ignored hundreds of years of judicial precedent in order to invent a new constitutional right – choice – which they deemed so paramount, that it could override one of our original inalienable rights – life. Thus, in *Roe v. Wade*, the Supreme Court started down a judicially created path that now allows a mother to choose to take the life of her own baby, so long as she chooses before it is born. In fact, the mother's choice is the primary determination as to whether a law is broken when the baby is killed. If the mother chooses not to keep the child, the baby is magically renamed a "fetus," and the act of deliberate killing of the child is likewise renamed "abortion" rather than "murder". Because it ignored the moral absolutes that law had always been founded upon, the Court was free to say what the law was without regard to past precedents or moral standards. As a result, today choice has become a more valued principle than life itself.

The Supreme Court did this by introducing the artificial concept of "viability," meaning that once a "fetus" or baby has reached sufficient growth to be able to sustain itself, then it is "viable" and cannot be aborted, but prior to reaching "viability" a baby can be legally aborted. This legal invention was not derived from the express language of the Constitution, which places legal limits upon what kinds of issues the Court is authorized to decide. Nor was the concept consistent with the Biblical spirit or founding intent behind the Constitution. It is completely contrary to both Biblical principle and the Constitution's separation of powers.

First, Biblical principles are clear on this point. The Bible teaches that God and only God creates life. It also teaches that God forms us while we are still in the womb, and that we have a distinctive personal identity even before birth (Psalm 139:13). Geneticists have confirmed that everything a person needs for life is in place at the moment of conception, not birth.[2] Life starts at conception, then through a process of growth that is initiated, directed, and controlled by God, results in a live birth of a baby. Even then, the growth of that life is not over. It continues throughout childhood, adolescence, and beyond. Under either common law or natural law founded on the Bible, abortion could never have been declared legal, let alone a constitutional right, since it is in direct conflict with God's revealed law. Moral and legal absolutes do not change with the latest fad; they are solid and constant, providing society with an anchor that maintains a strong culture. Yet we as a nation have discarded our Biblical anchor long ago, and so now we have lost the constitutional limitations upon which moral and legal absolutes rested.

Second, the Court's decision in *Roe v. Wade* transgresses the Founders' limitations on judicial power. Under the Constitution, it is the legislative branch that has the authority to make new laws, not the judicial branch. Once the Court found nothing in the Constitution to provide guidance, they should have indicated it was a question for the legislative branch and made no ruling against the status quo; then such a volatile issue would have been handled by the branch most responsive and accountable to the people, rather than the Supreme Court, which is completely unaccountable to anyone. Ideology should not have determined the result in *Roe v. Wade*, the Constitution should have. The end should never justify the means if we are to truly be a nation under the "rule of law."

The danger of an activist court not tied to constitutional limitations is that while a Court can create new rights, it can also take old rights away. Fifty years ago, abortion, homosexuality, and adultery were all illegal. Under the common law, rooted in Biblical truth, they would stay illegal. Under the evolutionary, evolving judicial standard of today, all these acts are now legal. In fifty more years, perhaps they will be illegal again, or other rights that are legal now will become illegal, such as the free speech and free exercise right of a pastor to preach that homosexuality is a sin. Law becomes unpredictable without an anchor. Today's Court loss could be tomorrow's victory. Such judicial waffling to the Pied Piper of public opinion disposes the Court system to political influence and public demonstrations. Lady Justice is no longer blindfolded to the influences of the day, sacrificing long-standing judicial principles to ever-changing circumstances.

Herein lies the real danger of evolutionary, judicial activist courts. Judges are as fallible as anyone else. If what they say is the law of the land, regardless of a Biblical standard to the contrary, or a Constitution to the contrary, then the judicial branch has become a place of legal tyranny. The Founders were concerned about the powers of the judicial branch becoming too great, because it is the only branch that does not have direct accountability to the public. Judges at the federal level are appointed for life, and impeachment, the only mechanism for holding them accountable, is rarely invoked.

Activist Courts Ignore the Separation of Powers

By ignoring constitutional restraints, the Supreme Court has also usurped the power of the legislature, thereby violating the separation of powers principle. Examine what the Supreme Court did in *Griswold v. Connecticut.*[3] The Court searched mightily to find a right to privacy in the Constitution. In spite of their efforts, Justice William O. Douglas, who authored the majority opinion, admitted that the right of privacy could not be found in the Constitution, but, the majority on the Court clearly wanted to find such a right and were determined to sanction it regardless of whether it could actually be found. That is the action of an unconstitutional activist court. Ultimately, the Court concluded that the right to privacy was to be found in the "penumbra" of other constitutional guarantees.[4] According to Webster's Dictionary, a "penumbra" is a partial shade or obscurity on the margin of the perfect shade of a shadow. In other words, the Supreme Court found a constitutional right lurking in a fuzzy shadow. This was a desperate Court decision that stretched far beyond the bounds of judicial authority and reason.

Instead of being intellectually honest and concluding that there was no right of privacy in the Constitution, the Court decided the right should exist, so they created it themselves. Such an "end justifies the means" type of attitude has made a mockery of our constitutional separation of powers framework. Properly, where there is no right explicitly mentioned in the Constitution, yet no prohibition on such a right, the legislative branch is free to act. If they wanted a constitutionally protected right to privacy, they could have proposed an amendment to the Constitution, following appropriate democratic procedure.. There were several constitutional and legal options available to provide for a right to privacy, but none of those legal options involved the courts acting as a legislative body.

There is an ironic twist to the Court's action to find a right of privacy in *Griswold v. Connecticut.* Had the judicial branch not previously forsaken our common law heritage that recognized Scripture as the source and authority for all law, the justices would have found more than a "fuzzy shadow" or "penumbra" to rely on. With its principles of the dignity of man made in the image of God, examples such as Noah's son's sin in publicizing to his brothers his father's nakedness while asleep in his tent, and other perspectives, the Bible could have helped them find the right to privacy they desired. However, had it been rooted in the Bible as it properly should have been,[5] the right would likewise have been appropriately limited to support activities consistent with other Biblical principles. The legislative branch could have then used that basis as found by the court to pass laws that would have been constitutionally supported, while retaining the integrity of the separation of powers principle.

Holding the Judicial Branch in Check

The judicial branch itself is not above the law, any more than the executive or legislative branches. Therefore, when acting unconstitutionally, the Court must be checked by Congress if we are to preserve a true republic. Congress has been given the power to impeach members of the judiciary when they are found guilty of undermining the Constitution. Congress also has the power to restrict the Court's jurisdiction.

There is one final limitation Congress possesses once a judge is appointed. Under Article III, Section 1, judges can only continue to hold their office "during good behavior," a broadly defined term that is meant to provide Congress with optimum discretionary authority. Unfortunately, Congress has only invoked this power twice in the last 210 plus years – once for drunkenness and once for disloyalty during the Civil War.

Of course, another check upon such unconstitutional actions by any of the three branches of government can be exercised by the people through their state legislatures. Amendments to the Constitution can be proposed by a convention called by two-thirds of the state legislatures and then ratified by three-fourths of them,but this procedure has never been exercised by the states since the Bill of Rights was added to the Constitution; all of the 17 subsequent amendments to the Constitution have been proposed by Congress.

Amendments to the Constitution should be cautiously proposed, however, since not all amendments are necessarily beneficial. For example, as discussed earlier, the Fourteenth, Sixteenth and Seventeenth Amendments altered our form of government for the worse, despite the good intentions of those who proposed and voted for them. Many times amendments can be poorly worded, allowing evolutionary minded courts to construe the words in ways that further expand the powers of the national government. When not drafted by people who clearly understand and support our constitutional, republican form of government, amendments will more likely create mischief than solve problems.

Yet in the hands of godly men and women who do understand our originally intended form of government, the state initiated amendment process can be a precious power left to the discretion of the American people as a means of restoring our national heritage as a true republic.

ELEVEN

"IF CONGRESS CAN APPLY MONEY INDEFINITELY TO THE GENERAL WELFARE...THEY MAY UNDERTAKE THE REGULATION OF EVERYTHING": An Unconstitutional Expansion of the Federal Government

During the ratification debates, James Madison assured skeptical Americans in *Federalist no. 45* that the powers of the federal government under the proposed Constitution were to be "few and defined." As one of the principal authors of that document, he was clearly in a position to know. He understood that the Constitution established a unique system of government based on delegated, enumerated, and limited powers. Only those powers delegated to the national government can be constitutionally exercised at the federal level; that left the great bulk of powers to be exercised by the states. This "American experiment in limited government generated a degree of liberty and prosperity that was virtually unimaginable only a few centuries before."[1]

Today that "experiment in limited government" is gone. The power differential between the states and the federal government has been reversed from the Founder's intentions. State governments, which were intended to be strong, are now weak administrative extensions of Washington D.C., whereas, our federal government, which was intended to be limited and restrained, has become extremely powerful.

The federal government will spend more than $2,100,000,000,000 (2.1 trillion) in fiscal year 2003. After taking out the government's core functions of national defense and justice, it will still spend more than

$1,700,000,000,000 (1.7 trillion). That amounts to roughly $16,000 for every household in the United States. Clearly, the federal government has taken on a huge range of spending programs beyond its basic responsibilities.[2]

The federal government has grown from three original departments and a handful of employees to fifteen cabinet-level departments, hundreds of federal agencies, and millions of employees. The federal government has usurped nearly every power originally left to the states.[3] Like Pinocchio before he was brought to life, the states are now just marionettes dancing at the direction of federal strings. How has this happened?

The general answer is that Americans lost sight of the spirit of our Constitution. We have forgotten or ignored the Biblical basis upon which our Constitutional structure is founded. That Biblical basis relied on a common core of beliefs built upon religion, morality, and faith in God. Our Founders warned us that the strength of our Constitution was dependent upon that Biblical basis. Those Biblical principles warned Americans of the dangers inherent in unbridled government and the need to keep its most numerous powers at the lower levels, where it would be more accountable to the people. Indeed, our first President referred to religion and morality as "indispensable supports" to our government structure.[4] Religion and morality based on Biblical principles provided government with much needed limits and controls and helped keep it within its proper role. Once those supports began to crumble, so did its original structure of limited government under the control of enumerated Constitutional powers.

There were numerous ways in which the federal government broke free from its Constitutional restraints, but all entailed a misapplication of Constitutional language. The misapplications of the following four provisions caused the most damage: (1) the "general welfare" clause, (2) the commerce clause, (3) the "necessary and proper" clause, and (4) the incorporation doctrine of the 14th amendment. Each of these will be examined separately below.

Misapplication of the "General Welfare" Clause

The "general welfare" clause of the Constitution is found in Article I, Section 8, which deals with the specific powers of the legislative branch. According to the views of Madison and most other Founders, it was intended as a limitation upon the power of Congress to tax and spend in furtherance of the enumerated powers listed immediately following. In other words, the spending that occurred in the exercise of an enumerated power had to be for the *general* welfare and not for specific persons, groups of persons, or regions of the country.[5] The words of James Madison are instructive to those who argue for a broader interpretation:

> If Congress can apply money indefinitely to the general welfare, and are the sole and supreme judges of the general welfare, they may take the care of religion into their own hands; they may take into their own hands the education of children, establishing in like manner schools throughout the Union; they may undertake the regulation of all roads, other than post roads. In short, everything from the highest object of State legislation, down to the most minute object of policy, would be thrown under the power of Congress; for every object I have mentioned would admit the application of money, and might be called, if Congress pleased, provisions for the general welfare.[6]

Not everyone adhered to the Madison view, however. Alexander Hamilton believed that there was an "independent power to tax and spend for the general welfare,"[7] in addition to the enumerated powers, but such a view would render meaningless the listing of enumerated powers. In effect, Hamilton's view, the minority position during the founding era, would have given Congress a "blank check" authorization to tax and spend, in direct contrast to the Founders' desire for limited federal government.

> But as South Carolina's William Drayton observed on the floor of the House in 1828, Hamilton's view would make a mockery of the doctrine of enumerated powers, the centerpiece of the Constitution, rendering the enumeration of Congress's other powers superfluous: whenever Congress wanted to do something it was barred from doing by the absence of a power to do it, it could simply declare the act to be serving the "general welfare" and get out from under the limits imposed by enumeration.[8]

The practice of federal lawmakers for nearly 150 years under the Constitution was to treat the "general welfare" clause as a significant limitation upon its power, consistent with the views of Madison. For example, in 1794, Congress appropriated $15,000 to aid French refugees from the St. Domingo revolt.[9] Congress justified the appropriation as within the enumerated powers since it would offset the United States' debt to France. But James Madison, a member of the House of Representatives at the time, opposed the appropriation, stating, "I cannot undertake to lay my finger on that article of the Constitution which granted a right to Congress of expending, on objects of benevolence, the money of their constituents." In 1796, William Giles of Virginia opposed a relief measure for fire victims on the floor of the House of Representatives because it was not the purpose of Congress to "attend to what generosity and humanity require, but to what the Constitution and their duty require."[10] In 1854, President Franklin Pierce vetoed a bill that sought to assist the mentally ill because he could not find any authority in the Constitution for "public charity."[11] One of the best known examples of a Congressman objecting to a bill for a lack of "general welfare" or an enumerated power is that of Davy Crockett, who served in Congress from 1827 to 1835. A fellow Congressman of his told the story of a bill taken up to appropriate money for the benefit of a widow of a distinguished naval officer. No one opposed the bill until Mr. Crockett rose to speak against it. Excerpts of his speech follow:

> We have the right, as individuals to give away as much of our own money as we please in charity; but as members of Congress we have no right so to appropriate a dollar of the public money. . . . We cannot, without the grossest corruption, appropriate this money as the payment of a debt. We have not the semblance of authority to appropriate it as a charity. Mr. Speaker, I have said we have the right to give as much of our own money as we please. I am the poorest man on this floor. I cannot vote for this bill, but I will give one week's pay to the object, and if every member of Congress will do the same, it will amount to more than the bill asks.[12]

As a result of that speech, the bill ended up being defeated. What is noteworthy however, is the result of Davy Crockett's challenge for each of the Congressmen to put up their own money for the charitable act of paying the widow. None did. That is the problem today. It is much easier to spend other people's money than it is to spend our own.

In 1936, in the case of *U.S. v. Butler* (297 U.S. 1), the Supreme Court sided with the Madison view, as well as congressional practice. It ruled that the "general" welfare implies that government may not tax and spend for the "specific" welfare of individuals, regions, or socioeconomic groups. It noted in doing so that "the power to confer or withhold unlimited benefits is the power to coerce or destroy." However, it opened the door for future expansion of the clause's interpretation when it also noted that there is an independent power, separate from those enumerated in the Constitution, to tax and spend for the general welfare, along the lines of what Hamilton argued.

A year later, in *Steward Machine Co. v. Davis* (301 U.S. 548) (1937), the Supreme Court walked through the door left open in *Butler* to uphold the constitutionality of the new Social Security program, which benefited only certain portions of the population, noting that Congress may tax some groups and subsidize others because the subsidized groups will spend more and thus stimulate the general welfare. In so ruling, the Supreme Court effectively amended the Constitution through judicial fiat, writing out a significant limitation on Congressional spending power. Today, as a result, the distinction between "general" and "specific" welfare has been virtually obliterated. Congress now passes legislation to spend money on bailouts for airlines, prescription drugs, education, Social Security, various welfare programs, subsidies for farmers, and thousands of similar items that go beyond the enumerated powers of Article I, Section 8 and do not provide for the "general welfare" as the Founders intended.

There are many who claim that welfare and various assistance programs are based on the Biblical principle of charity. The parable of the Good Samaritan is an obvious example of this Biblical principle. Yet those who make this claim are missing two very important distinctions. Nowhere did God expressly state in the scriptures, let alone even imply, that such charity is to be a function of government. The Biblical emphasis has always been on individuals or groups of people assisting the poor and downtrodden of society on a voluntary basis and for the purpose of showing the love of God. In fact, showing the love of God is the whole point of acts of charity from a Biblical perspective. 1 Corinthians 13, verse 3, says that we can do all sorts of great "works" but if they are not done in love for the purpose of demonstrating God's love, everything we do is worthless. Those who assert that government poverty programs are consistent with the Biblical principle have missed the point: the end is not to help the poor, that is the means to the end. The Bible teaches clearly that the true end is glorifying God by showing His love for people so that through acts of kindness and charity, they will be motivated either to begin to serve God themselves, or to strengthen their relationship with God. The Good Samaritan acted voluntarily on his own initiative, to show the love of God. He paid for the wounded man's stay at the inn out of his own pocket; he wasn't forced to do so by government decree, nor did he compel others who were not so inclined to pay "their fair share." He certainly did not advocate that government should take care of the problem, as many people would argue today. When the federal government gets involved, we lose both aspects of the Biblical principle of charity because the monetary assistance is from coerced tax money, and it is distributed by government workers who, more times than not, are not motivated by the love of God, but are just doing their job. Even assuming that many government workers administrating these programs genuinely care for the people they are assisting, the current misapplied doctrine on separating the church and state precludes the demonstration of God's love to the people being assisted.

There is another aspect to government charity that confirms that it is not Biblically based. When the government provides the assistance, the focus is not on God or the recipient's need for God, the focus is on the government. Indeed, over time, government is looked upon as our artificial "savior" and provider. Yet those are the roles of God alone, not government, and our Founding Fathers understood those separate roles and were careful to keep them distinct. Today's social reformers do not. Thus, while they are often the first to vehemently argue that church and state should be separate when the issue is a religious activity in government, they often blur the separation by attempting to usurp the role of the church on behalf of government in their advocacy of more government programs that are more properly the role of the church.

The result has been an exponential increase in government spending, federal largesse, and overburdening the American citizens with inordinate taxes which they resent paying. Instead of creating an atmosphere of love and compassion for the poor and needy through private, voluntary charitable programs, the government's welfare state has created division, resentment, dependence, and animosity that has deteriorated into "class warfare."

Misapplication of the Commerce Clause

A second cause of expansive federal government is the misapplication of the commerce clause. The Constitution, in Article I, Section 8, Paragraph 3, gives Congress authority to "regulate commerce with foreign nations, and among the several States, and with the Indian Tribes." The intent of this commerce clause was to eliminate trade barriers between the states. It was not intended to be a means for federal government intrusion into and regulation of every area of life, though that is how it is often applied today.

As with the "general welfare" clause, for most of America's early history and until the 1930s, the Courts adhered to the original intent of the commerce clause. However, they began to waver in the 1930s, and in 1942, the U.S. Supreme Court provided for future Congressional tyranny in its ruling in *Wickard v. Filburn* (317 U.S. 111) (1942). Filburn was an Ohio farmer who harvested 12 acres of wheat above the government production quota set by the Department of Agriculture. Filburn argued that since he grew the wheat for his private use, his excess wheat harvest had nothing to do with commerce "among the several States," and thus the federal government regulation of his excess wheat crop was unconstitutional. The Supreme Court disagreed. It held that had he not grown the extra wheat, he would have had to purchase the wheat, probably from another state, and thus he indirectly or

potentially affected interstate commerce. Therefore, even the *potential* affect upon interstate commerce was enough to allow Congress to regulate it at
the federal level.

That decision destroyed the distinction set forth in the Constitution between interstate and intrastate commerce, thereby greatly expanding the
power of Congress beyond the confines of the express language of the document. For decades after the *Wickard v. Filburn* decision, Congress was able
to exercise nearly unfettered power in regulating what historically would
have been deemed unconstitutional interstate commerce.

However, in the case of *U.S. v. Lopez*,[13] the U.S. Supreme Court finally
drew the line. In that case, the Court addressed the constitutionality of the
1990 Gun-Free School Zone Act which made it a federal offense "for any individual knowingly to possess a firearm at a place that the individual knows,
or has reasonable cause to believe, is a school zone." The government made
two arguments that possession of a gun in a school zone substantially affected interstate commerce. First, they alleged that such possession *may
result* in violent crime and that the costs of crime raises insurance rates and
crime impairs incentives to travel to unsafe areas of the country. Second,
they said that possession of guns in school zones threatens the learning environment, which results in a less productive citizenry and thus reduces the
nation's economic well-being. The Court, in an opinion by Justice
Rehnquist, rejected both arguments by noting the government's position
would give Congress unlimited authority since nothing could fail to have
some effect on interstate commerce.

> The Government admits, under its 'costs of crime' reasoning, that Con-
> gress could regulate not only all violent crime, but all activities that might
> lead to violent crime, regardless of how tenuously they relate to interstate
> commerce. Similarly, under the Government's 'national productivity' rea-
> soning, Congress could regulate any activity that it found was related to the
> economic productivity of individual citizens: family law (including mar-
> riage, divorce, and child custody), for example. Under the theories that the
> Government presents . . . it is difficult to perceive any limitation on federal
> power, even in areas such as criminal law enforcement or education where
> States historically have been sovereign. Thus, if we were to accept the Gov-
> ernment's arguments, we are hard-pressed to posit any activity by an
> individual that Congress is without power to regulate.[14]

The Court drew a distinction that a criminal statute, such as the Gun-Free
School Zone Act, has "nothing to do with 'commerce' or any sort of economic enterprise, however broadly one might define those terms."[15] In doing

so, the Supreme Court deferred, at least partially, to the concept of state authority in this matter.

> Under our federal system, the 'States possess primary authority for defining and enforcing the criminal law.' 'Our national government is one of delegated powers alone. Under our federal system the administration of criminal justice rests with the States except as Congress, acting within the scope of those delegated powers, has created offenses against the United States.' When Congress criminalizes conduct already denounced as criminal by the States, it effects a 'change in the sensitive relation between federal and state criminal jurisdiction.'[16]

While the *Lopez* decision recognized that the brakes needed to be applied to recognize that the interstate commerce clause was not limitless in its application, it did not seek to overturn the myriad of prior cases that still allow the great expanse of Congressional regulation to march on. For example, left standing were decisions that authorized federal regulation of maximum sales prices of timber confined within one state,[17] application of railway labor regulations to a railroad owned by a state,[18] application of wage and hour regulations to state employees of public schools and hospitals,[19] intrastate coal mining,[20] intrastate credit transactions,[21] intrastate restaurants,[22] intrastate hotels,[23] and of course, the production and consumption of home-grown wheat found in *Filburn*. Therefore, the *Lopez* decision appears to have been a minor bump in the road in the continued use of the commerce clause as a means to justify greater federal interference in state and local jurisdictions.

Misapplication of the "Necessary and Proper" Clause

Another clause that Congress uses to justify its exercise of powers nowhere mentioned in the Constitution is the "necessary and proper" clause. Article I, Section 8, Clause 18 permits Congress to "make all Laws which shall be *necessary and proper* for carrying into Execution the foregoing Powers. . . . " The clause was added by the Committee on Detail without any prior discussion in the Convention, nor any debate prior to its final adoption as part of the Constitution.[24] There is still some legislative history useful in ascertaining its intended meaning. A prior proposed clause offered by Gunning Bedford but rejected by the Committee provided for "an almost completely open-ended grant of power to Congress" that was rejected in favor of the enumeration of powers and the present "necessary and proper" clause.[25]

In the ratification debates that followed within the various state ratification conventions, further clarification on the clause's meaning was provided. At the Virginia Convention, George Nicholas argued that the clause did not give Congress any new powers not already enumerated.[26] Likewise, the President of the Virginia Convention, Edmund Pendleton was adamant that the clause did not go "a single step beyond the delegated powers."[27] Similar sentiments were voiced in the ratification debates throughout the other states.[28]

Further meaning was provided during an early constitutional show down on a proposed national bank bill in 1791. In opposing the bill as being beyond the enumerated powers of the Constitution, James Madison offered a crucial distinction between interpreting the necessary and proper clause in terms of "necessity" versus those of "convenience." He determined that while the bank would certainly be convenient for the government, it was not necessary to carry out any of its enumerated powers.[29] The Attorney General and former delegate to the Constitutional Convention, Edmond Randolph, and Secretary of State Thomas Jefferson conveyed their formal opinions to President Washington that the bank bill was unconstitutional for the reasons articulated by James Madison. In the words of Jefferson:

> The constitution allows only the means which are "necessary," not those which are merely convenient for effecting the enumerated powers. If such a latitute of construction be allowed to this phrase, as to give any non enumerated power, it will go to every one; for there is no one, which ingenuity may not torture into a convenience, in some way or other, to some one of so long a list of enumerated powers; it would swallow up all the delegated powers"[30]

Washington's Secretary of the Treasury, Alexander Hamilton, who initially proposed the idea of the national bank, defended its constitutionality based on the popular use of the term "necessary" as meaning useful or conducive to. Hamilton asserted the need for Congress to be given discretion in applying the clause to its delegated powers. His view ultimately prevailed, and President Washington signed the bill into law.[31] Nonetheless, the controversy surrounding the national bank bill illustrates how seriously lawmakers of the day took the protection of the enumerated powers.

Chief Justice John Marshall and the U.S. Supreme Court first became involved in the debate over the meaning of the phrase "necessary and proper" in the 1805 case of *United States v. Fisher.*[32] In that case, Justice Marshall interpreted the clause to give nearly complete discretion to Congress, writing, "Congress must possess the choice of means, and must be empowered to use any means which are in fact conducive to the exercise of a power granted by the constitution."[33]

While the *Fisher* case was the first Supreme Court interpretation of the necessary and proper clause, it certainly was not the most famous. That distinction goes to Justice Marshall's later decision in *McCulloch v. Maryland*,[34] a case familiar to virtually every law student in America. In that case, Justice Marshall contrasted the term "necessary" with that of "absolutely necessary," found in Article I, Section 10, and concluded from the lack of the prefix "absolutely" that the necessary and proper clause gave Congress much greater latitude to "accommodate its legislation to circumstances."[35] Unfortunately, Justice Marshall practically ignored concerns about how an open-ended grant of discretionary power conformed with the overall constitutional principles of limited government and enumerated powers. Therefore, legal scholars of the day were highly critical of this opinion. In fact, John Taylor, a contemporary of Madison and Marshall, wrote an entire book arguing against the reasoning of the *McCulloch* decision. In that book, *Construction Construed*, and *Constitutions Vindicated*, Taylor argued that Marshall's interpretation would lead to the corruption, if not outright destruction of the principles upon which the government was established.

> When necessity is taken to mean expedient, this mode of construction completely establishes the position, that Congress may pass any internal law whatsoever in relation to things, because there is nothing with which, war, commerce and taxation may not be closely or remotely connected.[36]

Madison's concern for the integrity of the enumerated powers framework being undermined by the necessary and proper clause has been borne out. Much of the basis for doing so has been Marshall's opinion in *McCulloch*. However, the decision in *McCulloch* has also been interpreted by many current law professors even more expansively than it should be, given Justice Marshall's clarifying comments. In response to the "torrent of condemnation"[37] following the opinion, Justice Marshall published a defense of the decision by noting the following:

> In so single instance does the court admit the unlimited power of congress to adopt any means whatever, and thus to pass the limits prescribed by the constitution. Not only is the discretion claimed for the legislature in the selection of its means, always limited in terms, to such as are appropriate, but the court expressly says, 'should congress under the pretext of executing its powers, pass laws for the accomplishment of objects, not entrusted to the

government, it would become the painful duty of this tribunal. . . to say that such as act was not the law of the land.' [38]

Thus, arguably Justice Marshall himself clarified the opinion to reduce its application back within the powers delegated to Congress. To do less would be to render meaningless the care taken in the Constitution to enumerate certain and specific powers of Congress. It is also consistent with the term "proper" of the "necessary and proper" clause that the act in question must still be within the jurisdiction granted to Congress. Therefore, "necessary and proper" refers to something much more than the mere convenience of Congress with no relation to its enumerated powers. However, Justice Marshall's clarification, along with the overall context in which it was made, has been largely lost by most present day legal scholars, who tend to lean heavily towards an activist view of law that resists being tied to any limits in the Constitution's text. It is ironic that today's courts have used the McCulloch decision in a manner that is even contrary to Justice Marshall's own language in that decision, namely, as a mere "pretext . . . for the accomplishment of objects not entrusted to the government."[39]

As a result, in recent decades the clause has been interpreted by the federal courts to give Congress additional, if not outright unlimited power to legislate in areas not specified in the Constitution.[40] In fact, the clause has been stretched so far beyond what was originally envisioned by the Framers of the Constitution that the "necessary and proper" clause is now often referred to as the "elastic" clause.[41]

Misapplication of the 14th Amendment through the Incorporation Doctrine

The incorporation doctrine of the 14th amendment is the fourth of the primary ways in which the federal government has expanded its previously limited powers under the Constitution. It is common today to hear someone talk about how a certain state or local law violates the First Amendment or one of the other ten amendments of the Bill of Rights. However, it was not until the 20th century that the idea of imposing the Bill of Rights on the states was even seriously considered.[42]

James Madison had proposed that portions of the Bill of Rights should be applied to the states, but his idea was rejected. The U.S. Supreme Court, in *Barron v. Baltimore*[43] held that the Bill of Rights did not apply to state governments. Instead, the Bill of Rights was intended to protect the specified rights only against intrusion by the federal government. Following enactment of the Fourteenth Amendment in 1868, some people argued that the

Bill of Rights was incorporated into the amendment's "privileges and immunities" clause, thereby becoming applicable to the states,[44] yet this argument was rejected by the Supreme Court in the *Slaughter House Cases*.[45] For 57 years after the adoption of the Fourteenth Amendment, the Supreme Court consistently rejected its application to the states, with only one exception.[46] But in 1925, all that changed when the Supreme Court, in *Gitlow v. New York*,[47] ruled that freedom of speech and of the press were among the "liberties" protected from the states by the due process clause. To do so, the Court had to ignore judicial precedent from a long string of prior decisions.

From the *Gitlow* decision of 1925, the incorporation doctrine arose, and the idea that the Bill of Rights was a restraint only upon the federal government faded away. Yet it was actually Justice Hugo Black's dissent in the 1947 case of *Adamson v. California*[48] where the doctrine was articulated more specifically. In a dissenting opinion, Justice Black noted that "no state could deprive its citizens of the privileges and immunities of the Bill of Rights," and therefore the Fourteenth Amendment "incorporates" the Bill of Rights and applies it to the states. While the Supreme Court did not endorse a complete incorporation of the Bill of Rights, it did incorporate individual components under the revised doctrine of "selective incorporation."[49] Through this mechanism, activist courts are free to direct the further expanse of the federal government, regardless of constitutional language limitations. In the journal *This World* in 1993, legal scholar Douglas Bradford made this observation:

> This interpretative device [selective incorporation], many writers argue, allows the Supreme Court to transform the Bill of Rights from its original status, namely as a limitation on federal authority, into a specification of the constitutionally guaranteed rights incident to national citizenship. Upon this rock rests the authority of the federal judiciary to oversee busing, quotas, school district boundaries, abortion, Miranda warnings, probable cause for arrest, prison and asylum standards, libel, pornography, subversive speech, and the separation of church and state. Incorporation has emerged as the linchpin of judicial activism in the twentieth century.[50]

The incorporation doctrine has not only been used as a means of extending federal legislation and regulation beyond the boundaries imposed by the Constitution, it has also allowed activist judges to go beyond the intentions of the drafters of the Fourteenth Amendment. In a highly supportive tribute to the Warren Court, Charles Murphy, a "liberal legal scholar," revealed that the Warren Court "had utilized the judiciary as a constructive policy-making instrument in a wide range of areas. Intent more upon social ends than upon legal subtleties and refinements, and candidly prepared to say so, he had pushed the nation, through his Court's legal rulings, to take public actions that Congress was unprepared to recommend and the executive was incapable, unilaterally, of effectively securing."[51]

Mr. Murphy captures the problem in the judiciary branch's misapplication of the Constitution in extending the Bill of Rights to the states. On its surface, the idea of extending the protections of free speech rights to the states, for example, seems benign, if not outright positive. However, the courts are the branch of the federal government least democratic and least responsive to the desires of the citizens. By distorting the true meaning of the Constitution, the Court can "impose [its] policy preferences on the country" and convert the Constitution into an instrument for achieving political goals it could not attain through the proper democratic process.[52] Such judicial activism turns the judicial branch into a policy-making branch that can push an extreme agenda upon the entire country, even when it is opposed by the majority of the population. Individual state legislative bodies, accountable to their citizens, are the proper origins of laws extending federal Constitutional protections to their own citizens. That way, should the citizens oppose such an action, they can vote the responsible legislators out of office. However, when a federal court takes such action, the citizens have no easy recourse to change the outcome if they disagree.

The evidence is quite clear that the Framers of the Fourteenth Amendment had no intention of expanding the Bill of Rights to the states. According to Professor Charles Fairman, who authored one of the seminal law review articles on the subject, the objective of the Fourteenth Amendment Framers was to insure the constitutionality of the 1866 Civil Rights Act, which had as its sole purpose to guarantee black men certain civil rights that were being denied, such as the right to contract, sue, testify, travel, and own property.[53] This conclusion is consistent with the Congressional debates, wherein there was no mention of the Bill of Rights.

The strongest evidence by far of the Framers' intention not to extend the Bill of Rights to the states was the Blaine Amendment, which was first introduced in Congress in 1875, seven years following adoption of the Fourteenth Amendment. The Blaine Amendment contained language virtually identical to the First Amendment, providing that "no State shall make any law respecting an establishment of religion or prohibiting the free exercise thereof." It failed to pass twenty different times, despite the fact that the Congress that considered the Blaine Amendment contained 23 members of the Congress that wrote the Fourteenth Amendment. Not one of those 23 drafters of the Fourteenth Amendment stated that the Bill of Rights was incorporated.[54]

They certainly could have saved themselves a lot of work if it had been, since it would have rendered the Blaine Amendment redundant.

Finally, the U.S. Supreme Court itself, in *Bartkus v. Illinois*,[55] ruled that the Due Process Clause of the Fourteenth Amendment did not apply the Fifth Amendment's double jeopardy clause or "any of the provisions of the first eight amendments" to the States.[56] The Court could not have been more direct when it declared that "the relevant historical materials . . . demonstrate conclusively that Congress did not contemplate that the Amendment was a short-hand incorporation of the first eight amendments making them applicable as explicit restrictions upon the States."[57] So, once again, the U.S. Supreme Court today is charting a judicial path that earlier Courts declared off-limits. It has overruled itself, and as a result, federal legislation and regulations are nearly unlimited in their reach. The result has been to transplant the original Constitution into the "dead letter office."[58] In their book *Judicial Dictatorship* Professors Quirk and Bridwell speak of the real dangers of a Court that no longer adheres to the language of the Constitution. They noted that the Supreme Court "routinely overrules the actions of the local police, boards of education, and the state laws under which they act. The beneficiaries of the Court's protection are criminals, atheists, homosexuals, flag burners, . . . illegal entrants, including terrorists, convicts, the mentally ill and pornographers."[59]

The federal courts have long since abandoned the practice of referring to the actual language and text of the Constitution as they have produced judicial edicts that have brought instant change in the legal and cultural composition of "every neighborhood in the country."[60]

Today we have reached the point in our constitutional transformation that the national government can override nearly any law passed by the states. The carefully erected wall of 18 limited federal powers found in Article I, Section 8 of the Constitution, not to mention the overriding principle of limited government, have been ignored and left in the dust. It is no coincidence that this development coincides with the fact that the moral and religious basis that undergirds our Constitution has also been ignored.

Specific Erosions of Intended Constitutional Limitations

Do we think that today, more than 215 years since its authorship, we somehow know better than the original authors how to maintain and interpret our Constitution? Only the height of arrogance would suggest that we do. Yet consider some of the specific actions in each of the three federal government branches that have replaced original intentions with modern ideology.

The Legislative Branch

The most fundamental duty of the legislative branch is to make laws. Some people feel they do this job too well, giving the American public an excess of laws and regulations. However, there are several instances in which Congress has exercised legislative power contrary to the Constitution.

a. The Graduated Income Tax

Clearly Congress has the authority to tax, but the Constitution limited the means by which it was to do so. In Article I, Section 8, Paragraph 1, the Constitution provides that all taxation will "be uniform throughout the United States," yet it is difficult to argue that today's graduated income tax system is "uniform." Those citizens who labor more diligently so as to earn more money are penalized by a different and higher tax bracket. The constitutional provision calling for a uniform tax was consistent with Biblical principles. In referring to what was called the head tax, used to support the civil order, Exodus 30:15 states that *"The rich shall not give more and the poor shall not give less."* Discriminatory taxation was forbidden.[61] Thus the practice of a graduated tax schedule is contrary to the initial system that taxed all citizens at the same rate, it is contrary to the express language of the Constitution, and it is contrary to the Biblical example.

b. The Power to Borrow Money

The Constitution also gave Congress the power to borrow money, but the intent of the Founders was for this power to be exercised sparingly. Compare the spirit of the Constitution in the area of borrowing money with today's practice. We have clearly ignored the warnings of Jefferson not to saddle posterity with our debts. Now we lack the moral courage required to make the tough decisions to reduce spending. Deficit spending and graduated taxation were virtually unheard of until passage of the Sixteenth Amendment setting up the federal income tax in 1913. Now the federal government taxes approximately 35% of an average American's income.

c. Automatic Tax Withholding

In 1943, a further encroachment upon the Constitutional power to tax occurred when the federal government began to withhold taxes automatically from employees' paychecks. The effect of this automatic withholding has been to artificially hide the heavy tax burden the government places on its citizens. Since the money is never received, it is as if we never had it in the first place. The effect is tranquilizing; through automatic withholding, people become numb to the pain of having their own money taken out of their pockets. That numbing effect has removed much of the pressure on Congress to reduce the tax burden because the number of people complaining stays small. Now Congress refuses to balance the budget as a routine practice. In fact, when Congress finally did balance the budget in 1998, the event was newsworthy.

d. The Constitutional Limit to "Coin Money"

In Article I, Section 8, Paragraph 5, the Constitution explicitly states that Congress only has the power to "coin money." That means that they are not constitutionally authorized to print paper money. In case this seems like an unreasonable interpretation of the provision, the legislative history confirms it. In James Madison's notes from the Convention, he says that the delegates originally considered allowing Congress to "emit bills of credit" or paper money, but the phrase was struck out in order "to shut and bar the door against paper money." Later, in Section 10, Paragraph 1, it states that only "gold and silver coin" would be legal "tender in payment of debts."

For about 80 years, that is what we had, a currency consisting entirely of precious metals. During the Civil War, an emergency situation, America began using paper money, and the federal government has never stopped since. Initially, the "greenbacks" issued by Congress could not be redeemed in gold or silver, but in 1878, Congress changed that situation so they could be redeemed in gold.[62] This enabled our currency to remain tied to a gold and silver standard. The constitutional mandate was being followed at least in spirit, if not by the letter of the law. Yet all pretense of adhering to the Constitution was tossed aside in 1933, when President Franklin Roosevelt used economic "emergency" powers to abolish the gold standard.[63] This promotion of the constitutionally unauthorized "bills of credit" continued until the transformation was completed in 1968. That was the year, when on June 24, the President proclaimed Federal Reserve silver certificates merely *fiat* legal tender, since they could not be redeemed in silver.[64] That proclamation terminated what was left of the silver standard, and our currency became completely loosed from the constitutional constraints that tied it to a precious metal anchor.

Now any time Congress wishes to pay off some of its excessive spending, instead of facing the public with higher taxes and hearing the inevitable howls that would keep them in check, they simply order more money to be printed and borrow from it. In the process, everyone's money is devalued and retains less purchasing power. This solution is politically expedient, encourages irresponsible spending, and has the effect of being a hidden, nonconsensual tax. It is nothing more than glorified theft by government from its own citizens. It is also constitutionally groundless, because to this day, the requirement to coin money remains. Instead of lawfully amending the Constitution to allow for the issuance of paper money, government has unlawfully ignored the limitation.

e. Foreign Policy Matters

It is in this area, perhaps as much as any other, where we have ventured beyond the original intentions of our Founding Fathers and the spirit behind the Constitution. We had been warned by our Founders against entangling alliances, such as our current association with the United Nations. Jefferson said in his inaugural address as President that we should have "peace, commerce, and honest friendship with all nations, entangling alliances with none." The Founders understood that in order for America to be morally right in any foreign involvement, we must be free from any preconceived arrangements and be able to make an impartial judgment as to what is right to do. We should never have an alliance or treaty that commits us to militarily or economically support a nation that might be at fault.

Any alliances we do have should be for a short term, and even then they should be terminated as soon as possible. Governments can quickly change direction by virtue of coups, insurgencies, and even regular elections. We must have the ability to withdraw quickly from prior commitments for the same reason. Trade should be completely without political connections. Indeed, economic trade should not go through government channels at all. Moreover, we should never intervene militarily in support of a revolution unless it is just and capable of leading to self-government or unless a government directly threatens our nation's security. This was how our foreign policy was originally designed to be carried out, and it's the approach most consistent with Biblical principles.

Failure to abide by such principles has diminished our nation's ability to successfully conduct the armed conflicts in which it has been engaged during the 20th century. For example, international commitments to the UN and the Southeast Asian Treaty Organization actually limited our ability to conduct the Korean and Vietnam wars at our own discretion, and was partially responsible for the stalemates in both conflicts. Most recently, the NATO-led Kosovo air campaign required that the United States conduct its bombing campaign in accordance with the consensus of the 19 separate governments that were then represented in NATO![65]

Until this century, America largely maintained a Biblical approach to foreign policy, under which we were concerned about the moral implications of our alliances. Today, however, our nation enters into alliances with little or no consideration for the moral consequences; politics and economics have become our primary concerns. A perfect example of this recently came when the executive branch recommended and pushed for free trade status with China, and the Congress approved it in the late summer of 2000. Economics overrode the human rights atrocities of forced abortions, religious persecutions, and government crack downs on political expression, such as the slaughter at Tiananman Square.

Our membership in the United Nations was also begun without considering the moral consequences. As a result, the United States is aligned with many nations that reject Christianity and are repressive towards it. For example, before it was invaded by Iraq in 1990, Kuwait used much of its monetary wealth to purchase Bibles around the world for the sole purpose of burning them.[66] Iran, another U.N. member nation, has publicly executed former Muslims who converted to Christianity and refused to renounce their new-found Christian beliefs.[67] In July, 1996, an Islamic court in Saudi Arabia sentenced a Christian man to execution because he had converted to Christianity from a Muslim faith and he refused to deny Christ. More recently, in 2003, a court in northern Jordan ordered a Christian widow to jail for 30 days if she refused to hand over her two minor children to be raised as Muslims.[68] Through our alliance with the U.N., America has aligned itself with such practices. In the early part of this century, America was far more respected in the eyes of the world. Since we have compromised our Christian principles and Biblical focus, we are constantly ridiculed in the foreign press and the public at large for our apparent support of oppressive regimes around the world.

The Executive Branch

The President of the United States is not only the Commander-in-Chief of the armed forces, but also our chief diplomat. He establishes foreign policy and proposes treaties, but they must be approved by Congress. However, the process is not always carried out the way it was designed to be. For example, in 1945 President Roosevelt negotiated a secret treaty at Yalta with Churchill and Stalin which was never submitted to Congress.[69] In retrospect, it should have been. In that secret alliance, America consented to allow the

Soviet Union to take control of Eastern Europe, including East Berlin. As a result, Americans and the world could only watch in horror as a barbed wire and concrete wall of separation was built up in Berlin, and desperate souls running for freedom were shot and killed. Thanks to President Roosevelt's secret treaty at Yalta, millions of people were ruthlessly enslaved in Eastern Europe under the heavy yoke of Soviet-style communism. Only the ceaseless and persistent prayers of many faithful believers throughout the world eventually brought down the oppressive Iron Curtain that atheism and the Yalta alliance created.

a. Expansion of Executive Powers

The primary function of the executive branch is to enforce the laws made by Congress. Today, in order to carry out this task, the President appoints 15 secretaries to preside over 15 executive departments; these individuals are referred to as the Cabinet. Additionally, there are over 60 other executive offices and independent agencies. Many of these additions were made necessary by the expansion of presidential power beyond what is constitutionally provided for.

As intended by the Founders, the office of President was limited to six areas of responsibility under the Constitution: (1) the chief of state, (2) the commander-in-chief over the military, (3) the chief diplomat over our foreign relations, (4) the chief executive officer of the executive branch, (5) the chief architect for needed legislation, and (6) the conscience of the nation in granting pardons or reprieves when the President feels justice requires it.[70]

Since the days of our Founders, the executive branch roles have been greatly expanded with no expansion of constitutional authority. For example, today the executive branch supervises all radio and television broadcasting in the U.S., administers nearly 40% of the nation's land area and its resources, oversees a network of health agencies, administers a national welfare program, provides federal relief for victims of natural disasters, supervises the distribution of atomic energy resources, and has a myriad of other responsibilities nowhere included in the authority granted by the Constitution.[71]

Unfortunately, the original Biblically-based concerns of the Founders about the dangers of excessive power in a national government have been pushed aside in our never-ending quest to place more of our reliance upon the shoulders of our federal government "provider." Where our Founders saw God as their provider, today's Americans see national government as their provider. This was especially evident during the 1992 presidential campaign. News clip after news clip showed children and adults asking candidate Bill Clinton what the government could do to solve their various individual problems. Not once did Mr. Clinton ever say that the national government was not designed to solve most of those problems, instead, he told them what they wanted to hear, the politically expedient answer, and the voters rewarded him for it. Mr. Clinton was not the first, nor will he be the last politician to feed the lie that government is the answer to all our problems.

b. Legislating By Executive Order

There has always been a temptation for the President to cross over the constitutional boundary of the executive into the legislative function constitutionally reserved for Congress. This can occur through presidential orders and directives referred to as executive orders. There are three basic types of executive orders, and it is important to distinguish among them when trying to determine whether a President has usurped a legislative function. The first type of executive order implements an international agreement under the President's foreign policy authority. Clearly those type of agreements are constitutional, since they are a proper function of the chief diplomat of the nation. A second type of executive order is that used to implement a legislative act. These, too, are constitutional if they are consistent with the legislation, since they are a proper function of the President's duty to take care that the laws are faithfully executed. Of course, if the executive order is written to undermine the legislation, then the executive order has no constitutional authority. The third and last type of executive order is that issued under the general inherent power of the executive. These are the most controversial and constitutionally questionable since they are often likely to intrude into the legislative function properly reserved for Congress. An example of this last type of order is executive order 11748, dated December 4, 1973, which created the Federal Energy Office, an entirely new administrative agency with powers over energy matters that affected the lives of all U.S. citizens.[72] There is no executive function related to such an order that would make it anything other than an unconstitutional intrusion into the legislative function of Congress.

Executive orders are nothing new. They have been issued since the tenure of our first President in 1789.[73] However, they have gone a long way since 1789 into frequent trespasses into the legislative function. Arguably, today it is the President, not Congress, who makes the most laws by the means of executive orders. They were originally intended to be administrative instructions or policies that only affected federal departments and agencies of the second type described above. Over time, though, the federal courts began to consider them as legally binding as congressional legislation.

The expansion of presidential power into the domain formerly left to Congress has been mind-boggling. For perspective, consider that prior to President Teddy Roosevelt, no President had issued more than 70 executive orders in his entire term. Teddy Roosevelt changed that prior pace dramatically. In his term alone, he issued more than 1,000 executive orders.[74] By 1935, the trend became so great that Congress required that they be published in the Federal Register.[75] Today there are over 13,500 executive orders on the books. Because many such orders are not numbered and only numbered orders are published, no one knows exactly how many executive orders have been issued. Former Secretary of the Interior Harold L. Ickes once estimated that the number of *unnumbered* executive orders alone exceeded 15,000, while some have placed the figure as high as 50,000![76] Through the use of the third type of executive orders, the executive branch has unconstitutionally encroached upon the responsibility of the legislative branch, undermining the separation of powers.

The Judicial Branch

The judicial branch is responsible for guarding the constitutional separation of powers and is composed of the nine member Supreme Court, 11 Circuit Courts of Appeal, and 144 other federal courts. The judicial branch has as its primary purpose the interpretation of the laws of Congress in light of the Constitution and higher law. Yet not only have the courts failed to check both Congress and the President in the areas discussed previously, they have themselves been guilty of encroaching into the other branches' responsibilities, as we have noted.

The evolution of the judicial branch has been consistently moving in the wrong constitutional direction, away from those early intentions of the Founders. In his book, *The Constitution of the United States*, Edwin S. Kirwan describes four distinct stages in the history of the Supreme Court. The first two stages, the era of "national supremacy" (from 1800 to 1835) and the era of "Constitutional supremacy" (from 1835-1895), Kirwan describes as generally good stages, consistent with the Court's constitutional design. That all changed with the era of "judicial supremacy" from 1895 to 1950, when the decisions of the Court were no longer considered mere interpretations of the laws. During this period, Court decisions rose to a new height; they were considered "the law of the land" in place of the Constitution itself when they conflicted. This era culminated in the arrogant attitude best exemplified in 1907 by Chief Justice Charles Evans Hughes, that "the Constitution is what the judges say it is." The final stage described by Kirwan is our present era, which he calls "judicial activism" or "judicial legislation." In this stage, the Court no longer limits itself to settling disputes between parties; it now strikes down laws in all fifty states, usurping both legislative and executive powers.

The American republic today is far different from that originally established by our Founders in 1787, but a remnant of Biblical principles continues to hold the threads of union together. Now is the time, before these threads completely unravel, to start re-sewing the fabric of government that was entrusted to our care and return to the overriding principle that the powers of the federal government were intended to be "few and defined."

TWELVE

"MAKE NO LAW PROHIBITING THE FREE EXERCISE OF RELIGION": An Unconstitutional Separation

Traditional images of justice at work bring forth certain traditional expectations. For example, from a traditional image of Supreme Court justices toiling amidst age-old books of prior decisions, under the subdued light of green shaded brass lamps, attempting to craft interpretations of the religion clauses and the liberties they entail, one would expect caution and restraint before justices ever chose to toss out 340 years worth of religious liberty principles. One would expect each new decision to be closely intertwined with earlier crafted principles of law, so that a long stream of measured consistency and predictability would be evident.

Given such rational expectations of our highest court, most people would probably assume that the Supreme Court's current interpretation of the establishment clause is quite old. Perhaps they would assume that it is well-rooted in more than 200 years of carefully crafted precedent, spanning the entire duration of the Court, and that the justices had dutifully sought to remain loyal to the original intentions and principles of the Framers. Sadly, those assumptions would be wrong. Contrary to reasonable expectations, after generations of decisions based on long-standing religious liberty principles in this country, and interpretations of the Constitution based on those principles, the Supreme Court justices made a major shift in their interpretation. Given the length of time our religious liberty principles have stood, it is shocking how new and different the Court's establishment clause interpretation really is.

The current Court view was not born until February 10, 1947, in the case of *Everson v. Board of Education*.[1] It was a dramatic turning point in this country's history. On that day, 157 years after the First Amendment was adopted, the U.S. Supreme Court applied for the first time[2] the phrase "wall of separation between church and state."[3] That phrase, so casually thrown about today, was virtually unheard of even 60 years ago. Before 1947, the Supreme Court had ruled on numerous religious cases and never found such a phrase in the First Amendment. Is it reasonable to believe that prior to 1947, the Supreme Court justices did not properly understand the First Amendment, or that Supreme Court justices since 1947 are wiser than their predecessors? Not likely. The more reasonable explanation is that since 1947 the Supreme Court has chosen to substitute its own version of what the religion clauses should be while presenting a false view of the intent of the Founders who drafted them. Thus, the Supreme Court, armed with an improper application of the concept of separation of church and state, has acted as a juggernaut, mowing through 340 years of this country's moral fabric, so carefully sewn by principles of religious freedom. The judicial pen has thus succeeded in destroying what sword-wielding enemy armies have failed to destroy.

The 1947 Everson Decision: The Establishment of the Secular Viewpoint in Constitutional Law

The *Everson* Court considered whether state tax money could be used to reimburse parents for the cost of bus transportation to parochial schools. Although they upheld the state statute that allowed reimbursement to the parents, the Court warned that their decision carried them to "the verge" of forbidden territory under the religion clauses.[4] It represented the outermost limit to which the judges were willing to go. While that in itself was noteworthy, the real significance of the decision was that it was the first application of the term "wall" in reference to church and state relations, and the language of the Court was emphatic. Justice Black found the term by borrowing a metaphor from a letter of Thomas Jefferson's, thus engaging in some very questionable and selective historical analysis.[5]

> The First Amendment has erected a wall between church and state. That wall must be kept high and impregnable. We could not approve the slightest breach.[6]

Justice Wiley Rutledge, in his dissent, was even harsher. He wrote that the clause "was to create a complete and permanent separation of the spheres of religious activity and civil authority . . . ."[7] In sweeping language, the Court effectively broadened the establishment clause at the expense of the free exercise clause and the intentions of the Constitutional Framers.

Improper Legislative History

It is now well known that the Jefferson metaphor the Court used came from a letter he wrote in 1802 to the Baptists in Danbury, Connecticut. It was written in response to their concerns that the federal government would promote a particular religion. In that context, Jefferson mentioned his understanding that the First Amendment built a "wall of separation between church and state."[8] In some respects, it is understandable that the Supreme Court would cite Jefferson's opinion; after all, as noted earlier, he was the co-drafter, along with James Madison, of the Virginia Statute of Religious Liberty of 1786, making Virginia the first state to formally disestablish the state church in the colonial period.

Nonetheless, as a means of establishing the legislative history on the First Amendment, its use was entirely improper and inexcusable for several reasons. First, if the Court sincerely wanted to ascertain the meaning of the religion clauses as found in the First Amendment to the federal Constitution, they should have checked the writings of one of its authors. Thomas Jefferson was an "outsider," a non-participant in the drafting of the Constitution. He was not a delegate to the Constitutional Convention, he wasn't in Philadelphia as an interested observer, nor was he even in the country during the course of the Convention! According to just about any criteria one could choose for finding an "expert" on the meaning of the religion clauses to the federal Constitution, Thomas Jefferson was the wrong man.

Second, Supreme Court justices know better than anyone that, in terms of the judicial weight to be assigned to the documentary evidence, there is a vast difference between personal correspondence from a non-participant in the drafting of a legal document and the actual language of the document itself.[9]

Finally, even if it were deemed proper to quote Jefferson to ascertain his views on the subject, the justices were intellectually dishonest in their selective use of his "wall of separation" metaphor in the face of all his other writings on church-state matters, and in their misrepresentation of his other views. It is interesting that the Supreme Court ignored Jefferson's many other writings and actions as a governmental official that contradicted the conclusion of absolute separation drawn by the *Everson* Court. Ironically, had the Supreme Court reviewed all of Jefferson's writings, they would have found an admonishment by the man himself against their act of questionable constitutional interpretation. On June 12, 1823, Thomas Jefferson had this to say in a letter to Justice William Johnson on the subject of constitutional interpretation:

On every question of construction, carry ourselves back to the time
when the Constitution was adopted, recollect the spirit manifested in the debates, and instead of trying what meaning may be squeezed out of the text,
or invented against it, conform to the probable one in which it was passed.[10]

Citing a non-participant of the debates is the type of squeezing out of the
text that is not ascertaining its "probable" meaning.

Jefferson's Views Improperly Represented

As we noted in Chapter 5, if the Supreme Court justices insisted on using
Jefferson's views, then they had an obligation to at least represent them accurately. Granted, Thomas Jefferson was one of the Founding Fathers more
committed to the concept of separation between church and state, but his
views would not "measure up to the standards of absolute separation which
the *Everson* Court attributed to him."[11] Some of the points from our earlier
discussion of this issue bear repeating here.

While Jefferson did coin the term "wall of separation between church
and state," his later pronouncements demonstrate that he intended his phrase
to mean a wall of separation around the institution of the church to prevent
the government from infringing upon religious practices.[12] Perhaps a more
accurate metaphor would have been a moat of protection surrounding the
walls of the church.

Moreover, Jefferson was only concerned about federal government intrusions. He recognized that while the federal government had no authority
to establish a church, there was nothing unconstitutional about individual
states doing so.[13] Jefferson was very aware that the Constitution's First
Amendment only proscribed government intrusions on the church and not
the other way around, a distinction lost on most separationists today. He was
not at all hostile to religion, or religious influence in the public arena. His actions confirm his beliefs on church and state separation. In fact, as the
founder of the University of Virginia, he recommended that the University
students be allowed to meet on the campus for prayer and worship, along
with their professors, and he designated space in the Rotunda of the University for chapel services.[14] In the first plan of public education Jefferson
developed for the city of Washington, he included the use of the Bible and
the Isaac Watts Hymnal as the main textbooks for teaching reading.[15] As
Governor of Virginia, he issued a public Thanksgiving proclamation calling
for prayer and fasting and encouraging the citizens of Virginia to reflect on
the blessings of God. Most astounding of all, as President of the United
States, Jefferson approved several appropriation bills authorizing the expen-

diture of federal funds to pay for Christian missionaries to the Indians![16] Imagine the irony of the Supreme Court decision in *Everson* in light of this more complete and accurate perspective on Jefferson. The Supreme Court justices ruled that they were on the verge of forbidden territory in allowing *state* tax money to reimburse parents for bus transportation to religious schools, citing as an authority a man who previously approved the use of *federal* tax money to teach the Indians about Christianity!

Despite the inappropriateness of using Jefferson as an authority on the meaning of the First Amendment, had the Supreme Court represented his views accurately, we would have a much less "impregnable" wall of separation between church and state than we do today. That fact alone speaks volumes on the effects of historical distortion on our religious liberty jurisprudence. Thomas Jefferson was, as most historians concur, one of the more staunch proponents of a separation between church and state of all our Founding Fathers (with the possible exception of James Madison). Yet even his views, let alone those of the actual drafters of the First Amendment, have been greatly overstated by current Supreme Court opinions. It is obvious that the Supreme Court has wandered far from the original intent of those who actually authored the amendment.

Actions of the Framers are the Best Evidence of Their Intent

If the Supreme Court had been serious in its effort to ascertain the intent of the Constitutional Framers, there was a far better source of their intent than the views of a non-participant expressed in a personal letter. The Framer's actions, taken both before and immediately after passing the First Amendment, provided the best evidence of their intent concerning the relationship of religion and government.

Action taken before passage of the amendment as we know it included James Madison's competing proposal on the same topic. His language was as follows:

> The civil rights of none shall be abridged on account of religious belief or worship, *nor shall any national religion be established,* nor shall the full and equal rights of conscience be in any manner, or on any pretext, infringed.[17] [emphasis added]

The floor debate in the House over the religion clauses made it clear that the concern of the Framers was accurately reflected by Madison's draft: to prevent Congress (i.e. the *federal government*) from establishing a national religion by compelling citizens to worship God in any manner contrary to their conscience.[18] Their concern was far more limited than what staunch separationists express today. For example, encouragement of religion in general was not a problem to them, especially since so many of the Founders felt that religion was a critical support of government.

On September 3, 1789, the Senate reported this language back to the House:

> Congress shall make no law establishing articles of faith or a mode of worship, or prohibiting the free exercise of religion.

The version that emerged from the conference between the House and Senate was the one we know today. Both the final version and the Senate proposal omit Madison's reference to the prohibition against a national religion. Many historians use that omission to conclude that the Framers purposely changed the language because it didn't accurately reflect their intentions for the religion clauses, but such a conclusion clearly does not coincide with the historical record. In fact, much of the debate thereafter was about whether subsequent generations, not understanding the Framers' main purpose of proscribing a national church, might actually over apply the so-called "establishment clause" to prohibit all, or nearly all religious influence in government.

During the opening speech in the First Congress on the proposed religion clauses Peter Sylvester of New York expressed a fear that has turned out to be prophetic and well founded. He was concerned that the establishment clause "might be thought to have a tendency to abolish religion altogether."[19] Hence, he wanted to retain the Madison language that more accurately reflected the primary concern of the Framers. He was not alone in those fears. The religion clauses were clearly designed to "facilitate the encouragement of religion and positive religious influence, not to isolate the interests of religion behind a delimiting wall of separation."[20]

Moreover, only one day after the House of Representatives voted to adopt the First Amendment in its ultimate form, Representative Elias Boudinot proposed a resolution asking President Washington to issue a Thanksgiving Day Proclamation, which the President agreed to do. These are hardly the actions of a Congress committed to absolute neutrality of the government between religion and non-religion, nor are they the actions of a Congress committed to absolute separation of religion and state.

Neutrality between Religion and Non-Religion Not Intended

For our purposes here, James Madison's original language prohibiting a national religion, and the debates on the amendment, including the concerns of Peter Sylvester, do not indicate an intent that the government should consider religion and non-religion as equal goods, as today's courts now insist. Their desire was clear: freedom of religion for all, and no establishment of a national church like the one their forefathers fled from in England.

Action taken immediately after proposing the First Amendment was once again a better indicator of the Framers' intent than Jefferson's private correspondence. On the same day that Madison proposed the amendments which became the Bill of Rights, the First Congress re-enacted the Northwest Ordinance for the governance of the Northwest Territory. That ordinance provided that "religion, morality, and knowledge, being necessary to good government and the happiness of mankind, schools and the means of education shall forever be encouraged."[21] Note carefully the meaning of that provision. Congress sought to encourage education because of the need for "religion, morality, and knowledge" as necessary tools of good government. Religion and morality were considered to be important influences for government! They were concepts that were not intended to be kept behind the four walls of a church, or in the private confines of an individual's heart and mind. No, religion and morality were seen as so important to good government that the legislators of the day made sure that religion and morality were taught in the public schools, and established them for just that purpose.

Current Separation Doctrine Ignores First Amendment Language

Due to the distortion made by current judicial doctrines in the area of religious liberty, we have completely lost the ideas conveyed by the language in the First Amendment itself! That language was initially quite clear, seeming not to require an elaborate examination of constitutional history, let alone a selective and distorted one. Ask any American, even those not familiar with the law, what the first clause of the First Amendment is about. Nearly everyone is quick to say that the First Amendment entails the "separation of church and state," a phrase not even found in the amendment. Sadly, most of those same people are unable to recall its actual language. The first clause states that "Congress shall make no law respecting an establishment of religion. . . ."

Let's look at the actual criteria established by the language in the First Amendment for determining whether the establishment clause has been violated.

a. There must be a "law" involved

Because of the distorted reliance on Jefferson's metaphor, courts don't even look to see if there is a "law" involved, let alone an "establishment of religion" in a particular activity to determine whether it is constitutional. A common sense reading of the amendment should lead a court to exactly that issue. The controversial Ten Commandments monument displayed in the foyer of the Alabama Supreme Court building was not placed there as a result of any "law" passed by Congress or any other legislative body. Nor was there any "law" that required persons to worship the monument, revere it, or even pay attention to it, nor one that penalized any person for not doing so. No coercive influence existed whatsoever. The simple requirement of the First Amendment's language that a law be involved was ignored by the Federal District Court of Appeals when it found an establishment clause violation, because today's establishment clause jurisprudence has substituted its own standard of "separation," which is not found in the First Amendment, for the requirement of a "law," which is found there. The courts are no longer applying the Constitutional language when interpreting the Constitution! That, of course, is a recipe for disaster.

b. A Religion Must Be Established

In order to "establish" a religion, there must be a strong element of coercion involved. Without coercion, people are free to ignore the activity, or respectfully tolerate it while adhering to their own viewpoints. Nothing is "established" through a display such as the Ten Commandments monument. As the litigants entered the federal district Court of Appeals that decided the Alabama monument case, they had to walk by a statue of the Greek god of Justice, Thebes, that was sitting outside above a fountain. That statue represented a pagan god and a pagan religion, but it no more "established" that religion than the monument of the Ten Commandments that was the object of litigation inside. The statue of the Greek god of Justice did not force or coerce Christians or anyone else to worship it, and so it stands today, being tolerated by people of other faiths and no faith. The monument of the Ten Commandments is no different in its lack of coercive effect and resulting failure to "establish" a religion.

The issue decided by the *Everson* Court would have been easy to determine if the Court had applied the language of the First Amendment. The issue was whether state money to support the costs of bus transportation of children could also be used to support the costs of transport to religious schools. Did such practice "establish" any religion? To determine that issue,

look to see if any American was *coerced* into a certain type of religious belief. Were Catholics forced to be Methodist, or Jews forced to be Christian,
or atheists forced to be Presbyterian? If not, then where was the "establishment" of a religion, or the coercion of a religious belief? Since the law
merely provided the costs to pay for bus transportation to religious schools in
the same way that it provided for non-religious students, no religion was "established" by the law, it merely put religious and non-religious students on
an equal footing.

Indeed, no particular religion was even favored, quite the contrary. The
law actually served to even the playing field, so that if a parent chose to send
their child to a religious school, they would not be penalized by having to pay
for bus transportation that parents sending their children to secular schools
did not have to pay for. The legal analysis, if we stick to the actual language
of the First Amendment, is quite simple, and far more reflective of the intent
of the Framers. Most importantly, such an interpretation better protects the
liberties of those who choose to exercise their religion.

c. Congress must be Involved for an Establishment Clause Violation

The clear language of the First Amendment evidenced an original intent
by the Founders to limit only "Congress," yet that carefully limited focus has
now been unconstitutionally broadened to include federal agencies, state
legislatures, state agencies, universities, and even personal activity.

Consider some recent cases. An individual teacher with a personal Bible
on his or her classroom desk is told to remove it, while a kindergarten student
in a New Jersey public school is told he cannot distribute pencils that say "Jesus loves the little children" or candy canes that have an attached card that
refers to the birth of Jesus.[22] Where is Congress in these cases? Indeed,
where is the church in these cases, and where is one organized religion?
More importantly, what religion was "established" by the acts of an individual teacher and a kindergarten student? Finally, what "law" was involved
that was coercing people into believing in the Bible or Jesus based on these
individual actions? The courts don't even ask such relevant questions anymore, yet they are clearly part of the express language of the First
Amendment.

We have long since abandoned the language of the First Amendment or
its common sense framework of looking for the "establishment of a church"
in a questioned activity. Now our decisions seem part of a "witch hunt" of
sorts, like the out-of-control McCarthy-ism of the 50's, or a "religious apartheid" of the present day, looking for any evidence of religion attempting to

sneak into a public school or a government building. The scarlet "A" that so many people accused zealous Christians of placing on the adulterers in the past is now a scarlet "R" that the secularists are placing on those who seek to exercise their religion in public. This pressure has become a very effective means of eliminating all religious expression and influence from the public square without admitting what it truly is: censorship.

The Effects of Jurisprudence Based on a Metaphor

Through this misapplication of the separation concept, the Supreme Court has determined that religious expression, no matter how innocuous, is equivalent to the establishment of religion. The effect of the *Everson* Court's new phrase has been shocking. Since 1947, under the guise of the "separation of church and state" clause, U.S. Courts have held that allowing a voluntary, non-denominational prayer establishes a religion;[23] that students praying over their own lunch out loud establishes a religion;[24] that a Board of Education using or referring to the word "God" in any official documents establishes a religion;[25] and that hanging the Ten Commandments on a school house wall establishes a religion.[26] It doesn't take much these days to "establish" a religion.

The public schools have been especially harsh on religious expression. For instance, a teacher in Colorado was ordered by his superiors to remove his personal Bible from his desk on pain of disciplinary action.[27] The teacher was not even allowed to read it silently while his students were working on their lessons. He was also told to remove two books on Christianity from his 250 book classroom library, even though books on Native American religious traditions and books on the occult were allowed to remain. His offense? He had created a "religious atmosphere." Where is that criteria found in the language of the First Amendment?

A sixth grade boy in Tempe, Arizona wanted to sing the song "Shepherd Boy" in his public school's talent show, but school district officials told him no because of the separation of church and state.[28] His humiliation and embarrassment at the rebuke was the price to be paid for a secularized society. A senior at an Atlanta public high school was suspended for passing a handwritten note to another student in the school hallway. The note merely told the recipient the time and place of the next Fellowship of Christian Athletes meeting. The student who received the note was given a written reprimand by school authorities and told that any further possession of "Christian material" could lead to his suspension.[29] Where is the "church" that is being "established" in these individual acts and where is the coercion to believe in that church?

These are not isolated cases. They occur on a regular basis in all school districts throughout the country. Indeed, the Court's misapplied metaphor is now so well entrenched in our minds that it is often the local school administrators or school boards who act as the official censors of religious expression or activity without the courts even having to make a ruling. Likewise, it is often enough to halt a religious expression by one lone voice of dissent to a school board or other official. Indeed, as voluminous as the case law is, the decided cases are only the tip of the iceberg. There are thousands of other instances where religious expression is quashed that never make it to the courts, and there are thousands more that are initially quashed and only after the expenditure of much time and money in litigation are the cases settled or ultimately won. The mere threat of expensive litigation is often sufficient to keep the religious voice silent. The significance of this is that the amount of suppressed religious activity and expression is far greater than even the vast number of court cases would suggest.

Thomas Jefferson intended his phrase to protect religious expression and activity, yet today's courts, ignoring his intent, have used it as a weapon against religious expression and activity. The cases are endless in which the so-called wall of separation concept has been used to deny public religious expressions that were never even challenged prior to 1947.

Religion Separated From the Public Square

Liberal ideology prides itself on its tolerance of the free expression of ideas and speech. It embraces the idea that only with a free flow of all ideas in the public square can truth spring forth. Yet this same liberal ideology has targeted religious expression for special exclusion from that marketplace of ideas through the Court's application of the "separation of church and state" concept. It is clear that this misapplication has become a new method of censorship of particular religious ideas. According to Franky Schaeffer:

> It has been convenient and expedient for the secular humanist, the materialist, the so-called liberal, the feminist, the genetic engineer, the bureaucrat, the Supreme Court justice, to use this arbitrary division between church and state as a ready excuse. It is used, as an easily identifiable rallying point, to subdue the opinions of that vast body of citizens who represent those with religious convictions.[30]

During the 1994 elections, this one-sided application of "separation of church and state" was obvious. For instance, when Senatorial candidate Oliver North, a conservative Christian, spoke at a Virginia church, the act was decried as a violation of the "separation of church and state." Yet when President Clinton spoke to a Baptist church to gain their support for his troubled health care plan, not a word was mentioned by the media or liberal church and state guardians about a possible violation of that impenetrable wall. Likewise, when Pat Robertson, a conservative Christian and former clergyman, ran for President in 1988, he was pilloried for trying to "force" his religious views on everyone else. Yet when Reverend Jesse Jackson, a liberal Christian, ran for President, those same voices of loud protest were strangely silent. Similarly, Vice President Gore and Senatorial candidate Hillary Clinton used liberal church podiums during the 2000 election to advance their partisan political agenda without a word of protest from the religious separation community. Most recently, Senator John Kerry criticized President Bush's re-election campaign for consisting of the "politics of last resort," a clearly political speech, from the podium of a church in Jackson, Mississippi in March, 2004.[31] The application of the separation concept is far from neutral.

The *Everson* Court's misapplication of Jefferson's metaphor has created much confusion and divisiveness in this country. Those who oppose its present application are accused of wanting to force their beliefs on others and establish a theocracy. Strict separationists are accused of being "anti-religious" or atheists. The truth is lost in the battle of pejorative accusations. Meanwhile, the true intention of the Founders who drafted the First Amendment is ignored.

The Intended Application of Church and State Separation

Although the phrase "separation of church and state" is not found in our Constitution, the concept was relevant for the Framers, albeit in a much more limited form than we see applied today. To the Framers, it meant that the *institution* of the state should be kept separate from the *institution* of the church.[32] Indeed, this is a Biblical concept recognized in the Old Testament;, the Hebrew kings were traditionally selected from the tribe of Judah, while the priests were chosen from the tribe of Levi. Moreover, as originally approved in America, this limitation was intended to apply only at the federal government level. The Framers did not intend, nor does the Constitution require, that religion and government be kept separate at the state and local level.[33] The individual practice of religion was not part of the Framers' fear of the establishment of a national church. It would have been unthinkable to the Framers to suggest that a "wall of separation" meant that Christians, or any other religious group, should be excluded from expressing or practicing their faith except behind the closed doors of their churches or homes.[34] To read the separation language in this way changes our constitutional protection of religious liberty from freedom *for* religion to freedom *from* religion.

Hostility Towards Christianity

Yet, as applied by our courts, the infamous "wall of separation" has, in less than 50 years, changed the soul of America from that of a Christian nation to that of a secular state hostile towards our religious heritage. The phrase has become a thoughtless, knee-jerk reaction to any attempt at including religious matter in the public realm.

There is far more concern for the lone atheist who might be offended by a graduation prayer than there is for the many Christians who might be offended by the absence of any public acknowledgment of God at such an important event.Does anyone care about the thousands of Christians who are deeply offended about the dogma of evolution that is "forced" on everyone in our public schools, supported by federal tax dollars whether it runs contrary to their religious belief or not? Why is a lone voice of Christian dissent not enough to halt a particular secular practice that is offensive to the Christian when a lone atheist voice is so quickly heeded? If we are so concerned about offending non-believers by including references to God in our public schools, where is the equal concern for offending believers by *not* including God in our public schools? If believers in God are expected to pay taxes to support schools that omit all references to God, why aren't non-believers expected to likewise pay taxes to support religious schools that include references to God? The constitutional principle has been turned on its head, from an open encouragement by government of voluntary religious activities to an open suppression by government of voluntary religious activities.

Moreover, the exalted virtue of tolerance is not equally applied today. Christians are expected to be tolerant of the atheist's viewpoint and of a secularized atmosphere, yet the atheist is not expected to be tolerant of the Christian's desires or of any religious reference in the public domain. Not even out of respect for the religious desires of others do we ask the lone atheist to sit quietly and exercise tolerance while the others pray at a school graduation. No one forces the person to pray, no one forces the person to believe in something contrary to his beliefs, and no one forces his or her views on him. It is merely a matter of mutual respect for the views of others. In this current age of "tolerance," such an expectation that non-religious citizens respect the views of the religious does not seem unreasonable

Yes, the "wall of separation between church and state" is the correct concept. But its wrong interpretation and application, divorced from the language of the amendment, has birthed a society far different from what the Constitutional Framers intended, and one that does not protect religious liberty. Now in America, a nation founded by Christians, unbelief is favored over belief.

The Lemon Decision: Secularization Secured

Where the *Everson* Court gave birth to a secularized America, the case of *Lemon v. Kurtzman*[35] ensured its permanence. The Lemon case set forth a three-pronged test to determine whether a statute or government activity violated the establishment clause of the First Amendment.

Every analysis in this area must begin with consideration of the cumulative criteria developed by the Court over many years. Three such tests may be gleaned from our cases. First, the statute must have a secular legislative purpose; second, its principal or primary effect must be one that neither advances nor inhibits religion; finally, the statute must not foster 'an excessive government entanglement with religion.[36]

It is this three part test that has ensured a secular society, primarily by virtue of the first two of these prongs, further considered below.

a. The Statute Must Have a Secular Legislative Purpose

This first prong effectively blocks the door to religion in public, except by special invitation. It puts religion and religious believers on the outside looking in. The obvious question is, why must there be a secular purpose? Such a requirement presumes that a religious purpose must be wrong and is always to be avoided merely because it is religious. It conveys the impression to the American public that a secular purpose is better than a religious purpose, leading to the logical conclusion that secular ideas are to be preferred and trusted over religious ideas. Such an assumption is completely contrary to the words and actions of the drafters of the Constitution. It is ironic that such a clearly unconstitutional standard requiring a secular purpose is now used by our courts to determine what is constitutional in the religious liberty arena.

The first prong forgets the distinction that it was the institution of the Church that was meant to be separate from the institution of the State. Requiring that all laws have a secular purpose changes the equation to separate religion itself from the state,rather than just the administrative functions of particular churches. Once the equation changes, the result changes. Thus, under the "secular purpose" prong, it no longer matters if the religious activity in question is voluntary, if the government action shows no preference for any particular religious group, or if the activity only involves individuals instead of "churches" and "states." If a public activity does not have a non-religious purpose, it is unconstitutional under this first prong of the *Lemon* test. Jefferson's metaphor has been converted into a wall of separation between any religious activity and state, not church and federal government. There is an enormous difference between those two standards.

The Court used this first prong of the *Lemon* test to strike down an Alabama law which allowed a one-minute period of silence in public schools for meditation or voluntary prayer.[37] Even though the Supreme Court admitted that the activity of silence was otherwise constitutional, they could not get around the secular purpose prong.[38] Since the Court found the purpose of the law to be an effort to return voluntary prayer to the public schools, the law was deemed invalid as an effort of the State to "encourage" a religious activity.[39] Here, the"secular purpose" prong was used to prohibit religious motives even if the activity itself a moment of silence, was constitutional. Moreover, this requirement shifts the focus of the court from looking for an establishment of a national church by a state activity, to looking for mere state encouragement of individually exercised religious expression or activity. No "church" is involved in the moment of silence issue, let alone an "established" Church; but a changed equation, always yields a different answer. Indeed, government can manipulate the answer by changing the equation.

The requirement for a "secular purpose" not only removes the Framers' intent from consideration, it also removes all common sense. In a case decided by a federal appellate court,[40] the court held that a kindergarten teacher who had her class recite a poem that didn't even mention God[41] had violated the Establishment Clause. How? The court feared that the poem might cause the children to think about God. As the dissenting judge wryly noted, such an application of the "secular purpose" test led the court to conclude it was unconstitutional to think about God.[42] Actually, that isn't completely true; free speech protections allow anyone to curse God publicly and to think bad thoughts about God. So, extending the dissenting judge's logic, the court's test really only placed limits on thinking and expressing good thoughts about God.

Requiring a secular purpose for a statute to be valid effectively requires all but the remotest vestiges of religion to be removed and censored out of the public square. It leads to the ridiculous point of not allowing creches at

Christmas unless the religious message is totally diluted and rendered ineffective by reindeer, Santas, and other secular symbols. Once again the tolerance for others' beliefs is one-directional. Christians must tolerate the secularists' Santa Clauses and reindeer at Christmas and witches at Halloween, but the secularists need not tolerate a lonely creche with a baby Jesus. The end result is the silencing of religious influence in society.

b. Laws Must Neither Advance Nor Inhibit Religion

This second requirement from the *Lemon* decision undermines religion because it perpetuates a myth. By requiring statutes to neither advance nor inhibit religion, it proposes that it is possible to be neutral towards religion. There are two problems with such a notion. First, it runs directly counter to the intent of the Constitutional Framers, who envisioned a government encouragement of religion. Second, neutrality toward religion is not feasible. The consequences of such efforts at neutrality have been to create hostility toward religion.

1. The Founding Fathers never intended for government to be neutral towards religion. According to historian Rousas John Rushdoony, the concept of a secular state did not exist when our nation's founding document, the Declaration of Independence, was written. It still did not exist during the Constitutional Convention, nor in 1791 when the Bill of Rights was ratified. Thus, for the Supreme Court to interpret the Constitution as the "charter for a secular state is to misread history, and to misread it radically. The Constitution was designed to perpetuate a Christian order."[43]

The men at the Constitutional Convention were Christians; many of them had to be in order to qualify for public office under their state constitutions. That is how deeply many states believed that Christianity was fundamental to good citizenship and leadership in society. As part of the censorship of religion in our public schools since the late 1940s, Americans are no longer familiar with what was obvious to all back then. Patrick Henry summarized what was generally well-known:

> It cannot be emphasized too strongly or too often that this great nation was founded, not by religionists, but by Christians, not on religions but on the gospel of Jesus Christ! For this very reason peoples of other faiths have been afforded asylum, prosperity, and freedom of worship here.[44]

Nor did the Framers see any contradictions in keeping church and state institutions separate while government provided overall encouragement of religion in general. They did not intend or desire to "expunge Christian moral influence from society or even foster a climate of detached neutrality towards religion."[45] According to the University of Houston study noted earlier, which examined an estimated fifteen thousand writings by the Founding Fathers in the period 1760-1805, the book the Founders cited by far most frequently was the Bible.[46] Indeed, the religious influence in our civil institutions was so well known and accepted that less than thirty-five years after the Constitutional Convention, Daniel Webster made this observation:

> Finally, let us not forget the religious character of our origin. Our fathers were brought hither by their high veneration for the Christian religion. They journeyed by its light, and labored in its hope. They sought to incorporate its principles with the elements of their society, and to diffuse its influence through all their institutions, civil, political, or literary.[47]

2. Furthermore the second prong of the *Lemon* test is based on a false presupposition. Government cannot be neutral towards religion. The Supreme Court has tried to appear objective about religion by declaring a "benevolent neutrality" towards it, but as John Whitehead asserts, the Court has used the idea of neutrality as a "sugarcoating to make palatable to us the bitter pill of the abandonment of Christian values . . . ."[48]

Although many people would disagree, there is strong evidence that another religion, or philosophy of life, has filled the void left by the removal of Christianity. It is called secularism, or in the words of the Supreme Court, who declared it in *dicta* a religion, "secular humanism."[49] It is a belief system in which man, not God, defines what is right and wrong. Even the charter document of humanism, the "Humanist Manifesto I", written in 1933, declares that humanism or secularism is a religious point of view.[50] Whether one agrees it is a religion or not, clearly secularism presents a world view that is contrary to a traditional theistic world view.[51] Therefore in promoting a secular environment, the court system has not been neutral; through its rulings, it has replaced the predominant religion in America, Christianity, with that of secularism. Now traditional religion is portrayed as the unwelcome intruder into any public discussion, and the other religion or world view of secular ideas is seen as the neutral voice of reason.[52]

There are really only two choices for a state that seeks to be neutral. It can either promote all religion by including God in the picture, or it can promote atheism or secularism by excluding God from the picture. The American courts have tried to straddle the fence and not mention God one way or the other; yet that awkward stance is no different than the one that promotes atheism, since both end by excluding God from the picture. A true middle ground does not exist, and we fool ourselves if we believe it does.

If God and all religious practices are excluded, then the government has, in a de facto sense, effectively "established" the religion of atheism. In so doing, the Court has violated its own standard of neutrality between religion and non-religion. So the atheistic viewpoint is promoted at the expense of the traditionally religious viewpoint that was responsible for founding the nation in the first place. Where is the neutrality in that? We are merely promoting religions based on unbelief over religions based on belief. It is a substitution of religion, but it is not neutral. Ironically, it is often the secularists who are the first to cry that the Christians are trying to force their views on everyone else. The reality is that the secularists have already succeeded in taking over many of our public institutions, and they are enforcing their views against Christians to protect their turf.

Attempts at neutrality have created a tremendous double standard. A public school teacher can promote the atheistic ideas of Karl Marx or Freud, but cannot promote the principles of the Bible. Schools can teach the atheistic concept of evolution and Darwinism, but are not allowed to teach the Christian concept of creation science.[53] Carl Sagan was allowed to teach that the cosmos is all there is or ever will be,[54] but others cannot refute him or teach about who created the cosmos. Our marketplace of ideas has become a closed system intolerant towards religion in general and Christianity in particular. Children can read about and make little witches and goblins for Halloween, but cannot read about or make a creche at Christmas or a cross at Easter. That is not neutrality.

The Effect of Neutrality Efforts is Actually Hostility toward Religion

Examples of current hostility toward religion in America are rampant. Americans have been led to believe that society must be secular and that efforts to bring religion into the public realm are somehow wrong. The result is predictable.

In September, 1980, Mayor Tom Bradley of Los Angeles proclaimed that "[a] Bible study would not be a permissible use in a single family residential area."[55] Christians meeting in two home study groups were told to "cease and desist" since the homes had not been zoned for "church purposes."[56] Similar zoning laws have led officials in Seattle and Atlanta to question home Bible studies in those cities, as well. Attorney Jay Sekulow sums up the attitude:

> When it comes to free expression of just about anything on the radical fringe, some school administrators and most courts have taken the broadest

interpretation of the First Amendment. But when traditional religion is involved, a knee-jerk, heavy-handed application of the establishment clause has been the rule of thumb.[57]

An example of this attitude arose in the firestorm over public tax dollars used to support photographer Robert Mapplethorpe through a grant by the National Endowment for the Arts (NEA). Mapplethorpe used the money to blatantly offend Christian believers by placing a picture of Jesus Christ on a crucifix in a jar of urine. He entitled his "artwork" "Piss Christ." His work was strongly supported by the free speech advocates as protected speech under the First Amendment. Yet where are those same free speech proponents when artists or other public figures wish to praise the Deity? One commentator noted the hypocrisy, pointing out: "Place a crucifix in a jar of urine, pose it in a public gallery, and you get a federal subsidy. Place a figure of the Christ in a manger, pose it on a public lawn, and you get a federal lawsuit."[58]

The obsession with obtaining secular purity has reached extremes. In Manassas, Virginia, a ten-year old girl, who brought her Bible to read on the bus ride to school was told by her principal that she was not permitted to do so because of church-state separation.[59] In Massachusetts, a fourth-grade girl placed crosses on her art project and was told by her teacher they had to be removed.[60] Again, we have lost sight of the purpose of the First Amendment- to prevent the establishment of a national church. How does a little girl "establish a church" by placing crosses on her art project or by bringing her Bible to read on the bus?

Today, any attempt to restore or maintain religious activity in public is fought as a violation of "separation of church and state." Religion continues to be pushed out of the public arena in an ever-growing effort to secularize society. It has forced believers to artificially take off their "religious cloak" when entering the public domain and pretend, against their deeply held beliefs, that God doesn't exist. For the sake of those who don't believe and who might be offended, America has decided it is better to offend the believers. Non-believers are allowed to bask in their religion-free society, while believers are forced to accept it.

Unfortunately, there is a price to be paid for this one-sided tolerance. A growing number of skeptical citizens are being led to think that religious beliefs are not relevant to rational decision making, that religious belief is no different than a hobby people pick up for fun in their spare time, after their serious work is done. The inevitable conclusion many will draw is that God, if He does exist, must not be very important since He is never talked about in public. That alone has a chilling effect on religious liberty.

Prior to the 1947 Supreme Court decision in *Everson*, there had been little confusion over the meaning of the First Amendment. Since then, for the past fifty years, church-state relations have been governed not by the actual language of the First Amendment, but by a misapplied metaphor, the "wall of separation." It has served to demonstrate the truth of Benjamin Cardozo's observation that "[m]etaphors in law are to be narrowly watched, for starting as devices to liberate thought, they end often by enslaving it."[61] This metaphor lies at the center of an improper application of the First Amendment based on bad historical analysis. It must be discarded and replaced by the actual language of the Constitution itself if we ever expect to restore religious liberty to its intended position in society. What could not be achieved by the swords of our enemies has been accomplished through the pens of our own legal guardians.

PART IV

RESTORING THE FOUNDATIONS

THIRTEEN

Recognizing the Secular Assaults on the Constitution

The stifling hot Philadelphia summer had past. A hint of approaching autumn was rustling through the trees outside the convention hall where so much toil and intellectual wrestling had gone on. The persistence of those constitutional convention delegates would pay dividends for more than two centuries. The bonds of friendship crafted on the anvil of intense give and take during that summer would endure for the rest of the delegates' lives. Now, with their labors of statesmanship completed, the delegates began saying their farewells and heading back to their homes, where long neglected families anxiously awaited them. A woman spotted the easily recognizable old statesman Benjamin Franklin and quickly approached him. Gaining his attention, she asked the question that no doubt was on the minds of many people: "What kind of government have you given us, Sir?" It was a reflective, solemn answer the old sage gave her. "A republic, madam, if you can keep it!"

"If you can keep it." The words contained an inferential warning that it wouldn't be easy. Indeed, it hasn't. It has now been over 215 years since Ben Franklin spoke those words, and the concerns he had then are even more appropriate today. Can we preserve the cherished gift for which our Founding Fathers worked so arduously? Or perhaps we have already allowed that gift to be lost, and now we must seek to restore it. In either case, Ben Franklin and his esteemed colleagues were well aware that the Constitution was far more than a mere document. It was a document that astutely reflected the wisdom of Biblical principles and a Biblical world view. Therefore it could only continue to flourish if those principles continued to undergird its future application. Without those Biblical principles and the virtue of the people necessary to implement them, our Constitution is little more than fancy parchment paper containing flowery, yet empty words.

That is why, though, other nations have tried to copy our Constitution in various ways, they have never been able to replicate America's success. The former Soviet Union is a good example. Their constitution was filled with great words of liberty and individual freedom, yet their nation, founded on principles of Marxist atheism and outright assaults upon Christianity, was a nation of horrible oppression, suppression, and hopelessness. They copied much of the form without copying the spirit underlying that form. So what is the spirit behind America's Constitution? As we have tried to stress throughout these pages, the spirit of America's Constitution is the principles of God's laws found in the Bible and written on the hearts of mankind. Without those two ingredients, America's Constitution is no different than any other. With those two ingredients, however, America's Constitution is a model for all nations for all time here on earth. Along with the Declaration of Independence upon which it is based, it is a perpetual charter for human liberty that will never become obsolete.[1]

America Needs a Course Correction

Ben Franklin's admonition unfortunately no longer applies. As we have attempted to demonstrate in this book, what he and his fellow convention delegates so wisely provided for America is now largely gone. The issue is no longer "keeping" our republic, but rather restoring it. The call for Americans today is not to pursue the status quo. We can no longer "stay the course" if we hope to return this nation to the principles our founders gave us, because the course our Founders set for this nation has already been changed.

This book has attempted to illustrate that the views of our Founding Fathers were deeply rooted in Christian principles that, for the most part, are no longer followed by our schools, our courts, or our government institutions. The course our founders set, and the course our nation followed for approximately 150 years since becoming a nation, and well over 150 years before that, encouraged the influence of the Bible and Christianity upon all of the nation's institutions. That course brought forth great liberty and a beacon of hope for the world that drew millions of immigrants to our shores. It was the course that allowed a backward, poor, and disorganized group of settlers in the New World to transform themselves into the most freedom loving, prosperous, and accepting nation on earth. The United States did not reach perfection, but no nation ever has. The United States has had various moral problems to deal with, but every earthly nation does. Yet when compared to every other course nations have taken, the fruit of liberty this nation has produced stands as an achievement unique in world history.

Yes, America has had her critics over the years, but perspective is in order. As strong as the Christian influence was in this nation, and as revered as the principles of the Bible were, this nation has never come anywhere close to the oppressive theocracy that many critics continue to warn against. Instead, the Christian influence has helped to restrain evil. No church has been allowed to take over the government. No church has been allowed to coercively dictate the policies of the nation. No political purges of thousands, if not millions of a nation's own citizens have occurred here, as they have in atheistic societies such as the former Soviet Union, Pol Pots's Cambodia, or communist China.

Previously, the courts, the schools, and our government institutions recognized the importance of religious influence on government, and even the need for government to encourage religion and the principles of the Bible. It was understood that the application of Biblical principles was part of good government, that Christian influence and virtue was a vital ingredient to the success of the nation. Our heritage was unique in recognizing that Biblical principles not only created an atmosphere in which liberty could flourish, it was directly responsible for the flourishing of liberty. And so from 1607 to 1947, a period of 340 years, Biblical principles were, in large measure, ingrained in our public schools, our judicial systems, and our government institutions, and for those same 340 years, liberty flourished.

But this is not the case today. As we noted earlier, the U.S. Supreme Court commandeered the tiller of our nation in the first half of the 20th century and set the nation on a new course with its 1947 *Everson* decision, which formally created an artificial separation between religious influence and the government. Not content with our Founders' desire to keep the government from controlling or being controlled by the institution of any one church, the Everson Court set a new course of hostility toward religion and Biblical principles, a course not supported by the Constitution. This course has sent our nation in a dangerous direction toward jagged rocks where there are no moral absolutes and where depravity, not liberty, flourishes. Furthermore, this was a course correction made without the benefit of a Constitutional amendment. Thus Americans, whose lives were affected by such a course correction, were never consulted or allowed to voice their opinions.

Creation of a "Religious" and "Secular" Dichotomy

Our public education system, as enabled by the Supreme Court, has taught and reinforced this new hostility toward religion by creating an artificial line between "religious" matters and "secular" matters. Instead of recognizing, as our Founders clearly did, that Biblical principles apply to all aspects of life and are appropriately applied to law, government, and all other institutions, today we teach that Biblical principles are "religious" in nature and therefore must be kept separate and distinct from these institutions, which can only be influenced by "secular" ideas. This compartmentalization ignores reality, namely the fact that all subjects and ideas are hopelessly intertwined. Even such a seemingly "secular" subject as mathematics is filled with religious principles — principles of absolute truth, principles of order, principles of right and wrong that do not change over the course of time. Math is completely contrary to the principles of an evolutionary world view being taught today, which emphasizes continual change as the appropriate response to changing conditions, yet no one seems to notice. Moreover, math is a subject that is completely consistent with a Biblical world view, a view that is consistent with the reality all around us, yet is not allowed to be taught in public schools today. The Bible clearly does not divide life between "spiritual" or "religious" matters and "secular" or "non-religious" matters. The divide we see in our culture today was artificially created by man, not by God.

Even more insidious than the creation of an artificial line between "religious" and "secular" matters is the implication, if not directly expressed teaching, that "religious" matters are based on subjective faith (some even call it "blind" faith), while "secular" matters are based on objective facts. Thus the theory of evolution is said to be based on objective facts, when in reality it is clearly based on subjective faith. Law is also supposedly based on the application of objective facts, when in reality it is clearly the application of subjective faith, at least when practiced without benefit of any objective criteria, such as the Bible.

We must recognize that, contrary to what we have been taught in our new secularized society, there are no facts that are viewed or judged objectively. Every person brings a subjective faith aspect to his or her view of facts, including atheists, agnostics, humanists, and other staunch secularists. One's view of every issue and subject in life is filtered through the lens of his or her subjective belief system. It is called one's world view. World views are the assumptions or presuppositions individuals use to guide their interpretations of any fact, concept or activity. It provides the filter through which we see life. By its nature, a world view is inherently subjective. Therefore, we must recognize that no one, not even secularists, has a corner on objectivity in viewing facts and circumstances. A secular or humanistic world view is not objective, neutral, or non-faith based, despite the assertions of the secularists to the contrary.

It is interesting to note that whenever an overtly Christian politician has run for the presidency, secular journalists are quick to ask that politician if he intends to bring his faith-based Christian views into his decision-making as President. The implication of the question is that somehow, to do so would be wrong. Yet those same secular journalists never bother to ask the overtly secular politician if he intends to bring his equally subjective, evolution-based, atheistic-based, or otherwise secular-based views into his decision-making as President. Such a question is certainly relevant, especially since the intellectual by-product of an evolution-based philosophy is a belief that all persons are mere biological accidents and therefore have little value. Unless they borrow from a Biblical perspective that highly values life as a creation of God, they may act in a manner that demonstrates the unimportance of individual life, as did the Marxist leaders of the former Soviet Union, Lenin and Stalin, who thought nothing of having thousands, if not millions of political opponents and dissidents permanently "removed."

The question posed by journalists to overtly Christian presidential candidates is also based on a false premise: that a people can and should separate their religious beliefs from their public opinions. Yet do so would create a nation of schizophrenics. Religious beliefs are part of who we are. Regardless of what our belief system is, it is nonetheless a belief system that shapes what we say and what we do. An atheist's belief that there is no God, that the physical realm is, all there is, and that we are here only as a result of chance affects his or her opinions on issues no less than does a Christian's belief in a sovereign God who created us in His image for a divine purpose.

To try to artificially divide the world's subjects and activities into "religious" and "secular" categories is to deny the fact that all of us are "religious" in our viewpoints. Our faith may be in God or in ourselves, but it is faith nonetheless. A "religious" viewpoint is therefore just as valid than a "secular" viewpoint, if not more so. If a "religious" viewpoint is to be dismissed, it should be dismissed based on facts that don't support a conclusion, not because it is "religious."

Continued Intolerance for a Biblical World View will Destroy America

Jewish Rabbi Daniel Lapin presents the situation succinctly and clearly, noting the critical choice our nation faces today.

> Only when we realize that there are two diametrically opposing nations struggling to gain ascendancy in America will we be able to have an open and honest examination of where each will lead. One acknowledges the Judeo-Christian tradition as necessary for America to survive, while the other defiantly insists that religion should stay in the churches and out of the public square. Note that we are not discussing whether Americans should attend worship services or belong to a religious organization. We are speaking instead of ideas that permeate and shape every decision of our lives. We are contemplating whether we should place God and biblical morality in a neat little box labeled "religion" or, as our founding fathers did, regard God and biblical morality as the core value for all of life.[2]

This question raised by Rabbi Lapin goes to the heart of this entire book in many ways. Our nation's adherence to Biblical principles and the values and standards of a Biblical world view is absolutely essential for the continued survival of this nation.

This conflict is what we mean by the "culture war" that is currently being waged in our land. On one side of the culture war is a world view based on evolution, that allows man to ignore God and try to live according to whatever standards he thinks is right. Yet an evolutionary world view could never have brought forth the fruit of liberty that is unique to America. To say otherwise is to be intellectually dishonest. There are consequences to a belief system that says the physical realm is all there is, and that people are here completely as the result of a biological accident, an impersonal series of "lucky coincidences" that allowed life to form out of non-life. Of course, to believe that, we must ignore or pervert several scientific principles, but let's review the logical consequence of such a world view.

First, such a belief leads to the conclusion that man has little to no value. We are no different than a rock or an amoeba swimming in a pond of primordial slime. Hence, we should have no feelings of greatness, no self-worth, no self-esteem. We are not alive for a noble purpose, nor do we have a calling for greatness from a loving Creator, nor are we even made in the image of God, as a Biblical world view teaches. Since there is no heaven and no eternity with God, this life is all there is. Therefore, wherever an evolutionary world view is taught, it is logical to expect the rates of suicide to go up significantly. This has been the experience in America over the past 50 years or so since evolution has been taught. A Biblical world view teaches that each person has value and worth and was specially created by a loving God for a special purpose. The person has great value, because of who Created him and because he was chosen to be created. He is not an accident. He has great value and thus his life is precious. The difference between the two world views is great. Human life is not sacred because 51% of the people say it is; it is sacred because life is from God and what God creates is sacred. Therefore, human life will continue to be sacred for all time, not just so long as a majority continues to believe it is. The sanctity of human life is one of the "self-evident truths" of our nation's founding. It is obvious that an evolutionary view of the importance of mankind was not the basis of America's founding.

As a natural consequence of an evolutionary world view, might and force are seen as appropriate means of control, and killing people is just another means to achieve a purpose. As a consequence, murder becomes an everyday occurrence. If a political opponent wants another's position, then it is more likely that the power holder will resort to killing or imprisoning his foe, a pattern we have seen from Lenin, Stalin, Castro, Pol Pot, and numerous other tyrants. History is replete with examples of the horrible consequences of an evolutionary world view. Since life has no inherent worth or value in this view, taking life is not as repugnant as it would be in a Biblical world view, where life is valued. This was not the position of the Founders of America.

In an evolutionary world view where we are all here by accident, there are no standards of right and wrong. Man is free to make his own standards based on anything he wants. The standards can even change, depending upon who is making the decisions. There are no moral absolutes, no eternal truths, no Biblical standards that govern all people at all times. The standards are whatever we say they are, and we can change them every other day if we so choose. In fact, if we can get enough people to agree with us, then we can even conclude that pedophilia is lawful, that the vilest pornography is lawful and should be supported by everyone's tax dollars, and that teaching that homosexual acts are sinful is unlawful. In an evolutionary world view, we make the standards without regard to any objective anchor or basis. This was not the view of our Founders, either.

In an evolutionary world view, there is no absolute basis to hold individuals responsible for their criminal or harmful acts, and even if they are, "right" and "wrong" labels are not applied. Someone who steals is not a thief or criminal who violated the law; he is someone who made some wrong choices. Moreover, his wrong choices were caused, not by any bad character in that person, but by the bad influence of society or his upbringing. Crime is therefore seen as the natural consequence of poverty or a lack of education, instead of a lack of moral character, as the Bible teaches.

Anyone familiar with the case of Nathan Leopold and Richard Loeb[3] knows the fallacy of believing the evolutionary lie that crime is the result of poverty or poor education. Leopold and Loeb were the sons of two of the wealthiest and most influential families in Chicago in the mid-1920s. Both were incredibly smart, Leopold spoke five languages fluently and had an IQ of 210. The two friends wanted to see if they could use their intellect to commit the "perfect murder," a scheme so devious that only a person with superior intellect could accomplish it and get away with it. On the afternoon of May 21, 1924, they drove past a school, randomly chose their victim, eleven-year old Bobby Franks, and enticed him into their car, and the boy was never seen alive again. Eventually Leopold and Loeb were caught, accused, and brought to trial. What made the case so repulsive to the Chicago community was the complete and total lack of remorse by either of the murderers. Despite pleading guilty to the charges in an effort to spare their own lives from the death penalty, no remorse for taking an innocent boy's life was demonstrated in their statements to the court or the press. According to one of the accounts, when Loeb was asked how he could justify such a cold, calculated murder and have no remorse, he replied "It was just an experiment. It is as easy for us to justify as an entomologist in impaling a beetle on a pin."[4] Such a statement is not from a Biblical world view, but instead is the logical outgrowth of an evolutionary view of life.

There is more to the Leopold and Loeb case that we should consider. Their parents had money and could afford to hire the best attorney possible to represent their sons and to ensure they did not receive the death penalty. They hired an attorney by the name of Clarence Darrow, who also believed in an evolutionary view of life. Darrow did his job well, for he successfully kept Leopold and Loeb from receiving the death sentence when the court sentenced both to life imprisonment plus 99 years.[5] In his argument to the court, Darrow argued:

> Why did they kill Bobby Franks? Not for money, not for spite and not for hate. They killed him as a spider would kill a fly — they killed him because they were made that way![6]

Despite seeing first-hand the destructive consequences of a belief system based upon evolution, Clarence Darrow would later go on to defend the right of public schools to teach that same destructive belief system to future generations of school children in the Scopes Trial. Crime is not the byproduct of poverty or a lack of education. It is, as the Bible says it is, a byproduct of a wicked heart.

The world view based on an evolutionary view of life is destructive and harmful to any nation. History demonstrates that wherever it was allowed to flourish without impediment, primarily in communistic countries, liberty was nowhere to be found. Despite overwhelming evidence as to the destructive nature of an evolutionary view of life, we continue to encourage our public school children to learn and adhere to this world view. It was not the world view that founded our nation.

On the other side of the culture war is a world view based on an acknowledgment that God is our Creator and that we will only have success in our endeavors if we apply Biblical principles to all areas of life. That was the view of nearly every single Founding Father involved in our Constitution. Consider just a few of the concepts we take for granted in this nation, and where the sources of those ideas are found.

The principle of equality before the law can be found in the following Bible passages: Exodus 12:49, Leviticus 24:22 ,and Numbers 15:15,16, and 29. The separation of powers doctrine is in Isaiah 33:22 and Exodus 4:29. The principle of having independent judges and juries is found in 2 Chronicles 19:5-10, Exodus 23:1-3, Deuteronomy 17:6, 19:15-19, and Leviticus 20. Free elections of representatives, essential to any republic, is found in Deuteronomy 1:13 and Exodus 18:17-27. The principles of consent of the governed, the right to vote, and the right to representatives in government are found in 1 Chronicles 28:1-8, 29:22, and 2 Chronicles 23:11. As Americans, we are familiar with every one of these noble principles of government found in the Bible, not because we know the Bible that well, but because our Founders did, and they chose to include them in our Constitution and our government institutions. A Biblical world view leads to liberty, while an evolutionary world view leads to destruction.

Eliminating the World View of the Founders

We noted earlier the strong Christian belief system of the large majority of our Founders, along with their equally strong application of Biblical principles to America's government structure and its public institutions. Yet, as a result of our change in course, this world view has been determined to be unwelcome in those same institutions today. Indeed, the views of our Founders are frequently taught as those of "dead white men" irrelevant to the needs of today's diverse, multi-cultural society. They have largely been eliminated from our public schools, leaving many children without a proper appreciation for the Biblical principles upon which our nation was founded upon and our Constitution is based.

Public school committees have supported the removal of books by Dr. James Dobson from their libraries because of the religious nature of his child rearing philosophy;[7] books donated to public libraries, such as The Closing of the American Heart, by Dr. Ronald H. Nash, have been refused because of their Christian perspective;[8] and public school textbooks have been a "fertile ground for the seeds of willful historical deception."[9] Gary DeMar refers to a study by Paul C. Vitz, a professor of psychology at New York University,which entailed a review of sixty textbooks used in elementary schools across the country. What he found was startling. In the books designed to introduce students to U.S. society, he found that "[n]one of the books covering grades 1 through 4 contain one word referring to any religious activity in contemporary American life."[10] Their coverage of history was revisionist in its omission of any reference to religious influence.

> Some particular examples of the bias against religion are significant. One social studies book has thirty pages on the Pilgrims, including the first Thanksgiving. But there is not one word (or image) that referred to religion as even a part of the Pilgrim's life. One mother whose son is in a class using this book wrote me to say that he came home and told her that "Thanksgiving was when the Pilgrims gave thanks to the Indians." The mother called the principal of this suburban New York City school to point out that Thanksgiving was when the Pilgrims thanked God. The principal responded by saying "that was her opinion" — the schools could only teach what was in the books.[11]

Indeed, sometimes religion, when it is mentioned at all, is portrayed in a derogatory way. Children in Seattle, Washington were also taught about the Pilgrims, but in one classroom they were told "the Pilgrims were narrow-minded bigots who survived initially only with the Indians' help, but turned on them when their help wasn't needed anymore."[12]

As a result of this systematic elimination of the strong and positive religious influences and the principles our nation was based upon, current and future generations of Americans have become ignorant of the importance of Biblical principles to the health of our nation. Concurrently, recent generations of judges have been interpreting our Constitution in a manner inconsistent with the principles upon which it was created. Even though they use the same document, their interpretations of the words and phrases of that document have essentially created a new and different Constitution without doing so through the consent of the governed.

The Founders Linked Biblical Principles to Liberty

To properly interpret the Constitution, we must once again teach the world view and the Biblical principles the Founders adhered to and followed. A document based on Christian principles and a Christian world view cannot properly be interpreted through the eyes of a secularist world view and the principles of evolution. To do so changes everything. The properly restrained liberty intended by our Founders under a Christian world view is changed to unrestrained license. The properly restrained freedom of speech becomes the unrestrained filth of obscenity and pornography. A right such as the freedom of speech, intended to ensure that a person is free to express his or her viewpoint, does not require society to support unabashed garbage. People can ably get their viewpoints across without needing to use obscene words or pornographic images. To conclude that a Constitution based on Biblical principles requires tolerance of obscenity is to interpret the document from the wrong perspective, which invariably leads to wrong interpretations. It fundamentally alters the meaning of the text in an undemocratic fashion, without going to the trouble of seeking a constitutional amendment.

A consistent theme throughout this book has been the direct correlation our Founders believed existed between a nation's adherence to Christian principles and the flourishing of liberty. Timothy Dwight, president of Yale College from 1795 to his death in 1817, explained the link between religion and liberty that used to be apparent to Americans.

> Religion and liberty are the meat and drink of the body politic. Withdraw one of them and it languishes, consumes, and dies. If indifference to either, at any time, becomes the prevailing character of a people, one half of their motives to vigorous defense is lost, and the hopes of their enemies are proportionally increased. Here, eminently, they are inseparable.
>
> Without religion we may possibly retain the freedom of savages, bears, and wolves, but not the freedom of New England. If our religion were gone, our state of society would perish with it and nothing would be left which would be worth defending. Our children, of course, if not ourselves, would be prepared, as the ox for slaughter to become the victims of conquest, tyranny, and atheism.[13]

At the bicentennial celebration of the Pilgrims' landing at Plymouth, the great orator Daniel Webster paid special tribute to the contribution of their religious influence, and he echoed the sentiments of so many leaders of that day and earlier who believed that religion and liberty were linked:

> Our ancestors established their system of government on morality and religious sentiment. Moral habits, they believed, cannot safely be trusted on any other foundation than religious principle, nor any government be secure which is not supported by moral habits. . . . Whatever makes men good Christians, makes them good citizens.[14]

True liberty can only be secured by interpreting our Constitution in the manner it was intended to be understood — through the perspective of Biblical principles.

On May 28, 1849, Robert C. Winthrop, former Speaker of the House, addressed the Annual Meeting of the Massachusetts Bible Society. His comments provide us a warning that we should heed before it is too late.

> The voice of experience and the voice of our own reason speak but one language . . . . Both unite in teaching us, that men may as well build their houses upon the sand and expect to see them stand, when the rains fall, and the winds blow, and the floods come, as to found free institutions upon any other basis than that morality and virtue, of which the Word of God is the only authoritative rule, and the only adequate sanction.
>
> All societies of men must be governed in some way or other. The less they may have of stringent State Government, the more they must have of individual self-government. The less they rely on public law or physical force, the more they must rely on private moral restraint. Men, in a word, must necessarily be controlled, either by a power within them, or by a power without them; either by the word of God, or by the strong arm of man; either by the Bible, or by the bayonet. It may do for other countries and other governments to talk about the State supporting religion. Here, under our own free institutions, it is Religion which must support the State.[15]

It is much more difficult for Americans today to reconcile the combining of religious principles with the apparently secular principles contained in government, law, politics, or other pursuits because, since 1947, we have been continually told that mixing the two is dangerous. In truth, mixing the two has been the norm since the founding of our republic, while separating them has been the exception.

Nonetheless, if we are to return to the principles upon which our Constitution is based, it is essential that our schools once again teach the religious influences of our Founders and the Biblical principles on which that document of freedom is based. To do so is not a prohibited "establishment of religion," but rather an accurate portrayal of our history and government. For private schools and home schools, the mandate is even greater, for they are not constrained by an improper interpretation of the First Amendment. Not only should they teach the religious influences and Biblical principles the founders incorporated into our government structure, they should also teach the Biblical principles entailed in every subject and sphere of life.

Secular Intolerance

We must recognize that all governments are based upon some philosophy, whether it be secular, Islamic, Jewish, Hindu or some other view. Every government structure in the world seeks to protect and encourage that philosophy upon which it is based. What we have failed to see is that secular governments, too, are ruthlessly protective of their own philosophy.

Since America has discarded her Christian heritage and become a secular state, America has ensured that the secular philosophy is encouraged over all other philosophies. Secularism is the primary paradigm taught in public schools, and any attempt to teach a world view based on the Bible or anything else is either excluded altogether, or limited to special religion classes. The same is true in our judicial system, where the Supreme Court's test to determine whether a given law violates the establishment clause includes the requirement that the law have a secular purpose.

Secularism in America has been fiercely intolerant of any contrary views being taught in school, demonstrated at graduation ceremonies, referenced by our government institutions, or otherwise used to influence public society.

For example, every year People for the American Way issues its report on censorship in the public schools. Never do they include in their definition of "censorship" efforts by themselves or others to keep children from writing school reports about Jesus Christ, or to keep teachers from assigning Christian-oriented history books, science books, or literature books. Nor do they include efforts to prevent the Bible from being read in school classrooms. Why? Because efforts to systematically remove Christian ideas from the public realm are consistent with their world view, thus, they do not recognize such actions as censorship. Yet the action of such groups demonstrates that secularism is a jealous, intolerant world view, a religion of its own.

It is important to point out that a secular government that excludes all other religious philosophies is not necessarily compatible with freedom of religion; but secularism is the religious philosophy and which predominates in the government and its laws. In the 1600's, 1700's, and 1800's, Christianity was the dominant religious philosophy encouraged by our government institutions. People were free to worship and believe as they pleased, but there was a greater deference paid to the Christian world view.

At public school graduation, for example, people were expected to tolerate a Christian prayer and invocation, even if they were not Christians themselves. No one was required or compelled to believe the prayer or to become Christians or to exalt Jesus Christ. They were merely expected to be tolerant of the Christian philosophy, since it in turn allowed free exercise for all religions.

Now that secularism is the dominant religious philosophy, at public school graduations, prayers of any type are being prohibited, and Christians are expected to be tolerant of secularism. Today, it is enough for one lone atheist to complain about religious activity, and the religious activity must cease. Why? Because the secularist philosophy dominates. To base a nation on the philosophy of the Bible and Christianity is no different, in this respect, than to base it on secularism; in both situations the nation is dominated by a religious philosophy, and in both situations there is an honest effort to provide for religious freedom. Yet in both situations, the philosophy that dominates will receive preferential treatment.

The blindness of secularists lies in their fear of Christian philsophies "taking over," yet they don't realize that secularist philosophies have "taken over" even more so. Remember the old examples people used to give to justify secularism? They would always refer to a poor atheist child who was inevitably humiliated and embarassed when the Bible was read or some Chrisitan principle was taught. Their example was intended to show that only by having a dominant secular philosophy are all children protected from such "religious intolerance." What they ignore are the Christian children and children of other religious faiths who are now the ones being offended when they are required to listen to teachers tell them they were created from primordial slime and evolved to human beings, with no reference to God in creation. Where is the same concern for Christian children and the children of other religious backgrounds being upset at the secularist philosophy they are required to learn? The same compassion for them does not exist as it does for the secularist adherents, yet secularist advocates are completely blind to this disparity.

Whether our nation is Christian or secular, a religious philosophy will dominate; there can be no neutrality. The idea that a Christian philosophy should be encouraged by the nation's government institutions should not scare anyone. Freedom of religion remains for other beliefs and non-beliefs in either case. However, our government was originally based upon the Biblical world view, and its laws have long reflected that philosophy. It was that philosophy that was responsible for a Constitution that provided for greater liberty than any other in the world. It was that philosophy that provided for greater religious liberty than anywhere else in the world. It is the philosophy America had when our Constitution was written, and that is what the delegates to that Convention intended would continue. Early movements to separate the church and the state were not intended to change the basic philosophy upon which America's government structure was based. They were never intended to remove the Biblical foundation of our laws and our institutions.

Yet the secularist philosophy of today is intolerant of any competitive viewpoint. So when it comes to examining our religious heritage, our Supreme Court and many others become very selective in their historical analysis. They become very discriminatory in which Founding Fathers they cite and which religious movements they emphasize. Apparently, it is not enough to merely be selective in their recitation of historical figures and events; they must misrepresent their selections. So, the Supreme Court has chosen to focus on Virginia at the expense of what was happening in other states; they focus on Jefferson and Madison while ignoring Roger Sherman, Gouverneur Morris, James Wilson, Fisher Ames, George Washington, and Patrick Henry; and they even tell the story they have selectively chosen in an incorrect manner. Jefferson was no advocate of removing religious influence from our government institutions; he was no advocate of the false idea of a religious neutrality; and he was no advocate of a secularist world view dominating the nation and its institutions, as it does today. If the Supreme Court insists on selectively focusing on Thomas Jefferson, then let them do so honestly. Then, despite their limited approach, we would not have the strict, unyielding wall of separation between church and state that our judicial branch insists upon today. Indeed, if the Court had been truly honest in its representations of Jefferson's religious liberty views, then our government institutions would still be allowed to encourage the Biblical world view upon which our Constitution rests and our liberty is founded.

In a book entitled *American Political Writings During the Founding Era*, Dr. Donald Lutz and Charles Hyneman collected 76 of the most representative pamphlets and essays written by our Founders. In these 76 essays, "virtue" is emphasized as vital over 300 times! In 1888, Philip Schaff wrote in *Church and State in the United States* that "Republican institutions in the hands of a virtuous and God-fearing nation are the very best in the world, but in the hands of a corrupt and irreligious people they are the very worst."

The visit to America by Frenchman Alexis de Tocqueville in the 1830's confirms these assertions. It was the intent of the Frenchman to identify the reasons our revolution was such a success when the French revolution was such a failure. The French had fought for their rights like we did in America and yet experienced a forty year reign of terror, anarchy, and bloodshed which led again to totalitarian rule under Bonaparte. In stark contrast, during that same forty year period, America enjoyed such peace and prosperity that we had already become the greatest nation on earth. It is little wonder De Tocqueville was curious about the difference in the two nations. What he found is now well-known but often forgotten. De Tocqueville discovered the foundation for America's success in the Christian faith and the righteous behavior that it produces in her citizens.

In his book *Democracy in America*, De Tocqueville candidly concluded that America's form of government would not work in France, because his own country lacked the virtue that arises out of "indispensible" Christianity. In 1870, another foreign statesman, Emilio Castclar of Spain, declared to the Constitutional Assembly there that America's government was a success because it was established on the Bible. It seems that America's Biblical foundation was obvious to those people in other nations who were watching the American experiment unfold.

In 1984, President Reagan reasserted these same observations to Americans, but America in 1984 was a nation that had forgotten its soul. Thus, ideas that were obvious and clearly accepted when our nation was young were now ideas many revisionists did not want to hear. Here is what President Reagan had to say, which met with a firestorm of uproar from the very secular and liberal press.

The truth is, politics and morality are inseparable. And as morality's foundation is religion, religion and politics are necessarily related. We need religion as a guide; we need it because we are imperfect. And our Government needs the Church because only those humble enough to admit they are sinners can bring to democracy the tolerance it requires in order to survive. . . . We establish no religion in this country nor will we ever; we command no worship; we mandate no belief. But we poison our society when we remove its theological underpinnings; we court corruption when we leave it bereft of belief. . . Without God there is no virtue because there is no prompting of the conscious. Without God we are mired in the material, that flat world that tells us only what the senses perceive. Without God there is a coarsening of the society. Without God democracy will not and cannot long endure.[16]

There is not one item in that 1984 speech by President Reagan that had not been stated emphatically many times over by our Founding Fathers. There isn't one Reagan conclusion that wasn't previously drawn by Alexis de Tocqueville of France, Emilio Castclar of Spain, and many other leaders of the day who saw for themselves the central role Christianity played in founding America. But unfortunately, many Americans today have rejected the truths of our founding. They don't want to admit how important Christianity is to our government because they are too busy trying to censor it out of public life. In the process, they are undermining the Godly foundations upon which our Constitution was built.

FOURTEEN

CONTENDING FOR THE CONSTITUTION

In Exodus chapter 18, verses 19-23, Moses is advised by his father-in-law to be "the people's representative before God," but also to command the people themselves to "select out of all the people able men who fear God, men of truth, those who hate dishonest gain; and you shall place these over them, as leaders of thousands, of hundreds, of fifties and of tens . . . . If you do this thing and God so commands you, then you will be able to endure . . . ." Similarly, the book of Deuteronomy 1:13 advised the people to "choose wise and discerning and experienced men . . . ."

The freedom to choose one's representatives is not an American invention, but a Divine plan for godly government that can work for any nation. John Jay, author of a portion of the Federalist Papers and the country's first Chief Justice of the Supreme Court, made this observation:

> Providence has given to our people the choice of their rulers, and it is the duty as well as the privilege and interest of our Christian nation to select and prefer Christians for their rulers.[1]

Thus, having representatives chosen by the people is not enough if the people do not choose virtuous representatives. Noah Webster clarified this distinction when he wrote:

> . . . let it be impressed on your mind that God commands you to choose for yourselves rulers, 'just men who rule in the fear of God.' The preservation of a republican government depends on the faithful discharge of this duty; if the citizens neglect their duty and place unprincipled men in office, the government will soon be corrupted; laws will be made, not for the public good, so much as for selfish or local purposes; corrupt or incompetent men will be appointed to execute the laws; the public revenues will be squandered by unworthy men; and the rights of the citizens will be violated or

disregarded. If a republican government fails to secure public prosperity and happiness, it must be because the citizens neglect the divine commands, and elect bad men to make and administer the laws.[2]

Today America is ruled by secularists and secular principles, dominated by an evolutionary world view. This state of affairs is neither neutral nor benign. It represents a significant change of course in the direction our ship of state is headed from the one so wisely charted during the founding of our nation. Our Constitution will not protect us from the evil that results when this occurs. We must turn back the rudder of our nation to the earlier charted course of a Biblical world view. Our Constitution was drafted by a virtuous group of leaders, the likes of which our nation has never seen since. They sought the guidance of their Creator and readily acknowledged His assistance in their endeavor. We must do no less if our nation is to continue to be a light to all nations. Charles Finney gave us this warning long ago:

> The Church must take right ground in regard to politics. . . . The time has come that Christians must vote for honest men, and take consistent ground in politics, or the Lord will curse them. . . . God cannot sustain this free and blessed country, which we love and pray for, unless the Church will take right ground. Politics is a part of religion in such a country as this, and Christians must do their duty to the country as a part of their duty to God . . . . He [God] will bless or curse this nation, according to the course they [Christians] take [in politics].[3]

We must be faithful to restore and uphold our Constitution, for in doing so, we can help to fulfill another important calling — that of our Lord Jesus Christ to "go therefore and make disciples of all the nations."[4]

While we clearly believe that a quest to restore the Biblical foundations of America is a holy one, a word of caution is in order. It is easy to lose our perspective as we endure the struggles of waging spiritual battle on the front lines to restore our land. Yes, it is a spiritual battle, but changing our governmental focus should not become our sole or ultimate goal. Our ultimate hope and salvation is not in government, but in Jesus Christ. Thus, while we should not forsake our duty to impact our government, we should not confuse it with the true source of our faith. Only with a changed and redeemed heart given by the merciful hands of God can man and the government in which he functions truly change for the good. Therein lies our true hope and our ultimate goal for all Americans, and all citizens of other lands.

The concern of the hour today remains the same as that expressed by Benjamin Franklin nearly 220 years ago on that pre-autumn day outside the Philadelphia Convention Hall. Whether our nation returns to a Biblical world view that openly acknowledges our Creator and follows His Biblical principles, as did our Founding Fathers before us, will be the primary factor in responding to the lady's question to Ben Franklin. "If we can keep" our republic or rather restore it, depends on each of us walking in that same Biblical world view.

Restoring the Spirit of America's Constitution

As we contemplate the awesome task of restoring God's vision for America and renewing our national purpose, the work may seem overwhelming. We might be tempted to think that we are not up to the task, and of course, we are not. Yet through Christ, we can do all things. Never forget that God does not call great men; He calls ordinary men to do great things.

When Moses was called by God to lead the Israelites out of Egypt, he initially must have felt overwhelmed. Why else would he make excuses and seek to avoid undertaking such a task by himself? Leading three million people across thousands of miles of desert and wilderness is a daunting task for any person. But who God calls, God equips, and Moses accomplished, through God, the task he was called to do. Moses was no different than you or I. Because Moses trusted completely in God's strength, and because Moses sought God's direction, he was able to accomplish a seemingly impossible task, not through his own strength, but through the strength of God. The formula of trust and obedience to God that Moses followed is the formula we, too, must follow.

Over 500 years ago, another ordinary man was called by God to use his navigational skills to spread the Gospel to a new land. Today he is ridiculed by revisionist historians, but Christopher Columbus knew he was called by God.[5] After God allowed him to reach the New World, Columbus reflected on the event with this inspirational thought:

> No one should fear to undertake any task in the name of our Savior, if it is just and if the intention is purely for His holy service.[6]

Yes, we are ordinary people, but as Christians, we serve an extraordinary God. As such, there is no task we should fear to undertake for His glory that God calls us to do. Indeed, just the opposite is true. If God calls us to do something, we should be fearful NOT to undertake it!

Where there is God, there is always hope. Where there is God, there is always power and authority to accomplish the changes God calls us to seek. We must not be afraid of the challenge. As Christians, we must be willing to get involved in the culture in which God placed us. We have neglected our duty for too long, but it is not too late. We must begin to reclaim the territory that the enemies of God have taken from us, and we must do it God's way. As Americans, reliance upon God is our duty and our heritage. Recall that as our Founders took that bold step of breaking away from England, they did so "with a firm reliance on the protection of Divine Providence." Recall also that their reliance upon God was not misplaced.

God's Way of Reclaiming Society

2 Corinthians 10:3-5 reminds us that our battlefield is not physical, although there is a physical dimension to it.

> For though we walk in the flesh, we do not war according to the flesh. For the weapons of our warfare are not carnal but mighty in God for pulling down strongholds, casting down arguments and every high thing that exalts itself against the knowledge of God, bringing every thought into captivity to the obedience of Christ.

We cannot escape the reality that changing society for the better is primarily a spiritual battle and it starts at our doorstep. We, as individual Christians, must get our own spiritual house in order before we can effectively engage in spiritual battle. We must repent of our sins, we must ask for God's forgiveness, and we must begin afresh to walk in the righteousness of Jesus Christ, with holy and pure motives. For God tells us what is required of us in 2 Chronicles 7:14:

> If my people, which are called by my name, shall humble themselves, and pray, and seek my face, and turn from their wicked ways; then will I hear from heaven, and will forgive their sin, and will heal their land.

If you are reading this book, chances are it is not by accident or coincidence, but by God's design. Perhaps He is calling you now upon a task to help restore His vision for America. Perhaps He is, through these pages, asking you to get involved. If that is the case, you need not be afraid. God will equip you. Ask Him what He wants you to do and how He wants you to do it.

Perhaps you are convinced that God does want us to bring His truth into the culture and institutions we live in, but you are not yet sure about the specific calling He has for you. While you await His calling, begin to prepare for it by seeking after God, seeking after His word, and seeking after His righteousness. There is no pursuit in life more important.

In seeking God, we must not neglect prayer. It is a simple activity, quite inexpensive, and something we can all do. When you pray, pray for our leaders, pray for our fellow citizens, and pray in general for America to be restored. Prayer is our secret weapon, and faith is its ammunition. Cry out to God with a humble heart, as Christopher Columbus did on the sea-tossed deck of the Santa Maria before land was sighted; as George Washington did in the snow at Valley Forge before victory was won; and as that small group of Convention delegates did at Independence Hall before our Constitution was brought forth. And once you start praying, don't stop, don't let up until you see the enemies of God on the run and in full retreat.

But don't forget the reminder contained in 2 Chronicles 7:14. Not just any type of prayer will do. We are told that we must first humble ourselves, seek God, and repent from our "wicked ways" before God will answer our prayers. Our Founders understood this need, as evidenced by the words of John Adams, as relayed by signer of the Declaration, Benjamin Rush:

> I sat next to John Adams in Congress, and upon my whispering to him and asking him if he thought we should succeed in our struggle with Great Britain, he answered me, "Yes — if we fear God and repent of our sins."[7]

Our hearts, our relationship with God, and our motives must all be aligned with God's word. We must not become arrogant or act self-righteously; God calls us to be humble. We must not act out of a motive to establish our "own ministry," that seeks to bring glory to ourselves. God calls us to seek His face and His glory through His ministry.

Nor can we continue in secret sin, hoping to step forward with the truth of God while leaving one foot in the carnal, sinful world which seeks its own pleasure. God calls us to "turn from [our] wicked ways." God must be our Lord, our Commander-in-Chief, our Master who directs all of our steps. We must die to our selfish interests and desire His interests. It is easy to say that Christ is our Savior, but it is much more difficult to let Him be our Lord. For us to have any effectiveness in being God's light to our land and people, God must be our Lord. Don't look for the easy way. Don't look for the expedient way. Look instead for God's way. Only then will He use us to bring godly change to America.

While prayer is a vitally important element in reclaiming America, we must not limit ourselves to that activity alone. We must also act upon the convictions that God places on our hearts, demonstrating the fruit of our beliefs, bringing the truth of God's word into all areas of society, wherever God may put us, at His direction. God's word is fit and intended to be proclaimed to all persons and institutions everywhere, not just behind a pulpit in a church building. There is no person, place, or organization which God's truth has no power to restore, uplift and rebuild what man has been tearing down.

Expect a Struggle

The Bible says in 2 Corinthians 10:3-5 that we are in "warfare." Wars, whether they be physical or spiritual, do not occur without a struggle, so we must not expect this fight to be easy. Moses, Columbus, and Washington all had their struggles; at times they seemed insurmountable. Don't expect it to be any different for us. Anyone who decides to speak out in accordance with the law of God will be ridiculed and persecuted in one way or another. People will say harsh, cruel, hate-filled things to you. They will lie about you, what you said, or what you are trying to accomplish. They will treat you unfairly. They will spit in your face, both figuratively and literally, and they will try to goad you into responding in kind. If you do, then they will cry out to the media about how "unchristian" your actions are. Don't be fooled. The enemy does not play by any rules, and those who would persecute you certainly won't play fair.

Talk to any Christian leader who is battling on the front lines of various social issues, and he or she will tell you it isn't easy. Nevertheless, if God is calling you to take action or to speak out in your community or social sphere, then you must not be deterred. God will see you through. In that truth, have no doubt. God has promised us that He will never leave us or forsake us, and God always keeps His promises.

Be confident that restoring God's vision for America is a noble cause, for without our adherence as a nation to the Biblical absolutes, our moral compass will never be repaired and America will drift aimlessly with the ever changing currents of man's godless standards. Instead of being a beacon of light and hope to the world, a city set upon a hill as the Puritans dreamed it would be, America will be covered in darkness with no hope to offer.

Sharing the Freedoms of Christ

It has been more than 225 years since the Continental Congress adjourned their gathering with a document we celebrate as setting forth our independence from England and establishing the freedoms this country would fight and die for — life, liberty, and the pursuit of happiness. Yet as great as those freedoms are, they pale in comparison to the freedoms we have as Christians. Those freedoms are unmatched by anything the world has to offer: the freedom we have over death; the freedom of eternal life; the freedom over the moral decay of our hearts; and the freedom to personally converse with our Creator, without appointment, without begging to be heard, but whenever we want.

Therefore, remember that while the spirit of America's Constitution brought forth political liberty to Americans, God's spirit also brings forth personal liberty to all people. It is very apparent, then, that the greatest freedoms this world has ever known, or could ever imagine, did not start at Independence Hall — they started in Jerusalem, at an empty tomb. As Christians, we must never forget the source of our truest freedoms — Jesus Christ.

END NOTES

Introduction

1. Charles C. Coffin, *Sweet Land of Liberty*, (Maranatha Publications, Inc., 1992, reprinted from 1881 manuscript), publisher's note.

2. Charles Francis Adams, ed., *The Works of John Adams - Second President of the United States*, (Boston: Little, Brown & Co., 1854), Vol. IX, p. 229.

3. 2 Corinthians 3:17

4. 2 Corinthians 3:4-6

5. James D. Richardson, *A Compilation of Messages and Papers of the Presidents, 1789-1897*, (Published by authority of Congress, 1899), Vol. I, pps. 52-53.

6. Letter of Thomas Jefferson to Justice William Johnson, dated June 12, 1823, *Jefferson Writings*, Merrill D. Peterson, ed., (NY: Literary Classics of the United States, Inc., 1984), p. 1475.

Chapter 1

1. W. Cleon Skousen, *The Making of America* (National Center for Constitutional Studies, 1986) p. 66.

2. Id.

3. John Fiske, *The Critical Period of American History 1783-1789* (The Riverside Press Cambridge, 1916) p. 98.

4. Skousen, supra note 1, at pps. 118-119.

5. Fiske, supra note 3, at p. 187.

6. Skousen, supra note 1, at p. 105; see also, Fiske, supra note 3 at p. 107.

7. George Washington letter to Colonel Lewis Nicola, Newberg, dtd 22 May 1782; *The Writings of George Washington*, vol 8, Jared Sparks, editor, Boston, 1835.

8. Skousen, supra note 1, at p. 106.

9. Fiske, supra note 3, at p. 110.

10. Fitzpatrick, *The Writings of George Washington*, Vol. 26, p. 227, quoted in Skousen, supra note 1 at p. 106.

11. Fiske, supra note 3 at p. 111. This was one of many instances of George Washington's selflessness of character that was evident to all his contemporaries.

12. Skousen, supra note 1 at p. 106.

13. Id. See also, Fiske, supra note 3 at p. 110. To Washington's credit, he immediately sent a letter to Congress explaining the urgency of the pay situation and proposing that Congress pass an act to commute the soldiers with half pay for life into a gross sum equal to five years of full pay, paid by certificates bearing interest at the rate of six percent. Congress accepted his proposal and the soldiers received their pay. Washington demonstrated with his actions that he was a man of honor.

14. Henry B. Watson, *George Washington, Architect of the Constitution*, (Patriotic Education Inc., Daytona Beach, FL) pps. 42-43, 1983.

15. Id. at . 43-44.

16. Catherine Drinker Bowen, *Miracle at Philadelphia* (Back Bay Books, 1986) p. 9.

17. Skousen, supra note 1 at p. 5. See also, Peter Marshall and David Manuel, *The Light and The Glory* (Fleming H. Revell Company, 1977) pps. 343-349.

18. Bowen, supra note 16 at p. 25.

19. Bowen, supra note 16 at p. 11.

20. Skousen, supra note 1 at p. 134.

21. Fiske, supra at note 3, pps. 180-183.

22. Ecclesiastes, chapter 3, verse 1.

23. Bowen, supra note 16 at p. 11.

24. Fiske, supra at note 3, pps. 224-229.

25. Id., at p. 228.

26. Id., at . 228-229.

27. Skousen, supra, note 1, p. 137.

28. Fiske, supra, note 3 at p. 225.

29. Letter from Thomas Jefferson to John Adams, August 30, 1787, reprinted in *The Works of Thomas Jefferson*, ed. H.A. Washington (New York: Townsend) 1884, vol. 2, p. 260.

30. Thomas Jefferson to M. Dumas, September 10, 1787, reprinted in, *The Works of Thomas Jefferson*, supra, note 29 at vol. 2, p. 264. Historian Alex H. Stephens, in his Pictorial History of the United States (Gately & Haskell, Baltimore, MD, 1882) described the participants at the Convention as follows: "It was unquestionably the ablest body of jurists, legislators, and statesmen that had ever assembled on the continent of America." p. 292.

31. John Eidsmoe, *Christianity and the Constitution: The Faith of Our Founding Fathers* (Baker Book House, 1987), p. 11. See also Fiske, supra at. note 3, p. 224. According to John Fiske, "In its composition, this group of men left nothing to be desired."

32. Mason Locke Weems, *The Life of George Washington: with Curious Anecdotes, Equally Honourable to Himself, and Exemplary to His Young Countrymen* (Cambridge, Mass: Belknap Press of Harvard University Press, 1809 edition, reprinted 1962), p. 182, quoted in John Eidsmoe, Christianity and the Constitution: The Faith of Our Founding Fathers (Baker Book House, 1987), p. 114; also quoted in Peter Marshall and David Manuel, The Light and the Glory (1977), p. 323.

Chapter 2

1. Mark A. Beliles & Stephen K. McDowell, *America's Providential History* (The Providence Foundation, 1992), p. 170. This portion is excerpted from that book.

2. John Fiske, *The Critical Period of American History: 1783-1789* (The Riverside Press Cambridge, 1916), p. 231. Historian John Fiske had this to say about Washington's speech: "[it] ought to be blazoned in letters of gold, and posted on the wall of every American assembly that shall meet to nominate a candidate, or declare

a policy, or pass a law, so long as the weakness of human nature shall endure." Id., at pps. 231-232.

3. Id. See also, Beliles & McDowell, supra note 1 at p. 170.

4. Fiske, supra, note 2 at p. 232.

5. Catherine Drinker Bowen, *Miracle at Philadelphia* (Back Bay Books, 1986), p. 17.

6. Id., at p. 18.

7. According to historian John Fiske, the decision to keep the Convention deliberations secret was quite wise. There was likely to be quite a bit of wrangling and spirited argument on many different points in which compromise would be necessary. They didn't need the extra pressure of the home constituents, who didn't have the benefit of the full discussion, clamoring for certain positions. Fiske noted that "... should their scheme be unfolded, bit by bit, before its parts could be viewed in their mutual relations, popular excitement would become intense, there might be riots, and an end would be put to that attitude of mental repose so necessary for the constructive work that was to be done." Fiske, supra note 2 at p. 230.

8. W. Cleon Skousen, *The Making of America* (The National Center for Constitutional Studies, 1986), p. 157. One of the more interesting rules was that each delegate was expected to pay attention to what was being said. They could not read any papers, books or documents while someone else was speaking. Id.

9. Skousen, supra, note 8 at p. 157.

10. William H. Wilbur, *The Making of George Washington* (Patriotic Education Inc., Alexandria, VA, 1973), p. 215.

11. John Eidsmoe, *Christianity and the Constitution: The Faith of Our Founding Fathers* (Baker Book House, 1987), p. 133, quoted by William J. Johnson, George Washington the Christian (Milford, Michigan: Mott Media, 1919, 1976), at p. 51.

12. Johnson, supra, note 11 at . 175-183.

13. Id., at p. 149.

14. Id., at p. 166-167.

15. B.F. Morris, *The Christian Life and Character of the Civil Institutions of the United States*, (Philadelphia, 1864), p. 428-29.

16. Bowen, supra, note 5, at p. 24.

17. Fiske, supra, note 2 at p. 232-233.

18. Bowen, supra, note 5, at p. 37, 39.

19. Id., at p. 239.

20. Id., See also, Skousen, supra, note 8 at p. 158.

21. Fiske, supra, note 2 at p. 240.

22. Id. at p. 242.

23. Id.

24. The Committee of the Whole was an "ancient device" brought over from England in which delegates were free to vote without binding themselves. It was a means of testing opinion. See, Bowen, supra, note 5, at p. 40.

25. Carl Van Doren, *The Great Rehearsal* (The Viking Press, New York, 1948), p. 34.

26. Id.

27. Fiske, supra note 2 at 245. See also, Skousen, supra, note 8 at p. 158.

28. Fiske, supra, note 2, at p. 250.

29. Bowen, supra, note 5, at p. 117; see also, Van Doren, supra, note 24, at p. 94.

30. Bowen, supra, note 5, at p. 127.

31. James Madison's *Notes of Debates in the Federal Convention of 1787* (New York, 1987), pp. 209-210, quoted in Beliles & McDowell, supra, note 1, at pps. 171-172; see also, Smyth, *The Writings of Benjamin Franklin*, Vol. 9, pps. 600-601.

32. Beliles & McDowell, supra, note 1, at p. 172, quoting from B. F. Morris, *Christian Life and Character of the Civil Institutions of the United States* (Philadelphia, 1864), p. 252.

33. Bowen, supra, note 5 at p. 127, see also, Van Doren, *The Great Rehearsal*, p. 102.

34. See *Notes of Debates in the Federal Convention of 1787*, p. 210.

35. Max Farrand, *The Records of the Federal Convention of 1787*, Vols 1-3, 1966, Yale University Press, New Haven and London. Volume one pages 450-452 has Franklin's speech as quoted by Madison and then in a footnote on page 452 it refers to differing accounts of the vote or lack thereof. Dayton's account is in appendix A in Vol 3 pps. 470-473. Madison later said that the matter was sent to a committee (p 531).

36. Id. Farrand, vol. 3, p. 472.

37. Bowen, supra, note 5, at p. 140; Fiske, supra note 2, at p. 252.

38. B.F. Morris, supra, note 15, p. 253.

39. Bowen, supra note 5, at p. 140.

40. Van Doren, supra, note 24, at p. 118.

41. Fiske, supra, note 2 at p. 251.

42. Id.

43. Id., at p. 252.

44. Id., at p. 254.

45. Fiske, supra, note 2, at p. 260.

46. Id., at p. 264. It is interesting to note the words of George Mason, a delegate from Virginia who became so disgusted by this compromise, he refused to sign the Constitution. He prophetically notes that this compromise will be judged by heaven and bring about national judgment.

They [slaveholders] bring the judgment of Heaven on a country. As nations cannot be rewarded or punished in the next world, they must be in this. By an inevitable chain of causes and effects, Providence punishes national sins by national calamities.

The Civil War would be the fulfillment of George Mason's prophetic words, clearly a national calamity to punish our national sin.

47. Benjamin Hart, *Faith & Freedom, The Christian Roots of American Liberty*, p. 334 (1990).

48. Skousen, supra, note 8 at pg. 728.

49. George Bancroft, *History of the United States,* Vol. VI, (D. Appleton & Col, NY, NY, 1891), p. 321.

50. Fiske, supra, note 2, p. 265. It is interesting to note that the northern states, while not having nearly the same large numbers of slaves as found in the south, indisputably maintained thousands of slaves as well. While certainly not excusing the south, the industrialized north did not have the same economic pressure, as did the south to maintain the institution of slavery. Their moral argument was therefore easier to make than in the south. According to the census of 1790, slaves were distributed among the states as follows:

North	South
New Hampshire 158	Virginia 293,427
Delaware 8,887	North Carolina 100,572
Maryland 103,036	South Carolina 107,094
Vermont 17	Georgia 29,264
Massachusetts 0	Kentucky 11,830
Rhode Island 952	Tennessee 3,417
Connecticut 2,759	
New York 21,324	
New Jersey 11,423	
Pennsylvania 3,737	
Total: 152,293	**Total:** 545,604

51. Fiske, supra, at note 2, p.264.

52. Fiske, supra, at note 2, pg. 265.

53. Van Doren, supra, note 24, at p. 143.

54. Fiske, supra note 2 at p. 303.

55. Id. at p. 305.

56. Id.

57. Id. at p. 304.

Chapter 3

1. John Fiske, *The Critical Period of American History:* 1783-1789 (The Riverside Press Cambridge, 1916) p. 307.

2. Id. at p. 310.

3. Rosalie J. Slater, "Noah Webster, Founding Father of American Scholarship and Education," contained in preface to *Noah Webster's First Edition of an American Dictionary of the English Language,* republished by Foundation for American Christian Education, 1995, p. 14.

4. Mark A. Beliles & Stephen K. McDowell, *America's Providential History* (The Providence Foundation, 1992), p. 173.

5. Id.

6. John W. Whitehead, *The Separation Illusion, A Lawyer Examines the First Amendment*, p. 41 (1977), citing to Frank Donovan, Mr. Madison's Constitution (New York: Dodd, Mead, 1965), p. 2.

7. Fiske, supra note 1 at p. 341.

8. George Bancroft, vol. VI, *The History of the United States* (D. Appleton & Co., N.Y., N.Y.) 1891, p. 380.

9. Id. at p. 310.

10. Id. at p. 314-315.

11. Id. at p. 315.

12. Id.

13. Id. at p. 316.

14. Id. at p. 316.

15. Id. at p. 330-331.

16. Id. at p. 332.

17. Id.at p. 334.

18. Id. at p. 338.

19. Id. at p. 338.

20. Id. at p. 337. Fiske's description of Marshall is interesting. "[He} was a tall and gaunt young man, with beaming countenance, eyes of piercing brillancy, and an indescribable kingliness of bearing....John Marshall, second to none among all the illustrious jurists of the English race."

21. Id. at p. 340.

22. Id. at p. 343.

23. Id. at p. 345.

24. Beliles & McDowell, supra, note 4 at p. 173.

25. Id. at p. 174, quoting from George Bancroft, *History of the United States of America* (D. Appleton and Co., 1891), Vol. 6, p. 420.

26. Id. at p. 174, quoting Bancroft, supra note 25 at p. 414.

Chapter 4

1. Clarence B. Carson, *Basic American Government* (American Textbook Committee, 1995), p. 18.

2. Peter Marshall and David Manuel, *The Light and the Glory* (Fleming H. Company, 1977), p. 343, quoted from, Annals of America, Britannica, III, p. 122.

3. W. Cleon Skousen, *The Making of America* (National Center for Constitutional Studies, 1985), p. 9.

4. Id.

5. John Fiske, *The Critical Period of American History: 1783-1789* (The Riverside Press Cambridge, 1916), p. 223.

6. Marshall and Manuel, supra, note 2 at p. 343.

7. *Noah Webster's Dictionary of the English Language* (1828).

8. Chief Justice John Jay's charge to the Grand Jury of Ulster County, New York, cited in Phil Webster, *Can a Chief Justice Love God? The Life of John Jay*, p. 58 (2002).

9. Fiske, supra, note 5 at p. 222.

10. Skousen, supra note 3 at p. 235.

11. Fiske, supra, note 5 at p. 222.

12. Marshall and Manuel, supra note 2 at p. 341.

13. Albert Henry Smith, ed., *Writings of Benjamin Franklin*, Macmillan Co., 1905-1907, Vol. 9, p. 702.

14. Robert A. Rutland, ed., *The Papers of James Madison*, University of Chicago Press, 1962, Vol. 10, p. 208.

15. Skousen, supra, note 3, at p. 5.

16. William J. Federer, *America's God and Country Encyclopedia of Quotations* (Fame Publishing, Inc., 1994), p. 273.

17. John C. Fitzpatrick, ed., *Writings of George Washington*, United States Government Printing Office, 1930, Vol. 29, p. 525.

18. Benjamin Rush, *Letters of Benjamin Rush*, L.H., editor (Princeton, New Jersey: American Philosophical Society, 1951), Vol.I, p. 475, to Elias Boudinot on July 9, 1788.

19. Id. at p. 345.

Chapter 5

1. Beliles & McDowell, supra, note 1 at p. 174.

2. Id., at p. 175, quoting B.F. Morris, *Christian Life and Character of Civil Institutions of the United States* (Philadelphia, 1864), p.273.

3. April 27, 1789, prior to the Inauguration of President G. Washington, see, Beliles & McDowell, supra note 1 at p. 174, quoting from *Annals of Congress*, 1789-1791 (Washington D.C., Gales & Seaton, 1843), Vol. I, p. 25.

4. Beliles & McDowell, supra, note 1 at p. 175, quoting from B. F. Morris, p. 274.

5. October 3, 1789. James D. Richardson, *A Compilation of the Messages & Papers of the Presidents 1789-1897* (published by authority of Congress, 1899), Vol. I, p. 64; quoted in Beliles & McDowell, supra, note 1 at p. 175.

6. Id.

7. Id., at p. 176.

8. A Resolution passed in the House. B.F. Morris, *The Christian Life and Character of the Civil Institutions of the United States* (Philadelphia:George W. Childs, 1865), p. 328.

9. March 30, 1863. James D. Richardson, *A Compilation of the Messages and Papers of the Presidents, 1789-1897* (Published by Authority of Congress, 1899), Vol. VI, p. 164.

10. June 14,1954. In a speech confirming the Act of Congress which added the phrase, Under God to the Pledge of Allegiance.

11. January 20,1961. In his inaugural address. Benjamin Weiss, *God in American History: A Documentary of America's Religious Heritage* (Grand Rapids, MI: Zondervan, 1966), p. 146.

12. 143 U.S. 457 (1892).

13. 143 U.S. at 471.

14. Quoted from John Adams, *The Works of John Adams, Second President of the United States*, collected by Charles Francis Adams (Boston: Little, Brown, 1854); cited in David Barton, *The Myth of Separation* (Press, 1989), p. 122.

15. Thomas Jefferson: Reply to John Thomas et al., 1807. ME 16:291.

16. June 20, 1785, James Madison, *A Memorial and Remonstrance* (Washington DC: Library of Congress, Rare Books Collection).

17. Selim H. Peabody, ed., *American Patriotism: Speeches, Letters & Other Papers Which Illustrate the Foundation, the Development, the Preservation of the United States of America* (NY: American Book Exchange, 1880), p. 142.

18. September 19, 1796, in his Farewell Address. James D. Richardson, *A Compilation of the Messages & Papers of the Presidents, 1789-1897* (Published by Authority of Congress, 1899), Vol. 1, p. 220.

19. Barton, supra, note 14 at p. 116; see also, Beliles & McDowell, supra note 1 at p. 148.

20. Federer, supra, note 9, at p. 677.

21. In *Everson v. Board of Education*, 330 U.S. 1 (1947), the decision included this reference to the separation movement in Virginia which culminated in the Virginia Statute on Religious Freedom.

"The Court has previously recognized that the provisions of the First Amendment, in the drafting and adoption of which Madison and Jefferson played such leading roles, had the same objective and were intended to provide the same protection against governmental intrusion on religious liberty as the Virginia statute. 330 U.S. 1, 13 (1947).

Thus the Court has tried to conclude that the motivations and objectives which were behind the separation movement in Virginia were the same as elsewhere. That is not an accurate conclusion.

22. *Engle v. Vitale*, 370 U.S. 421 (1962).

23. Supreme Court Justice Hugo Black in *Engle v. Vitale*, 370 U.S. 421, 427-428 (1962), cited in John W. Whitehead, *The Separation Illusion*, p. 35-36 (1977).

24. David Barton, *Original Intent, The Courts, the Constitution, and Religion*, p. 202 (Wallbuilder Press, Aledo, TX, 1996).

25. Perhaps the best insight into the views of Thomas Jefferson on the issue of church and state is provided by his own documents compiled in 1776 and found among his papers that are generally called his *Notes on Religion*. These papers include: (1) Resolutions for Disestablishing the Church of England and for Repealing Laws Interfering with Freedom of Worship; (2) A Bill for Exempting Dissenters From Contributing to the Support of the Church; (3) Outline of Argument in Support of His Resolution; (4) A List of Acts of Parliament and of the Virginia Assembly Concerning Religion; and (5) Notes on Acts of Parliament and of the Virginia Assembly Concerning Religion. (FN 192, Boyd, quoted in Mark A. Beliles, *The Influence of Christian Communities on Thomas Jefferson, James Madison and Early Republican Politics in the Central Virginia Piedmont*, 1736-1836, June 1999).

26. The case of *Godwin v. Lunen.* See Marie Kimball, *Jefferson: the Road to Glory,* 1743-1776 (Coward-McCann, New York, NY, 1943), p.94.

27. Bowers, *The Young Jefferson* 1743-1789, p. 53.

28. Isaac, p. 184ff, and 203, 218-236. Rev. Henley, although Anglican, was formerly associated with dissenters in England and thus opposed those in Virginia who wanted to punish dissenters. Henley himself refused to adhere to strict Trinitarian formulations of faith, but was wrongly accused of Deism. In reality, the opposition to Henley was rooted in his opposition to the creation of a Bishop for America.

29. Thomas Buckley, *Church and State in Revolutionary Virginia,* 1776-1787, (University Press of Virginia, Charlottesville, VA. 1977), p. 52. See also, Davis, p. 50; and for the whole document, see H. Shelton Smith, et al., eds. pps. 442-445.

30. William Irvin to Jefferson, pre-November, 1776. See also, *Petition of Dissenters in Albemarle and Amherst Counties* contained in the Jefferson Papers edited by Boyd.

31.Leland's *Declaration of Virginia Association of Baptists* to Jefferson, December 25, 1776. See also, Miss L.F. Greene, *The Writings of the Late Elder John Leland.* (New York: G.W. Wood, 1845).

32. Id

33. James, (FN 208 of Beliles thesis, supra at note 25).

34. Papers, Military and Political 1775-1778, of George Gilmer, M.D. of "Pen Park," Albemarle County, VA, *Miscellaneous Papers* 1672-1865 in the collections of the Virginia Historical Society, (Richmond, VA; Virginia Historical Society, 1887), pps. 71-139.

35. Samuel Smith to Jefferson, March and April, 1779. (where?)

36. Id

37. Jefferson's general revision of the laws, 1779; see also Beliles thesis, supra at note 25, at p. 12.

38. Beliles thesis, supra at note 25, pps. 12-13.

39. Id. at p. 13.

40. Buckley in Peterson and Vaughan's book on the Virginia Statute, p. 87.

41. Robert M. Healey, *Jefferson On Religion in Public Education;* see also Beliles paper, p. 16.

42. Notes on Virginia, Query 15, 1781; Beliles thesis, supra at note 25, fn 223.

43. Id.

44. Isaac, p. 65 (Beliles thesis, supra at note 25, fn 224).

45. Healy, p. 208. It should be noted that when this bill was later introduced in 1817 to the legislature by Joseph Cabell, all clauses concerning religion were omitted, even those which prohibited clergy from being teachers. When Jefferson served on the School Board for the District of Columbia while he occupied the White House, the Bible was used for teaching reading, and a Presbyterian minister was hired as the first teacher. John C. Proctor, ed., *Washington Past and Present* (New York; Lewis Historical Publishing Co., 1930), pps. 414-423. See also Wilhelmus B. Bryan, *History of the National Capital* (New York: MacMillan Co., 1914) (Beliles fn 225).

46. Beliles thesis, p. 18.

47. Beliles thesis, p. 20.

48. Id.

49. Barton, supra at note 24, p. 207, citing to Jefferson, *Writings*, Vol. XIX, pps. 449-450, at a Meeting of the Visitors of the University . . . on Monday the 4th of October, 1824.

50. Id.

51. Barton, supra note 24, p. 207, citing to Jefferson, *Memoir*, Vol. IV, p. 358-359, to Dr. Thomas Cooper on November 2, 1822.

52. Barton, supra at note 24, p. 207, citing to Jefferson, *Writings*, Vol. XVI, p. 291, to Captain John Thomas on November 18, 1807.

53. Id.

Chapter 6

1. Cotton Mather, *The Great Works of Christ ian America:* 1 (*Magnalia Christi Americana*) first published in 1702, (reprinted by Banner of Truth Trust from the 1852 edition, 1979), p. 45.

2. Id.

3. Peter Marshall and David Manuel, *The Light and the Glory,* (Fleming H. Company, 1977), p. 127.

4. Rosalie J. Slater, *Teaching and Learning America's Christian History: The Principle Approach* (Foundation for American Christian Education, 1965), p. XX.

5. Quoted from the Mayflower Compact, signed on the deck of the Mayflower on November 11, 1620.

6. Russell Kirk, *The Roots of American Order*, 3rd Ed. (Gateway, Washington, DC, 1992), p. 17, citing John Adams to F.A. , February 16, 1809, in C.F. Adams (ed.), *The Works of John Adams* (Boston: Little, Brown, 1854), Vol. IX, pps 609-610.

7. Id. at p. 45-46.

8. Id. at 12-13.

9. Id. at p. 14.

10. Id. at p. 28-29.

11. The account is recorded in the Bible at 1 Samuel 8:4-22.

12.James Madison, *The Federalist*, number 10 (New York: Tudor Publishing Co., 1937), p. 67; quoted in Foster, supra note 33, at p. 136.

13. The book of Acts 16:37.

14. Lydia is described in Acts 16:14 as "a seller of purple" who lived in the city of Thytira.

15. The book of Romans, chapter 15, verse 28.

16. Historian Russell Kirk is one who believes the Anglo-Saxon influence has been exaggerated. See, Kirk, *The Roots of American Order,* 3rd Ed. (Regnery Gateway, Washington, DC, 1992), pgs. 180-183. But see Charles E. Tucker, "Anglo-Saxon Law: Its Development and Impact on the English Legal System, 2

USAFA J. Leg. Stud. 127 (1991) for a strong analysis that favors the predominance of the Anglo-Saxon influence.

17. Tucker, supra, note 16 at p.132.

18. Kirk, supra note 6 at p. 177.

19. Tucker, supra, note 16 at p. 133. According to Tucker, even the Roman code played little to no role in British legal tradition since by the time it was written and reached Britain, the last grip of the Roman empire there had been released. "Thus, in spite of over 350 years of Roman occupation and administration, British governmental institutions seemingly internalized almost no Roman law and, even today exhibit almost no Roman influence." Id. at p. 134.

20. The Venerable Bede, *The Ecclesiastical History of the English Nation*, Ed. J.A. Giles (London: 1892), Book I, Chapter XXIII, p. 34, as cited in Tucker, supra note 16, at p. 139.

21. Bede, Book I, Chapter XXV, pps. 36-38; also Tucker, supra note 16 at p. 139.

22. Bede, Book II, Chapter V, p. 76, also Tucker, supra note 16 at p. 139. It is of interest to note that King Aethelbert was the great-grandson of Hengist, who some believed was a direct descendent of the Anglo-Saxon god Woden. See Tucker at note 16.

23. Sir Frederick Pollack and Frederic William Maitland, *The History of English Law Before the Time of Edward I*, 2nd Ed., Vol 1 (Cambridge: Cambridge University Press, 1952), p. 11; also Tucker, supra note 9, at p. 139.

24. Bede, Book I, Chapter XXXII, p. 58, citing a letter from the Pope to King Aethelbert in 601 A.D.; cited in Tucker, supra note 16, p. 140. While King Aethelbert was codifying his Dooms about the time Justinian was publishing the *Corpus Juris Civilus* codifying Roman law and this Roman experience of legal codification had been made known to Aethelbert, his code "bears little resemblance to the Roman code" in substance. Tucker, supra note 16 at p. 140.

25. Tucker, supra note 16 at p. 147-148. While the victim's social status was reflected in the amount of restitution required, that of the wrongdoer was completely irrelevant.

26. Tucker, supra note 16 at p. 149.

27. Mark A. Beliles & Stephen K. McDowell, *America's Providential History*,(The Providence Foundation, 1992), p. 41.

28. Id.

29. Tucker, supra, note 16 at p. 127. See also, H.G. Richardson and G.O. Sayles, *Law and Legislation from Aethelberht to Magna Carta*, (Edinburgh: Edinburgh University Press, 1966), p. 30.

30. Beliles & McDowell, supra, note 27, at p. 41.

31. Id.

32. Charles C. Coffin, *The Story of Liberty* (Maranatha Publications, 1987), p.21.

33. Beliles & McDowell, supra, note 27, at p. 42.

34. G.R.C. Davis, Magna Carta, p. 23-24 (The British Library, 1977).

35. Id. at p. 32.

36. Beliles & McDowell, supra, note 27, at p. 43.

37. Id.

38. Id.

39. Id., at p. 44.

40. According to Columbus's own words, "It was the Lord who put it into my mind — I could feel His hand upon me— the fact that it would be possible to sail from here to the Indies ." This quote is an excerpt from his *Book of Prophecies*, translated into English by Kay Britgham and published by CLIE publishers of Barcelona.

41. B. F. Morris, *Christian Life and Character of the Civil Institutions of the United States* (Philadelphia, 1864), . 41-42, quoted in, Beliles & McDowell, supra, note 27 at p. 46.

42. In 1834, Mr. Bancroft completed the first volume of his History of the United States, a 10-volume work which was the first comprehensive history of America, and was the best known and most widely read history of America for over 50 years. See, William J. Federer, *America's God & Country Encyclopedia of Quotaitons* (Fame Publishing, Inc., 1994), p. 36.

43. John Eidsmoe, "The Judeo-Christian Roots of the Constitution," Restoring the Constitution, 1787-1987 Essays in Celebration of the Bicentennial, p. 95 (H. Wayne House, ed., Probe Books, Dallas, TX) 1987.

44. Beliles & McDowell, supra, note 27 at p. 51.

45. Beliles & McDowell, supra, note 27 at p. 54.

46. Andrew C. McLaughlin, *Foundations of American Constitutionalism* (Fawcett Publications, Inc., Greenwich, Conn.), p. 18, 1966.

47. Id. at p. 19.

48. Id. at p. 20.

49. Quoted from the Mayflower Compact, November 11, 1620.

Chapter 7

1. Mark A. Beliles & Stephen K. McDowell, *America's Providential History*, (The Providence Foundation, 1992), p. 87.

2. Marshall Foster and Mary Elaine Swanson, *The American Covenant* (The Mayflower Institute, 1992), p. 95.

3. Marshall Foster and Mary-Elaine Swanson, supra, note 8.

4. Verna M. Hall, *The Christian History of the Constitution of the United States of America - Christian Self-Government* (Foundation for American Christian Education, 1987), p. 250-251.

5. From the text of the *Massachusetts Body of Liberties* as reprinted in Hall, supra, note 4 at p. 257.

6. Beliles & McDowell , supra, note 1at p. 90.

7. Id.

8. Beliles & McDowell, supra, note 1at p. 126.

9. 1983 Political Science Review.

10. *The Works of Rev. John Witherspoon* (Philadelphia: William W. Woodard, 1802), Vol. III, p. 46.

11. Samuel Adams, Rights of Colonists (1772), reprinted in Verna M. Hall, *The Christian History of the Constitution of the United States of America* (San Francisco: Foundation for American Christian Education, 1976), p.xiii.

12. Frank Moore, *American Eloquence: A Collection of Speeches and Addresses, By the Most Eminent Orators of America*, (D. Appleton and Company, 1858), p.324.

13. *McGowan v. Maryland*, 366 U.S. 420, at 562-63 (1961), (Douglas, J., dissenting)The North American Review, 1867.

14. Gary T. Amos, *Defending the Declaration*, (Providence Foundation, Charlottesville, VA, 1994), pps. 39-40.

15. Id., at p. 42.

16. Rufus King, *The Life and Correspondence of Rufus King*, Charles R. King, editor, (New York: G.P. Putnam's Sons, 1900), Vol. VI, p. 276, letter to C. Gore on February 17,1820).

17. James Wilson, *Of the General Principles of Law & Obligations*, Vol. I, p. 64.

18. John Dickinson, *The Political Writings of John Dickinson*, (Wilmington: Bonsal and Niles, 1801), Vol. I, pps. 111-112.

19. Samuel Adams, *Writings*, Vol. I, p. 269, Samuel Adams in the Boston Gazette of December 19, 1768 as "Vindex."

20.*The Daily Advertiser* (New York), May 1, 1789, p. 2. See also, *American State Papers: Documents Legislative and Executive, of the Congress of the United States* (Washington: Gales and Seaton, 1833), Vol. I, pps.9-10, April 30, 1789, cited in Barton, Original Intent, p. 324.

21. *The North American Review*, 1867.

22. *The Republic of the United States of America and Its Political Institutions Reviewed and Examined*, Henry Reeves, trans. (Garden City, NY: A.S. Barnes & Co., 1851), Vol. I, p.335.

23. Noah Webster, *History of the United States* (New Haven: & Peck, 1832), pps. 273-74, paragraph 578.

24. Herb Titus, *Constitutional Law Notes & Exams*, p. 8 (1994).

25. 12 Wheat, 213, 6 L. Ed. 606 (1827).

26. 12 Wheat, 213, 247, 6 L. Ed. 606, 652 (1827).

27. John Quincy Adams, *The Jubilee of the Constitution*, (New York: Samuel Colman, 1839), p. 54.

28. 165 U.S. 150, 160 (1897).

Chapter 8

1. Verna M. Hall and Rosalie J. Slater, *Teaching and Learning America's Christian History: The Principle Approach* (Foundation for American Christian Education, 1992), p. 240.

2. K. Alan Snyder, *If the Foundations Are Destroyed - Biblical Principles and Civil Government* (Principle Press, 1994), p. 114.

3. Id.

4. William J. Federer, *America's God and Country, Encyclopedia of Quotations*, at p. 410.

5. John 3:16: "For God so loved the world, that he gave his only begotten Son, that whosoever believeth in him should not perish, but have everlasting life." This scripture contains no exceptions to God's love. It doesn't matter if the person is handicapped, has a low IQ, or is not physically attractive. Jesus died for every person because God created every person.

6. Beliles & McDowell, supra note 1 at p. 23.

7. Id., at p. 24.

8. Gary T. Amos, *Defending the Declaration, How the Bible and Christianity Influenced the Writing of the Declaration of Independence*, (Charlottesville, VA, The Providence Foundation), p. 113, 1994.

9. Romans 13:1.

10. Romans 13:4.

11. K. Alan Snyder, *If the Foundations are Destroyed: Biblical Principles and Civil Government* (Principle Press, 1994), p. 30.

12. Id.

13. Id.

14. Amos, supra note 10 at p. 11.

15. Id.

16. William J. Federer, *America's God and Country Encyclopedia of Quotations* (Fame Publishing, Inc., 1994), p. 323, quoted from Jefferson's Notes on the State of Virginia, Query XVIII, 1781.

17. John 19:10-11.

18. John 19:11.

19. Richard J. Neuhaus, Preface, in William Bentley Ball, *Mere Creatures of the State? Education, Religion, and the Courts: A View from the Courtroom 4* (1994); see also, Douglas W. Kmiec, "Book Review: 'God's Litigator' A Review Essay of Mere Creatures of the State? Education, Religion, and the Courts: A View from the Courtroom," 70 Notre Dame L. Rev. 1247, 1250 (1995).

20. Kmeic, supra at n. 28.

21. Gary T. Amos, *Defending the Declaration: How the Bible and Christianity Influenced the Writing of the Declaration of Independence* (The Providence Foundation, Charlottesville, VA., 1994), p. 114.

22. See, James 2:1-4; 3:22; 3:11; Romans 3:22 and 10:12. Of course class distinctions remain, even amongst many Christians, not because the teaching of Jesus was wrong, but because sinful man does not always obey those teaching.

23. Peter Marshall and David Manuel, *The Light and the Glory* (Old Tappan, N.J.: Fleming H. Co., 1977), p. 370, note 10.

24. Amos, supra, at note 9.

25. Id.

26. Snyder, supra, note 8 at p. 34.

27. Federer, supra, note 9 at pp. 268-69.

28. Proverbs 23:7.

29. Hall, supra, note 2 at p. 265.

30. Quoted in Gary DeMar, *America's Christian History: The Untold Story* (American Vision Inc., Atlanta, GA. 1995), p. 191.

31. Class notes from Knox Theological Seminary, *The Foundations of American Christian History*, February 21, 1994.

32. D. James Kennedy, *Character & Destiny: A Nation In Search of Its Soul* (Publishing House, 1994), p. 162.

33. Class notes from Knox Theological Seminary, supra, note 16, April 25, 1994.

34. Id.

35. Snyder, supra, note 8 at p. 114.

36. Remarks of President John Adams at his address to the military on October 11, 1798. Charles Francis Adams, ed., *The Works of John Adams - Second President of the United States* (Boston: Little, Brown, & Co., 1854), Vol. IX, p. 229.

37. Marshall Foster, *The American Covenant: The Untold Story* (The Mayflower Institute, 1992), p. 135.

38. John Eidsmoe, *Christianity and the Constitution: The Faith of Our Founding Fathers* (Baker Book House, 1987), p. 369.

39. Acts 1:6.

40. Id.

41. Acts 1:7,8.

42. Acts 1:8.

43. See, 2 Corinthians 3:17.

44. See, Matthew 28:19,20.

Chapter 9

1. Quoted in Mark Beliles & Stephen McDowell, *America's Providential History* (The Providence Foundation, 1992), p. 172, citing James Madison's *Notes of Debates in the Federal Convention of 1787* (New York, 1987), pps. 209-210. Franklin's reference to the tower of Babel indicated his scriptural knowledge of the account in Genesis, chapter 11.

2. Mark A. Beliles & Stephen K. McDowell, *America's Providential History* (The Providence Foundation, 1992), p. 187-188.

3. See, Beliles & McDowell, supra, note 8 at p. 189.

4. Beliles & McDowell, supra, note 8 at page 189, citing, *Our Ageless Constitution*, p. 32.

5. Beliles & McDowell, supra, note 3 at p. 38.

6. Id.

7. Eidsmoe, *Christianity and the Constitution*, p. 372-373.

8. Noah Webster, *American Dictionary of the English Language* (New York: S. Converse, 1828).

9. This principle is admirably described in Snyder's book, supra, note3, at pps. 79-100.

10. Id., at p. 97.

11. Deuteronomy 17:6 states: "At the mouth of two witnesses, or three witnesses, shall he that is worthy of death be put to death; but at the mouth of one witness he shall not be put to death."

12. Deuteronomy 19:15; 24:3 provided the Biblical basis for these principles of justice.

13. Simon Greenleaf, former professor of law at Harvard University during the first half of the 19th century, concluded that the presumption of innocence and the requirement for proof beyond a reasonable doubt stemmed from "various places in the Mosaic code." He even found the outline for criminal procedure in Deuteronomy 17:4. 3 S. Greenleaf, Evidence, Part V, section 29, n.1 (1824), cited in Herbert W. Titus, *God, Man, and Law: The Biblical Principles*, (Institute in Basic Life Principles, Oak Brook, IL), p. 25 (1994).

14. See Beliles and McDowell, supra note 3 at p. 151.

15. Id., citing Robert B. Weaver, *Our Flag and Other Symbols of Americanism* (Alexandria, VA, 1972), p. 9.

Chapter 10

1. Thomas Jefferson to Charles Hammond, 1821. ME 15:331.

2. From the testimony of Dr. Jerome in the case of *Davis v. Davis and King, dba Fertility Center of East Tennessee*, Blount County, Tennessee at Maryville, Equity Division (Div. I), Case No. E-14496, p. 11, (1989).

3. 381 U.S. 479 (1965).

4. Ibid.

5. See, John W. Whitehead, *The Second American Revolution* (Crossway Books, 1982), p. 122.

Chapter 11

1. *CATO Handbook for Congress, Policy Recommendations for the 108th Congress*, CATO Institute, Chapter 2, "Limited Government and the Rule of Law," p. 15, Washington DC.

2. Id, supra at note 1, at Chapter 23, "The Federal Budget," p. 223-224.

3. In 1789, the three departments were Department of State, Department of the Treasury and the Department of War. The Post Office Department was created in 1789 but did not become an executive department until 1872 and was abolished in 1971. Although Congress had created the position of Attorney General in 1789, it did not form the Department of Justice until 1870. American Government in Christian Perspective, 2nd edition, p. 122, fn (A Beka Book, 1997).

The 15 executive departments today are: (1) Department of State, (2) Department of Treasury, (3) Department of Defense, (4) Department of Interior, (5) Department of Justice, (6) Department of Agriculture, (7) Department of Commerce, (8) Department of Labor, (9) Health and Human Services, (10) Housing and Urban Development, (11) Transportation, (12) Energy, (13) Education, (14) Veteran Affairs, and (15) Homeland Security.

4. From President George Washington's Farewell Address in 1796.

5. CATO Handbook, supra at note 1, Chapter 3, "Congress, the Courts, and the Constitution," p. 26.

6. Id., at p. 390, quoted from Thomas James Norton, *Undermining the Constitution: A History of Lawless Government* (New York: Co., 1950), p. 188.

7. Id. at p. 27.

8. CATO Handbook, p. 27.

9. Act of Feb. 12, 1794, 6 Stat. 13 (1794), cited in Jeffrey T. Renz, "What Spending Clause (or the President's Paramour): An Examination of the Views of Hamilton, Madison, and Story on Article I, Section 8, Clause 1 of the United States Constitution," 33 J. Marshall L. Rev. 81, 97 (Fall, 1999).

10. Walter Williams, Commentary, "Constitutional sleuthing," The Washington Times, December 17, 2003,
www.washtimcs.com/commentary/20031216-090337-3142r.htm.

11. Id. Washington Times Commentary.

12. www.garymcleod.org/davy.htm.

13. *United States v. Lopez*, 115 S.Ct. 1624 (1995).

14. Id at 1632.

15. Id at 1630-31.

16. Id. at p. 1631, fn. 3 (citations omitted).

17. *Case v. Bowles* , 327 U.S. 92 (1946).

18. *California v. Taylor*, 353 U.S. 553 (1957).

19. *Maryland v. Wirtz*, 392 U.S. 183 (1968).

20. See, *Hodel v. Virginia Surface Mining & Reclamation Ass'n*, 452 U.S. 264, 276-80 (1981).

21. See, *Perez v. United States*, 402 U.S. 146 (1971).

22. See, *Katzenbach v. McClung*, 379 U.S. 294 (1964).

23. See, *Heart of Atlanta Motel, Inc. v. United States*, 379 U.S. 241 (1964).

24. James Madison, *Notes of Debates in the Federal Convention of 1787*, p. 489 (W.W. Norton & Co., 1987) (1893); see also Randy Barnett, *The Original Meaning of the Necessary and Proper Clause*, 6 U. Pa. J. Const. L. 183, 185 (November, 2003).

25. Id. at 303; Barnett at 185.

26. Id. at 245-246; Barnett article, at p. 186.

27. Id. at 441; Barnett at p. 186.

28. Barnett article p. 186-187.

29. Annals of Cong. 1949 (Joseph Gales, ed., 1791); Barnett at p. 193.

30. *Opinion of Thomas Jefferson, Secretary of State, on the Same Subject* (Feb. 15, 1791), reprinted in *Legislative and Documentary History of the Bank of the United States*, at 93 (M. St. Clair Clarke & D.A. Hall., Augustus M. Kelley 1967) (1832); Barnett article, supra, note 24 at p. 196.

31. See, Barnett article, supra, note 24 at p. 198.

32. *U.S. v. Fisher*, 6 U.S. (2 Cranch) 358 (1805).

33. Id., at p. 396.

34. *McCulloch v. Maryland*, 17 U.S. (4 Wheat.) 316 (1819).

35. McCulloch, 17 U.S. at 414-415.

36. John Taylor, *Construction Construed and Constitutions Vindicated at 170* (The Lawbook Exchange, Ltd. 1998) (1820).

37. Barnett, supra, note 24 at p. 214.

38. *John Marshall, A Friend of the Constitution,* Alexandria Gazette, July 5, 1819, reprinted in John Marshall's *Defense of McCulloch v. Maryland* 186-87 (Gerald Gunther ed., Standford University Press 1969); also Barnett article at p. 215.

39. *McCulloch v. Maryland,* 17 U.S. (4 Wheat.) 316, 423 (1819).

40. *American Government in Christian Perspective,* 2nd Edition, p. 93 (1997).

41. Id. p. 93; see also, John Eidsmoe, *Institute on the Constitution,* a study on Christianity and the law of the land study syllabus, p. 47.

42. Samuel Francis, "Judicial Tyranny," vol. 13, No. 8, *The New American,* p. 5, April 14, 1997.

43. *Barron v. Baltimore,* 32 U.S. (7 Pet.) 243 (1833).

44. The pertinent portion of the 14th Amendment reads as follows:

All persons born or naturalized in the United States, and subject to the jurisdiction thereof, are citizens of the United States and of the State wherein they reside. No State shall make or enforce any law which shall abridge the privileges or immunities of citizens of the United States; nor shall any State deprive any person of life, liberty, or property, without due process of law; nor deny to any person within its jurisdiction the equal protection of the laws."

The language of the 14th Amendment only expressly incorporates the due process clause of the 5th Amendment.

45. *Slaughter House Cases,* 83 U.S. 36, 78-79 (1872).

46. The one exception was the case of *Chicago, Burlington & Quincy R.R. Co. v. Chicago,* 166 U.S. 226 (1897) dealing with a limited application of the 5th Amendment only. See, William D. Graves, "Evolution, the Supreme Court, and the Destruction of Constitutional Jurisprudence," 13 Regent U.L. Rev. 513, 542 (2000/2001).

47. *Gitlow v. New York,* 265 U.S. 652 (1925). Benjamin Gitlow was a Communist Party member convicted of violating New York's Criminal Anarchy Law that made it a criminal offense to advocate the violent overthrow of the government. Gitlow appealed his conviction, arguing that the New York law violated his First Amendment guarantee to freedom of speech that was incorporated by the 14th Amendment. While the Court upheld his conviction and the New York law, it also accepted his incorporation argument.

48. *Adamson v. California,* 332 U.S. 46 (1947).

49. Samuel Francis, "Judicial Tyranny," vol. 13, No. 8, *The New American,* p. 7 (April 14, 1997). Francis noted a liberal bias in the manner in which rights are selectively incorporated. "For example, the court-created "right" to abortion is incorporated; the constitutionally protected right to keep and bear arms is not." Id.

50. Francis, "Judicial Tyranny" at p. 8.

51. Francis, "Judicial Tyranny" at p. 9.

52. Samuel Francis, "Judicial Tyranny," at p. 9.

53. Charles Fairman, *Does the Fourteenth Amendment Incorporate the Bill of Rights?*, 2 Stan. L. Rev. 5, 134 (1949); see also William Graves, *Evolution, the Supreme Court, and the Destruction of Constitutional Jurisprudence*, 13 Regent U. L. Rev. 513, 543 (2000/2001).

54. See Michael A. Musmanno, *Proposed Amendments to the Constitution 182* (1929); see also William Graves, 13 Regent U. L. Rev. 513, 544.

55. *Bartkus v. Illinois*, 359 U.S. 121 (1959).

56. *Bartkus*, Id. at 125 n.3.

57. Id.

58. Charles E. Rice, "A Cultural Tour of the Legal Landscape: Reflections on Cardinal George's Law and Culture," 1 Av. Maria L. Rev. 81, 90 (Spring 2003).

59. Samuel Francis, Judicial Tyranny, at p. 11.

60. Charles Rice, supra, note 58 at p. 90.

61. Rousas John Rushdooney, *The Institutes of Biblical Law* (The Presbyterian and Reformed Publishing Co., 1973), p. 282.

62. W. Cleon Skousen, *The Making of America* (The National Center for Constitutional Studies, 1985), p. 424.

63. Id. On April 5, 1933, President Roosevelt, by declaration of a national emergency, ordered all gold coins, gold bullion, and gold certificates to be turned into the Federal Reserve banks by May 1. Later, on January 30, 1934, the Gold Reserve Act was passed, giving the Federal Reserve title to all gold which had been turned in by American citizens. Id., at p. 425.

64. Id.

65. On March 29, 2004, the 19 member NATO alliance expanded to 26 with the addition of the following seven member states: Bulgaria, Estonia, Latvia, Lithuania, Romania, Slovakia and Slovenia.

66. Patrick Johnson, Operation World (Publishing House, 1993), p. 339.

67. Id. at p. 305.

68. Barbara G. Baker, "Jordan Court Orders Christian Mother Jailed," Project Open Book, (January 24, 2003), at
http://www.domini.org/openbooks/jor20030124.htm.

69. Skousen, supra, note 62, at p. 255.

70. Id. at p. 508.

71. Id.

72. Congressional Research Service, *Executive Orders: A Brief History of Their Use and The President's Power to Issue Them*, (Library of Congress, 1977), p. CRS-5.

73. Id., at p. CRS-5 .

74. Skousen, supra, note 63, at p. 253.

75. Id., at p. CRS –8. The first executive order to be published in the Federal Register was executive order 7316 dated March 14, 1936 which concerned a bird refuge in South Carolina.

76. Id., at p. CRS-6.

Chapter 12

1. 330 U.S. 1 (1947).

2. The term had been used earlier by the Supreme Court in the case of *Reynolds v. United States*, 98 U.S. 145 (1878), in the following context: "Mr. Jefferson afterwards, in reply to an address to him by a committee of the Danbury Baptist Association, took occasion to say: 'Believing with you that religion is a matter which lies solely between man and his God; that he owes account to none other for his faith or his worship; that the legislative powers of the government reach actions only, and not opinions, — I contemplate with sovereign reverence that act of the whole American people which declared that their legislature should 'make no law respecting an establishment of religion or prohibiting the free exercise thereof,' thus building a wall of separation between church and state.'" 98 U.S. at 164.

3. David Barton, *The Myth of Separation* 11 (1989).

4. 330 U.S. at 16.

5. Id. See also, Daniel L. Dreisbach, *Real Threat and Mere Shadow, Religious Liberty and the First Amendment*, 47-48 (1987).

6. Id. at 18.

7. Id. at 31-32.

8. Id. at 16. See also, John W. Whitehead, *The Second American Revolution*, 99 (1982).

9. Jay Sekulow, *From Intimidation to Victory*, 33 (1990).

10. William J. Federer, *America's God and Country Encyclopedia of Quotations*, (Fame Publishing, Coppell, TX), p. 330-331(1994).

11. Dreisbach, *Mere Threat*, supra, note 5, pg. 114-115.

12. Whitehead, supra note 8, at 100.

13. See, Barton, *Original Intent*, p. 200 (fn 12).

14. Barton, *Original Intent*, p. 207.

15. Whitehead, supra note 8, at 100.

16. Barton, *Original Intent*, pg. 207.

17. See, *Wallace v. Jaffree*, 472 U.S. 38 at 94 (Rehnquist, J., dissenting); citing 3 J. Elliot, Debates on the Federal Constitution 434 (1891).

18. The floor debates in the Senate were secret, thus not reported in the Annals.

19. Joseph Gales, ed., *The Debates and Proceedings in the Congress of the United States, Compiled from Authentic Materials*, I (Wash. D.C., Gales and Seaton, 1834), 729, cited in Dreisbach, supra, note 5, at 51.

20. Id., at 52.

21. Sekulow, supra note 9, at 33. The provision was contained in the Northwest Ordinance, which set forth a government structure for the territories that had not yet become states.

22. See, *Walz v. Egg Harbor Township Board of Education*, 342 F. 3d 271 (3d Cir. 2003).

23. *Engel v. Vitale*, 370 U.S. 421 (1962). The Engel Court dealt with a New York state law that directed the school principal to cause the following prayer to be said aloud by each class before the teacher at the start of each school day:

"Almighty God, we acknowledge our dependence upon Thee, and we beg Thy blessings upon us, our parents, our teachers and our Country." 370 U.S. at 422.

The prayer was composed by state officials as part of their "Statement on Moral and Spiritual Training in the Schools." The New York Court of Appeals had sustained the power of New York to use the prayer "so long as the schools did not compel any pupil to join in the prayer over his or his parent's objection." 370 U.S. at 423.

24. *Reed v. Van Hoven*, 237 F. Supp. 48 (W.D. Mich. 1965).

25. *State v. Whisner*, 47 Ohio St. 2d 181, 351 N.E.2d 750 (1976). In this case, the parents were convicted of failing to send their children to public school because the school teachings were contrary to their religious beliefs. The Supreme Court of Ohio overturned the conviction based on the fact the school's minimum standards violated their rights to free exercise of their religion. The court noted however, that "[a]lthough appellants argue that no reference is made in those (minimum state education) standards to God or to Biblical instruction, we think it plain that to do so would constitute a violation of the establishment clause of the First Amendment." 351 N.E.2d at 764.

26. *Stone v. Graham*, 449 U.S. 39 (1980). The Court stated that it did not matter that the posted copies of the Ten Commandments were financed by voluntary, private contributions. 449 U.S. at 42.

27. Stephen L. Carter, *The Culture of Disbelief*, p. 11-12 (1993). The case went to the United States Court of Appeals for the Tenth Circuit, which upheld the removal of the Christian books. See, Jay Alan, *Re-evaluating Religion in Public Life, Law & Justice*, p. 4 (March, 1994).

28. *Docket List: Recent Victories and Other Legal Activities*, Law& Justice, p. 9, No. 6 (Jan/Feb. 1994).

29. Paul Thigpen, Christians in Court, *Charisma Magazine*, p. 66 (Dec. 1990). The facts of this case are shocking. On November 21, 1989, seventeen year old Scott McDaniel handed a note to his friend Matt Hinton in a hallway between classes at Henderson High School, near Atlanta. It was intercepted by the assistant principal who proceeded to suspend Scott for three days, and he threatened Matt with suspension. Matt had already been told by school officials earlier that day to put a jacket over his Christian T-shirt he wore to class so people couldn't see it. When Matt's father talked to the principal about what happened, he was told that if Matt or any other students brought their Bibles to school or wore religious T-shirts or buttons, they would be suspended. Additionally, the students were told by school officials that Fellowship of Christian Athletes could not meet on campus. Nor could they participate in any school activities or have a yearbook photo taken unless they removed the word "Christian" from their name. Only after a school board hearing and the threat of a lawsuit did the authorities back down. See, Sekulow, supra, note 9, at pps. 58-59.

30. Franky Schaeffer, *Plan for Action: An Action Alternative Handbook for Whatever Happened to the Human Race?* pps. 36-37 (1980).

31. MSNBC News Services, "Kerry marks 39th anniversary of Selma's 'Bloody Sunday,' by Jim Bourg/Reuters, March 7, 2004. Democratic presidential candidate Senator John Kerry spoke to the congregation during Sunday morning services at the Greater Bethlehem Temple Apostolic Faith Church in Jackson, Mississippi. According to The Boston Globe, Sep. 28, 2003, in a Patrick Healy article entitled, "Kennedy gives Kerry campaign a lift in Iowa," Senator Kerry spoke at another church. "Speaking at a predominately black church yesterday, Kerry praised affirmative action in college admissions and other race-based policies that he once questioned and pledged that, as president, he would invite Kennedy to the White House to write a new law making catastrophic health insurance a 'right' for all Americans."

32. Whitehead, supra, note 8, at p. 98.

33. See infra, note 112 about Story's Commentaries.

34. Whitehead, supra, note 8, at p. 98.

35. 403 U.S. 602 (1971).

36. Id., at pp. 612-13.

37. *Wallace v. Jaffree*, 472 U.S. 38 (1985).

38. Notice the words of the Court. "It is not the activity itself that concerns us; it is the purpose of the activity that we shall scrutinize." 472 U.S. at 48, n. 30.

39. 472 U.S. at 41.

40. *DeSpain v. DeKalb County Community School District*, 384 F.2d 836 (7th Cir. 1967).

41. The poem in question was quite innocuous:

We thank you for the flowers so sweet,
We thank you for the food we eat;
We thank you for the birds that sing;
We thank you for everything. 384 F.2d at 837.

42. "Despite the elimination of the word 'God' from the children's recital of thanks, plaintiffs maintain ...that that word is still there in the minds of the children. Thus we are asked as a court to prohibit, not only what these children are saying, but also what plaintiffs think the children are thinking... One who seeks to convert a child's supposed thought into a violation of the constitution of the United States is placing a meaning on that historic doctrine which would have surprised the founding fathers. 384 F.2d at 841. (Circuit Judge).

43. Rousas John Rushdoony, *The Nature of the American System*, 2 (1978).

44. Steve C. Dawson, *God's Providence in America's History*, 9:6 (1988), cited in Barton, supra, note 3, at p. 25.

45. Dreisbach, supra, note 5, at p. 50.

46. Donald S. Lutz, *The Relative Influence of European Writers on Late Eighteenth-Century American Political Thought*, 78 Am. Pol. Sci. Rev. 189, 192 (1984).

47. Mr Webster was speaking at the bicentennial celebration of the landing of the Pilgrims at Plymouth Rock, December 22, 1820. Barton, supra, note 3, at p. 134.

48. Whitehead, supra, note 8, at 87.

49. *Torcaso v. Watkins*, 367 U.S. 488, 495, n. 11 (1961).

50. Sekulow, supra, note 9, at 53.

51. A comment in *The American Atheist*, which linked secular education with the elimination of religion, noted, "[w]e need only insure that our schools teach only secular knowledge. . . . If we could achieve this, god would indeed be shortly due for a funeral service." G. Richard Bozarth, "On Keeping God Alive," The American Atheist, 7 November 1977, cited in Lynn R. Buzzard and Samuel Ericsson, *The Battle for Religious Liberty*, 96 (1982).

52. Sekulow, supra, note 9, at 38.

53. Attorney Jay Sekulow notes the inconsistency:

"Lawyer Clarence Darrow in the famous Scopes 'Monkey Trial' of 1925 argued for the right to teach evolution in schools. He contended that to allow only one version of creation history to be taught would be intellectual bigotry. Fair enough. But what do we hear from the so-called civil liberties lobby and the U.S. Supreme Court today? That teaching both evolution and a science-backed scriptural account of creation is a violation of the infamous 'separation of church and state.'" Sekulow, supra, note 9, at 70.

54. Francis A. Schaeffer, *A Christian Manifesto*, 44 (1982).

55. Buzzard and Ericsson, supra, note 44, at 9. Eventually Mayor Bradley announced that Bible studies would not be treated differently from other home meetings and the matter was resolved without court action. Id., at 10.

56. Id., at 9.

57. Sekulow, supra, note 9, at 60.

58. Tom Minnery, "Why the Left Needs Censorship," *Focus on the Family Citizen*, 4 (July 23, 1990).

59. Sekulow, supra, note 9, at 76. The little girl's name was Audrey Pearson and her family was able to get the principal to back down only after legal action was sought.

60. Id. Again, only after legal action was taken, did the teacher allow the girl to place crosses on her art project.

61. *Berkey v. Third Avenue R. Co.*, 244 N.Y. 84, 94, 155 N.E. 58, 61 (1926).

Chapter 13

1. W. Cleon Skousen, *The Making of America* (The National Center for Constitutional Studies, 1985), p. 6.

2. Rabbi Daniel Lapin, *America's Real War, An Orthodox Rabbi Insists that Values are Vital for our Nation's Survival*, p. 49 (Multnomah Publishers, 1999).

3. For an excellent resource on the trial, see "Famous American Trials, Illinois v. Nathan Leopold and Richard Loeb" 1924, by Professor Douglas , 1997 at www.law.umkc.edu/faculty/projects/ftrials/leoploeb.

4. Id.

5. Id. Although Loeb was later murdered in prison in 1936, Leopold was paroled after serving only 33 years. He later moved to Puerto Rico where he married and, at the age of 66, died with his wife by his side.

6. Id.

7. Gary DeMar, *America's Christian History: The Untold Story,* p. 22, (American Vision, 1995).

8. Id.

9. Id., at p. 24.

10. Id.

11. Id.

12. Id., at pps 24-25 citing Carey Quan Gelernter, "The Real Thanksgiving," *Seattle Post-Intelligencer* (November 23, 1986), L1.

13. Cited in Gary DeMar, *God and Government – Issues in Biblical Perspective* Vol. 2, p. xvi (American Vision, Atlanta, GA) 1998.

14. Cited in DeMar, supra at note 13, p. Xv.

15. Gary DeMar, *America's Christian History: The Untold Story,* p. 191-192 (American Vision, 1995), citing to Verna M. Hall, ed., *The Christian History of the American Constitution* (San Fransisco, CA: Foundation for American Christian Education, 1975), p. 20.

16. December, 1984, address given on the occasion of the enactment of the Equal Access Bill of 1984. *The Speech That Shook The Nation* (Forerunner, Dec. 1984), p. 12.

Chapter 14

1. Chief Justice John Jay in a letter to John Murray, Junior, October 12,1816, cited in Phil Webster, *Can a Chief Justice Love God? The Life of John Jay,* p. 86 (2002).

2. Noah Webster, *History of the United States,* (New Haven, 1833) pps. 307-308.

3. Revival Lectures (reprinted Old Tappan, NJ: Fleming Revell Co., 1970), Lecture XV, pps. 336-337.

4. Matthew 28:19

5. "It was the Lord who put into my mind (I could feel His hand upon me) the fact that it would be possible to sail from here to the Indies. All who heard of my project rejected it with laughter, ridiculing me. There is no question that the inspiration was from the Holy Spirit, because he comforted me with rays of marvelous illumination from the Holy Scriptures, a strong and clear testimony from the 44 books of the Old Testament, from the four Gospels, and from the 23 Epistles of the blessed Apostles, encouraging me continually to press forward, and without ceasing for a moment they now encourage me to make haste.

Our Lord Jesus desired to perform a very obvious miracle in the voyage to the Indies, to comfort me and the whole people of God." This quotation is from the Introduction of Christopher Columbus' *Book of Prophecies* cited in Catherine Millard, *The Rewriting of America's History,* (Horizon House Publishers, Camp Hill, PA, 1991), p. 3.

6. Kay Brigham, *Christopher Columbus - His Life & Discovery in the Light of His Prophecies* (Barcelona, CLIE Publishers, 1990); see also, Millard, supra, note 1 at p. 5.

7. Benjamin Rush, *Letters of Benjamin Rush*, L. H. , editor (NJ: American Philosophical Society, 1951), Vol. I, pp. 532-536, to John Adams on February 24, 1790.

Biblical Worldview University

Training leaders to transform their culture for Christ.

The Providence Foundation Biblical Worldview University (BWU) provides training for leaders of all ages and spheres of life in a curriculum of real-world topics, offered via distance learning and periodic live classes. BWU offers dozens of courses on providential history, the family and Christian education, the marketplace, and the state. Start your Biblical worldview training today.

Christian Education and a Biblical Worldview

This course examines for areas that are foundational for our worldview; contrasts the foundational principles of modern state education and the components of Kingdom education presents the need for education to have a Christian philosohpy, methodolgy, and curriculum; shows how to restore researching, reasoning, relating, and recording to education; and much more.

Order this and other BWU courses:

www.providencefoundation.com
Call: 434-978-4535
or email us and request a catalog:
university@providencefoundation.com

A Few Providence Foundation Resources

America's Providential History

Chronicles how the Lord guided our nation from the very beginning. Proof from history: our nation grew from Christian principles. How to bring them back into the mainstream.

Building Godly Nations

Lessons from the Bible and America's Christian History

Examines the mandate for building Godly nations and how to apply Biblical principles to governing the nations. Chapters include: Fulfilling the Cultural Mandate; Pastors and American Independence; Separation of Church and State; The Role of Women in History; The Bible, Slavery, and America's Founders; Biblical Principles of Business; Education & the Kingdom of God.

Become a Member and Receive Great Benefits.

Providence Foundation Basic Member: receive our newsletters, a 30% discount on all our books, videos, and materials, plus discounts to our seminars. **Premium Member:** receive Basic Member benefits plus a free book, $80 voucher toward one of our BWU Courses, personal coaching, and more.

To join or receive more information email us or visit our website: providencefoundation.com

35100053R00142

Made in the USA
San Bernardino, CA
15 June 2016